ADDISON-WESLEY EARLY CHILDHOOD EDUCATION

TAKE A LOOK

Observation and Portfolio Assessment in Early Childhood

Sue Martin

Professor of Early Childhood Education

Centennial College, Scarborough, Ontario

D0074121

Addison-Wesley Publishers Limited

Don Mills, Ontario • Reading, Massachusetts
Menlo Park, California • New York • Wokingham, England
Amsterdam • Bonn • Sydney • Singapore • Tokyo
Madrid • San Juan

Canadian Cataloguing in Publication Data

Martin, Sue
      Take a look: observation and portfolio assessment
in early childhood

(Addison-Wesley early childhood education)
Includes bibliographical references and index.
ISBN 0-201-58857-9

1. Child development – Research.   2. Child
psychology – Research.   3. Child development –
Evaluation.   4. Child psychology – Evaluation.
5. Observation (Psychology). I. Title. II. Series.

BF722.M37 1994   155.4'072   C94–930672–X

Printed and bound in Canada by Webcom

ISBN 0-201-58857-9

    C D E F   WC   99 98 97 96 95

Acknowledgments

I first thought of writing a book on child observations in 1986, when I taught at a college in England. Emigration left the idea on the back burner for several years. It was revived when Beth Bruder offered me a contract with Addison-Wesley. To her, and my editor Kateri Lanthier – who did a truly wonderful job with the manuscript – my thanks and gratitude for making *Take a Look* happen.

My colleagues at Centennial College have been encouraging throughout, and special thanks go to Pat Corson, Michael Pimento, Ira Lager, Lynn Haines, and the supervisors and staff of the college's child care centres. Contributions from my students have been invaluable and I have learned much from them.

Thanks also to my family (Andrew, Cassie, and Simon) for their support and help over the past eighteen months…and a mention of, but no thanks to, Jacob, our cocker spaniel, who ate the first batch of photographs.

Credits

Contents

◆ ◆ ◆ ◆ Introduction

Without effective observation you cannot have appropriate practice. Although elements of good practice can be clearly defined, unless care-givers and educators take a look at how the children are developing and the ways in which they respond to their environment they will not be able to provide developmentally appropriate programs.

Take a Look: Observation and Portfolio Assessment in Early Childhood offers the history, philosophy, and practice of observing, recording, and analyzing children's behaviour. Focussing on the individual child, the book explains the need to gather information about each young person, and then suggests a variety of techniques for recording the data.

This book differs from others in its approach to the observer's own skill development. Perceptions about what is seen are refined as the observer gains greater insight into why observation is the most effective means of evaluation. With practice, the observer acquires new techniques for recording information and learns to make valid and supported infer-ences about the child. A model for the validation process is a key feature of the text. It enables the observer to use information gathered in naturalistic settings in ways that allow for thorough evaluation. The emphasis on eval-uation is vital, as observations are often filed away without adequate exploration, with undue reliance on standardized test results to give devel-opmental information.

While adults responsible for young children may have known that observing was the most effective way to understand them, they often lacked the tools to do the job properly. *Take a Look* was written to assist the student or practitioner in building professional skills and becoming increasingly effective as curriculum designers, nurturers, facilitators of play and learning, providers of a healthy and safe environment, communi-cators, positive role models, program reviewers, self-evaluators, and team workers. The observer's take always leaves room for improvement, but the more you look the more likely you are to perceive objectively and make accurate evaluations.

Why, what, when, and how to observe are explored in the first chapter, with an overview of the principles behind the use of observation and port-folio assessment as developmentally appropriate evaluation.

Chapters 2-6 share a common pattern, as each explores a different style of recording. These chapters define the methodology, indicate features of the particular method, and demonstrate how it can be used.

Portfolios and child studies are addressed in Chapter 7. This chapter pulls together elements from each of the methods previously explained, and shows how collections of a variety of recordings and other information can provide the most detailed and effective technique for profiling the individual child.

Caregivers and educators may need to call on resources outside the agency to help make accurate evaluations of developmental progress. Chapter 8 gives an overview of the uses and limitations of standardized screening and assessment tools.

The final chapter shifts away from looking at the behaviour of individuals and groups of children and focusses on the child's environment. Lists of indicators of appropriate children's environments are based on a wealth of up-to-date research. These look at notions of quality, inclusivity, physical well-being, and nurturance. The lists can form an effective evaluation tool if used as the basis of a checklist, rating scale, or questionnaire.

Features of the book

Focus questions/answers: These enable readers to review their current understanding and skill level. The focus questions at the beginning of each chapter start the process of learning with reflection, and provide an overview of the content together with a method of checking that it was understood.

History notes: A brief historical perspective is offered at the beginning of each chapter, which explains the evolutionary stages that bring us to our current philosophy and practice. Views about how children develop have changed dramatically in a relatively short period. The history notes help us to understand these changes in how children are perceived and how records were kept to monitor their progress.

Definitions of the observation methods: A clear explanation of each method of observation and information gathering technique is essential to understanding, choosing, and using each. The definitions offered in each chapter assist the reader to access basic information quickly and efficiently.

Features of methodologies: The characteristics of each observation method are fully described in each chapter. The range of styles within each category is compared and contrasted so that the student or practitioner can appreciate their usefulness.

Advantages/disadvantages of observation methods: Concise information charts give a clear indication of the strengths and weaknesses of each observational method. All data collection techniques have positive and negative aspects; the selection of appropriate methods is assisted by thorough and objective analysis, while their effective use is supported by a list of common pitfalls to avoid.

Assignment options: The assignments are designed to aid appreciation of the philosophy of observation as developmentally appropriate evaluation, as well as to build skills in the use of observation methods. A variety of tasks is suggested to facilitate learning. Individual and group assignments will enable key issues to be understood and the relevant principles applied. The exercises have been devised and tried by large numbers of students and practitioners. This has resulted in some modifications, but the feedback has generally been positive, with most students reporting that the tasks helped them improve their perceptions, make more objective recordings, and analyze data more successfully. Instructors claim that the assignments supported the development of critical thinking skills.

Students and their instructors frequently request an "ideal" observation. As every observation is individual to the child, situation, observer, and chosen methodology, this is difficult to supply. No recorded observation is perfect, but we all aspire to record appropriate, objective, and useful observations. The assignment options include examples to critique. All have strengths that can be identified. Criteria for assessing the examples are also provided. This evaluation process is an essential learning tool. Instructors will find the evaluation criteria helpful for teaching and in assessing students' work.

The chapter on Screening and Assessment doesn't give assignments because the majority of readers will not normally administer standardized tests. The uses and limitations of such tests are discussed in this chapter. As they may form part of a portfolio, the educator must know their place, be prepared to consult with other professionals in their use, and be able to interpret the results, comparing them with other data from observational sources. As each testing procedure is different, particular tasks have not been set. There are benefits in becoming familiar with some of the tests used locally, and some commonly used screening and assessment tools are described briefly at the end of this chapter. You may want to examine the data indicating validity and reliability produced by the test publishers.

Key terms/glossary: At the end of each chapter the newly identified key terms are listed. Each is then defined in the glossary at the end of the book. As you become familiar with the format of *Take a Look* you will want to use the glossary as a quick reference tool to aid your understanding of the text. After reading each chapter you can check your learning by testing your knowledge of the listed terms.

Bibliography: To have included all of the works consulted in writing this book would have resulted in an extremely long bibliography. Only the references mentioned in the text are cited in the bibliography, and will assist further study in any given area.

Index: The index (which follows a simple structure and has been kept as straightforward as possible) includes the people and essential terms mentioned in the text.

Take a Look offers several new perspectives for students, instructors, parents, and early childhood educators:
◆ How naturalistic observation can offer the most reliable information about children, and form developmentally appropriate evaluation.
◆ That inferences drawn from objectively recorded observations can be validated.
◆ The way in which we understand how children develop affects our perception of them and how we record their progress.
◆ Skill development in recording observational information progresses with our ability to perceive the child's development.
◆ Professional teamwork is the most effective, fair, and appropriate way to evaluate children's progress.
◆ The most valuable way to gather information about a child is to use a number of data collection methods.
◆ Standardized tests offer only limited and often biased information about children, and should be used with caution.
◆ Children's behaviour is the key to understanding their development, and although you aim to understand the whole child you must accept you will never know everything!

1 Why, What, When, and How to Observe

You well know that the teacher in our method is more of an observer than a teacher, therefore this is what the teacher must know, how to observe.
Maria Montessori (1913)

Observation can lead to the collection of valid, reliable information without intruding on or transforming the daily classroom life and without constraining the children's behaviour so as to limit their demonstration of competence.
Tynette W. Hills (1992)

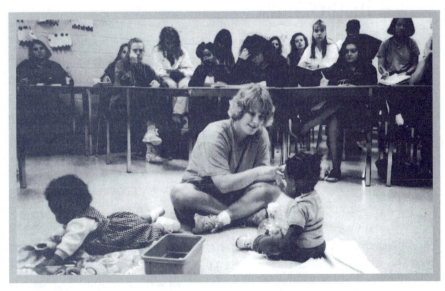

Early Childhood Education students use an in-class opportunity for non-participant observation of infants. Skill in objective recording needs to be gained from practice.

Focus Questions

1. Why do educators think that observation is important?

2. What can be learned from watching children involved in spontaneous activity?

3. How can observational information be recorded?

4. In recording any information about children, how can judgments and assumptions be avoided?

5. How can you reduce or eliminate personal biases that might influence your observations?

6. Can adults be sure that valid interpretations are made from objectively recorded observations?

◆ ◆ ◆ ◆ # History Notes

Observation of children in a systematic manner is a relatively new idea. Only in the last hundred years have our ideas evolved about how children develop to the point that we see any necessity for watching children's behaviours.

For centuries it was believed that children were ready-made miniature adults (Crain, 1980). This theory of **preformationism** meant that children were treated as small adults. It is possible that parents avoided acknowledging the individuality of children because of high infant and child mortality.

Locke's (1634–1704) view of children as being a blank slate, or "tabula rasa," came in the time of the "Enlightenment," the age of new democratic thought. The idea that children are empty vessels to be filled with information, although significant in the history of thought, does not acknowledge the notions of development that we have today.

A move towards the modern view of childhood emerged with Rousseau (1712–1778), who appreciated that children had individual ways of thinking and feeling. He believed that children were naturally good.

Rousseau's significant book *Emile* (1762) was a proposal for the education of a fictitious boy. Rousseau indicated four basic stages of development and a theory of how these occurred. He was not specific, however, about how the educator was to assess the child's stage of development other than by following a biological time plan.

The Edgeworth family, in Ireland (Whitbread,1972), was influenced by Rousseau's work. Having brought up one child according to the "Emile" method and having written detailed observations of his children, Richard Lovell Edgeworth wrote *Practical Education*. This work had a new focus on the importance of children's play, and was well-received in middle-class circles.

Pestalozzi (1745–1827) used Rousseau's methods to nurture his son but was disappointed with the outcome. He constructed his own theories, which were opposed to rote learning. He believed that children should determine their own ways of solving problems. His work drew on his brief experience as a teacher rather than on philosophy. From observing his own children, Pestalozzi came to believe that children learned from discovery.

Froebel (1787–1853) worked under Pestalozzi for two years. He evolved an educational theory based on what he observed in the development of the child. In a systematic methodology for unifying theory and practice in education, he devised his "six gifts." As creator of the "**kindergarten**" and father of current education practice, Froebel's place in child development history is central.

Rousseau, Pestalozzi, Froebel, and later Montessori (1879–1952), McMillan (1860–1931), and others made considerable advances in educational practice on both sides of the Atlantic. It was the Child Study Movement, however, that brought a completely new perspective to how children should be educated. The work of Hall, published in *The Content of Children's Minds* (1883), challenged the religious principles underlying the 17th and 18th century theorists. He presented the results of his observational experiments on learning in *Educational Psychology* (1910). A student of Hall, Gesell, carried out observational research based on the **maturation** of the child, which established norms for growth and development. These theorists presented a new scientific approach to education which, in part, challenged Froebelian principles and practice.

Increasing dissatisfaction with many aspects of education came with the growth of the middle class. The **child-centred** approach to education clashed with the scientific approach based on formal testing. These different views exist today.

The 1920s saw the growth of much child development research, particularly in the U.S. A wide range of behaviours were observed and studied to produce significant data about patterns of friendship, fears, aggression, and other features of development. These studies offered needed data to educators but many reacted with caution to the notion of studying children in a laboratory environment. They felt that observation techniques might be used for research but not in teaching.

The Progressive Education Movement was cross-fertilized between the U.S. and Britain. It did not represent one viewpoint on education but absorbed eclectic philosophies from a variety of theorists. In the U.S. its influence was not felt until the 1930s and 1940s (Wortham, 1992). In Britain, the mid 1930s were the time of the experimental school (Whitbread, 1972). Self-chosen activity, an understanding of the individual's patterns of development, flexible grouping, and the use of more open space characterized these schools.

To facilitate learning, teachers needed to become more aware of the individual's stage of development to work out what was needed for each child. Methods of observing and recording that information started to become more popular.

Watson's theory of **behaviourism** (1930) influenced thinking about how children learn. His belief that children could be made into whatever parents and society desired, by altering their learning environment, came from systematic observation of children in "set-up" situations.

Probably the most influential force in the child-centred approach to education was Piaget. Through observation of his own children he studied how children think. Development of the individual was seen as a **progression** through complex stages. American psychologists, particularly from the behaviourist school, argued against Piaget in an effort to undermine his explanations of behaviour, which he considered could be "proved" by observable behaviour (Boden, 1988).

Developmental psychologists use **naturalistic** observation to help them to appreciate the child's individual stage of development. Behaviourists use scientific methods of observation for research. Between those two extremes fall some further approaches to observation and assessment. Interpretive styles of recording information, using formats such as checklists and rating scales, came into use from the 1930s onwards (Irwin and Bushnell, 1980). They frequently combine a naturalistic approach to observation while relying on a structure that is theoretically acceptable or scientifically "proven."

The most recent developments in what is now called **developmentally appropriate assessment** are in the use of a combination of methods of observing and record keeping. While some disagree with any kind of standardized testing, others accept that formal assessments may be part of the child's evaluation. The collection of data may include naturalistic observation, in the form of narratives or samplings, checklists, and rating scales. The collection may also contain any of the following: video recordings, photographs of the child's activity, height and weight charts, formal test results, parental information and observations, a child's own record of achievement, examples of art work, tape recordings of **language** or music, teachers' reports on progress, or any other significant evidence of development. These are called **portfolios**.

◆ ◆ ◆ ◆ People Watching

A mother gazes at her newborn infant. The baby looks at her. At first the baby's sight is unfocussed yet attracted by the configuration of her face. The infant is, perhaps, "programmed" to have this interest. It encourages social interaction and leads to emotional bonding. Drawn to faces and signs of movement, the young infant learns by watching as well as through her other senses. All babies are born to be people watchers.

"Don't stare," says a mother to her young child, in the expectation that she can shape the child's instinctive behaviour. Socially acceptable behaviour requires that observation be subtle. Required behaviour is learned more by the example modelled than by verbal reinforcement; watching others is integral to the process of social learning.

Have you ever watched the hellos and goodbyes being said at an airport? If you have not been too caught up in your own emotions you might have sat and wondered about the demonstrations of feeling, the honesty of expression, or the social or cultural determination of particular behaviours. What are the stories behind all those faces? If you have done this kind of thing, then you, too, are an observer.

"I did not expect her to do that," "She must be frustrated to have that reaction," or "She is a very quiet person" are all examples of comments that people make from their informal observations. We all observe, deduce, and respond in all our communications with other people. The majority of adults go through this process without really considering what is happening.

The same process occurs when we are more conscious of making observations. The significant difference is that when we use observation as a method for collecting information we must do it carefully, systematically, and accurately.

◆ ◆ ◆ ◆ Why Observe?

Every adult involved with young children in any role or capacity will observe the children for somewhat different reasons. The adults in the child's life may be parents or other relatives, babysitters, caregivers, teachers, early childhood educators, psychologists, doctors, social workers, play therapists, students, child life workers (who work with children in hospitals), recreation leaders, camp counsellors, or any other interested party. All of these have some care duties, but the kind of responsibility varies. The following list gives some of the reasons that adults may observe children. (They are not in any particular order.)

To ensure safety
To see if the child is healthy
To notice changes in behaviour
To see what the child consumes
To learn about a child's interests
To see how long the child's attention span might be
To determine a child's physical skills and needs
To tune into the child's rhythms
To assess a program's effectiveness
To make inferences about cognitive activity
To notice social relationships
To deduce how the child is feeling
To help design a program plan for an individual or the group
To evaluate use of space
To make written records of a child's development
To assess the child for particular sensory disabilities
To help appreciate the individual's learning style
To learn about the ages and stages through which children develop
To help build skill in objective observation
To determine the progression through stages of development
To assess the behaviour with reference to "norms"

To report information to other professionals

To let a parent know how a child is developing

To enable parents to seek professional opinions about the child's progress or perceived concerns

To gain written documentation for legal purposes

To record any **regression** in behaviour

To confirm or contradict a formal assessment

To help change routines to be more effective

To determine appropriate guidance strategies

To determine when and how to "scaffold" (to extend the child's learning)

To establish the frequency of a particular behaviour

To acknowledge the complexity of the child's play

To determine the quality of interaction with an adult

To record activities undertaken

To look at a child's response to a new situation

To evaluate the effectiveness of play as therapy

To help determine the interaction between various aspects of development

To gain insight into the individual's personality and individuality

To evaluate the appropriateness of the learning environment

To determine the effect of the environment on the child

The observation may take many forms. Informal, unrecorded observation is frequently used as this can be done while participating with the children. Narrative accounts of behaviour do not rely on highly developed observation skill, and are open-ended. If looking for particular behaviours, methods that require a pre-written chart, checklist, or scale might be used.

The process of development

Assessment of development is decided on the basis of the assessor's beliefs about how that development occurs. In education, the focus has shifted from the content of what the child learns to the wider notion of the stages through which the child develops. Appreciating the process of development should not, however, be seen as being in opposition to what it is that the child learns. The two are interdependent.

If you agree that development is a dynamic, ongoing process involving stages of change in each of its aspects, then you will see that to assess that development is a complex task. Trying to see what is going on for the child is much more effective if you observe her in a natural environment rather than in a "testing situation." It is not that the lab experiment will not give useful data but that the child's behaviours will be more typical in her everyday setting.

With many theorists offering explanations of how children develop and learn, you need to select the most plausible and respond by maximizing the child's potential. This is not to suggest that you should "push" a child into accelerating development. The long-term effects of such programs, such as those run by Doman at "The Better Baby Institute," are heavily criticized by Elkind and others who appreciate the natural sequences of development and see how they can be damaged. You need to understand the stages of development through observation of the child undergoing the process, and do what you can to promote healthy development.

Piaget (1952) explained how the child creates his own knowledge through his experience of the world. By observing the child's responses to the world, you can make inferences about his thinking to supply the appropriate learning experiences. The "**zone of proximal development**," proposed by Vygotsky (1978), suggests that there is a gap between what the child can do presently in an independent manner and what the child can do in a supportive environment. This provides one of the strongest reasons to observe. The understanding of this concept underpins the validity of observation.

The term "**scaffolding**" comes from Bruner's work (1976) with infants. It describes the role of the mother in the infant's early interactions. Bruner believes that the mother provides the framework for these interactions. She connects with the child and provides bridges to make connections in the child's learning.

Both Vygotsky and Bruner's explanations indicate the necessity for careful observation to enable the adult to know when and how to intervene in the child's experience and therefore how to take responsibility for the child's development.

Focus on the individual

"Did they like the creative activity?" a teacher asked an ECE student as she came into the office. As she replied, the teacher realized that she hadn't asked a very useful question. Imagining that each child's response to a situation is identical can be a mistake. The focus must be on the behaviours of an individual child far more frequently than on the group.

If you can see only the general flow of action, you will not have insight into the set of individuals in your care. Without singling out children to observe closely, you are very likely to miss the particular skills that have been acquired and fail to acknowledge the areas of development that can be addressed.

Individuals do function within groups. Group dynamics can be better understood when the individuals in the group are first observed separately. For this reason, adults must learn to work at observing individual children and avoid making assumptions or generalizations. Later observations can centre on the interactions within the group.

Observation as developmentally appropriate assessment

The strengths of observation as a form of assessment are numerous. Observation:

◆ enables adults to take responsibility for the process of the child's development.
◆ of behaviour is the key to evaluating development.
◆ is significant because adults can bring about changes in a child's behaviour.
◆ focusses on what a child can do.
◆ forms the foundation of effective individual program planning and group planning.
◆ allows for variation and individuality of children in their development and needs.
◆ presupposes no curriculum theory but can support almost all types of program planning.
◆ can be more objective and tends to be less biased than standardized tests.
◆ allows for understanding of each interacting aspect of development.
◆ enables evaluation to be carried out in familiar surroundings.
◆ can be quicker and more effective then other methods of gaining information about development.
◆ encourages parental involvement and professional team work.

The Observer Role

"Watching the kids" is a phrase sometimes used to mean looking after or caring for children. It is interesting that the non-professional term accentuates a responsibility for observation.

There are conflicts in our jobs as caregivers, teachers, and parents. Consider a parent who spends a lot of his time watching his children and pointing out to everyone how advanced they are. He does not take responsibility for interacting or even being with them, but observes and expresses his pride in their accomplishments. Other parents and caregivers may be so busy doing practical domestic jobs that they don't take time to "stand and stare" – to watch with any sense of wonder or intrigue. Some are so involved with the children's activities that they do not notice their changing behaviours and increasing skills.

All adults involved with children need to observe constantly. Only a small amount of the information observed can be recorded or analyzed. Active involvement with the children can make more formal observations difficult. Some methods enable us to be interactive as we observe, but these require refined skill.

Non-participant observation

Early attempts at the more formal types of observing and recording need to be done while the observer is detached from the children. Students and skill-building teachers need to take themselves away from the children and become non-participant observers. In the practice of observation, the student educator's perspective will alter and he will gradually notice things that he missed, be more objective about what he does see, and be more analytical about the information recorded. This non-participant role is a necessary part of learning to observe effectively.

As a practising teacher, it will be necessary from time to time to remove yourself from direct contact with the children. This helps the teacher to see more carefully what is happening and usually leads to the teacher being more responsive. Taking the time to be a non-participant in the program does not mean prolonged time away from the children, however, and should never be an excuse to ignore a child's needs. Suitable supervision must always be made when the responsibilities change.

With young children, it is useful to be a non-interacting observer from time to time. As long as the children's needs are met, they may not be affected by you removing yourself just far enough that you are out of their personal space but within sight and earshot. Sitting on a small chair in a position that does not interfere with their activity or is not in a significant traffic area can be useful. Here are some suggestions.

◆ Avoid making the eye contact and facial expressions that initiate communications with the children.

◆ Wear comfortable but fairly plain clothes, avoiding anything that may be a lure to a child.

◆ Try to avoid obvious staring at a child, which could make her feel uncomfortable.

◆ Distance yourself so that you can see and hear the children but are not within their play area or personal space.

◆ Ensure that sufficient appropriate supervision is provided so that all the children's needs are met.

◆ If a child draws you into conversation, respond in simple sentences to explain what you are doing. Remember to follow through with any promises you make for doing activities with them later.

◆ Make regular times for non-participant observation so that the children get used to you doing it. Older children may learn to observe by imitating you.

◆ **Never use non-participant observation as an excuse for not being involved with the children when you should be responsible.**

Participant observation

The teacher who has gained skill in observing may make only brief recordings from time to time, but most of his observation will be done as he is involved with the children. If the teacher's skill has developed, this is quite acceptable; the teacher's level of operation will enable him to be responsive to casually observed information.

Student role

For training purposes, there are further ways of building skills in observation. Visiting child care agencies and schools may provide opportunities. Using a college's on-site lab school facilities can be particularly helpful.

There are several ways that a laboratory school can be utilized to help the student's skill development.

♦ Children can be brought to class for a set-up observation opportunity. The students would all see the same behaviour and can learn to record and analyze appropriately.

♦ Observations in the lab school can be pre-recorded for replay in class. Going over the material as a class can be a good practice when what is seen is the same for everyone.

♦ Students can go into the lab school and observe as non-participants. Situations can be set up so that students can focus on the same aspect of development.

♦ Observation booths can enable students individually or in groups to observe children. Ideally there would be a sound system to enable them to pick up language and other sound. This is a non-intrusive way of observing, which does not influence the recording. Students can observe while others set up activities for the children, taking the interactive role.

♦ If the centre is large enough, students may be able to do a placement at the lab school. As they get to know the children better than a visitor, the students can try out observation styles in non-participant and participant approaches.

The purpose for focussed observation for the students in a class situation may need to be explained to the parents and teachers of the children to be observed. Of course, permission should be gained.

♦ ♦ ♦ ♦ # Professionalism and Confidentiality

When you receive a psychological or medical report, it may arrive with a confidential sticker attached, making it clear that the report contains information to which there should be limited access. The circle of stakeholders involved in an observation, or those who require a degree of access to the information it contains, may be wider than you might at first imagine. This can present some challenges.

Who does, or should have, access to the formal records or informal notes that teachers and caregivers need to keep? While legal requirements vary, you need to ensure that you interpret and practise **professionalism**, and, when appropriate, **confidentiality**, in regard to all the information that is stored or shared. The basic principle is that information about a child is the concern only of that child and his custodial parent or guardian and of anyone with whom the parent consents to share it. In taking responsibility for the care or education of a child, you need to ensure that any legal requirements regarding access to information and privacy are met. Regarding the practice of recording observational and other information, it is necessary to be clear about with whom the information is shared and how that is to happen. Within the agency there needs to be a policy that determines who has access to information and in what circumstances.

All written records need to be kept in a secure, preferably locked, file. They should be labelled and dated. Files need to be updated regularly; all entries should be signed by their contributor. Any significant content must be communicated to the parents in an appropriate manner with any necessary explanations. Access to the child's file should be open to parents at any reasonable time. If you think that there is any cause to withhold information from a parent, it is quite probable that the content is inappropriate and possibly subjective.

It is easier to accept the need for confidentiality with formal documents. The challenge of the practising teacher is to maintain the same level of confidential treatment with all pieces of information regarding a child. The comfort level of parents in the degree to which privacy is an issue is very personal and may be culturally determined. Avoiding taking risks is essential and may require careful organization. While you may think that a posted chart recording the feeding, sleeping, and elimination pattern of the day is acceptable for an infant, you need to work out with a parent group what is appropriate practice in your setting.

In the days when all the children ran out of school clutching their readers of varying proficiency levels, it was quite clear to the parents (as well as the children themselves) who was at the "top" or "bottom" of the reading class. You can avoid this kind of practice, which lacks privacy.

Briefing parents about their child's challenging behaviour might be an excellent idea. While it is particularly useful to share daily observations, you must be sensitive about timing. Not only might the end of the parents' day be the "wrong time" to deliver seemingly bad news, but also offering the comments when others might overhear is inconsiderate.

The student is in a difficult position with regard to confidential record keeping. Observations made by a student about a child should not easily reveal the identity of the child to anyone who might accidentally come across the observation. As the student is a learner, the observations may not be as objective as they could be, and the inferences they contain might not be appropriate. Deductions made by the student may be based on insufficient information or analyzed on the basis of an inaccurate explanation of the behaviour.

Agencies have varying attitudes to students' access to the child's records. It may be understood at some agencies that the student is in a better position to appreciate the child's behaviour if some contextual information is offered, but to many in supervisory roles, this presents an unnecessary intrusion into the family's privacy. Centres working with students need to make some decisions about the way permission is sought to undertake the observation (see permission form) and the amount of information about the child that is offered. It is true that information may bias the observer's objectivity in recording. An agency might request that observations made by students are counter-signed by a member of their staff to indicate their acceptance that permission to make the observation was made. Feedback can be very useful for the student. Students may find that they have contributed new insights to the professional's knowledge of the child; the staff may give some idea of whether or not the observation represents a "true likeness" of the child.

◆ ◆ ◆ ◆ Objective Observation

You may be relieved to hear that it is impossible to be completely objective when observing children. It is a hard task to move beyond the "**objective**" and "**subjective**" and work towards an acceptable level of objectivity in all observation and recording. This idea is captured by Cohen and Stern:

> *For teachers observing the children with whom they work and live, absolute objectivity is impossible, and objectivity itself becomes a relative thing. As a matter of fact, it is to be hoped that no teacher would ever try for so much objectivity that she would cease to be a responsible and responsive adult to her group.* (1978)

No two people will see the same child in an identical way. Two open and honest teachers can be asked to observe the same child. What they will see and the sense that they make of it will depend on what they decide to look for and their particular perspectives. To the scientist this might appear to be an unacceptable variation. You need to decide on what is an acceptable degree of objectivity. According to the two teachers, each tells the "truth," or their version of it. How can you ensure that you keep to the

Permission Form

Child Observations, Case Studies, and Portfolios

Student and Parent Agreement

Without written permission I will not observe and record information about your child. Please sign in the space provided if you agree that I may make observations and study your child. It would be helpful if you could initial each of the boxes if you are willing for me to undertake any or all of the techniques of information gathering.

I _____ (student name) will not refer to the child in any written manner by his or her real name. Information recorded will be written objectively, treated professionally, and kept confidential.

_____   _____
(student signature)   (date)

I/We _____
       (parents' names)

agree to have _____
               (child's name)

observed ❑   photographed ❑   audiotaped ❑   videotaped ❑

by _____
   (student's name above)

at _____
   (agency/home)

for the purpose of study in child development at _____
(school/college) for a period of _____ (weeks/months) on the consideration that copies are made available to us, the parents, if we so request.

_____   _____
(parent's signature)   (date)

---

truth when others see the child's behaviour in a different light? How you see depends on your skill in observing, what you are seeking, and your own perspective. If these are the variables, you can improve observer reliability by increasing your skill, determining what you are looking for, and reviewing your personal perspective.

The Objectivity Continuum

Objectivity ————————— Subjectivity

- a demonstration of a concept that has no absolutes
- all observations fall between the two opposites
- objectivity is usually desirable
- subjectivity is not always "wrong"
- appreciation of the reasons for the degree of objectivity is always essential

---

Bias

Whatever stage you are at in your professional or adult life, you have had experiences that shape your perceptions. The way you take in information is determined by your previous experience and knowledge. You bring to situations previously acquired attitudes and beliefs. Some of these are well founded; others are born of some **bias** that comes from incorrectly understood information, negative experiences, or inappropriate generalizations. Most biases are subtle, and may be unrecognizable to others. Some biases may be much more blatant and recognizable to others and even considered to be acceptable.

The observer can eliminate many of his biases by acknowledging and confronting them. In due course, a practised observer will be able to analyze his recordings for bias. The observer will eventually realize that there is more to observation than seeing. What separates human observation from a mechanical means of recording is how you *perceive* what you observe. The selection of how, when, and what to observe is a skill.

You come to observe with some useful preconceived ideas as well as inappropriate biases. While you must build the background knowledge base, you have to avoid biases when you can and address them when they do exist.

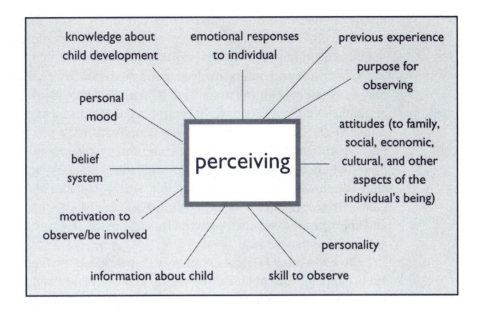

Perceptions

How you see is influenced by your experience, which has shaped your thinking.

Teamwork

Many people have a role in the caring, nurturing, and education of each child. Where there is responsibility for a child, there is a need for observation and assessment of that child.

Parents are the most significant stakeholders in children's lives. They may be the adults who take the leading role in observing their child and responding appropriately to her needs. Quite naturally and spontaneously, a mother or father will watch their child; it may elicit a wide range of feelings and responses. This informal monitoring of the child's behaviour, and noticing of changes in health or development, may well be the most significant assessment that is ever done. The professional involved in the child's care must never forget that the child is a member of a family and that family may be able to offer closer insights than the trained caregiver. No assessment could ever be complete without the inclusion of the parent's observations.

The front line caregivers need to consider their observations in the light of what is known about the child. This is done most usefully in discussion with co-workers and parents. Interested parties may be able to exchange observations in a relatively informal way – frequently at the start or end of the day or, perhaps, at nap-time for a younger child.

Supervisors and others involved in the delivery of care and education may add their own observations or help in making objective inferences about the child. When behaviour is observed that causes concern or is difficult to interpret, an "outside" professional, such as a psychologist, may be brought in. Legislation varies but professional principles and good practice indicate that this should be done after seeking parental permission, support, and involvement. Psychologists, occupational therapists, child care consultants, and social workers will not be able to make a fair and appropriate assessment without input from the day-to-day caregiver and the parents.

The TPBA model (Transdisciplinary Play Based Assessment) (Linder, 1990) offers the idea of holistic assessment, with the involved professionals working with the parents in a way that enables all parties to observe simultaneously and take the time to discuss deductions that have been made. Linder states, "Team discussion is critical, and having the same foundation improves team communication."

Not all observations are, or could be, conducted when all those who are involved are present. Communication systems need to be in place for the sharing of information in ways that are convenient.

The team approach increases the reliability of inferences that are made from observation. This model also encourages each adult to take responsibility in the process. An indicator of good quality child care is the practice of team work in observation and program planning.

◆ ◆ ◆ ◆ Choice of Observation Method

There is a wide range of methods of recording information. As you read this book you might want to try some new ways or practice some of those familiar to you. When choosing a method you will need to ask yourself the following questions:

1. Are you in a non-participatory role or do you have responsibility for the children as you observe?
2. Do you have the language skills to enable you to write detailed narrative descriptions?

3. Why are you observing? What are you looking for?
4. Is the purpose of observing to increase your skill or for the child's direct benefit?
5. Do you appreciate what the various methods of information collecting will tell you – and can you choose appropriately?
6. Have you developed strategies to summarize and make sense of the observational information collected?

If in doubt about where to start, work through the methods presented in this book. They are offered in a sequence that is appropriate for the observation student or skill-developing practitioner. As informal observation is what everyone has done without training, continue to do this. Your skill will improve as you record but your casual observations will gradually take on greater meaning as you continue the process. Narrative recordings require little interpretive skill and so may be a method of choice for the relatively unskilled. As you find new ways of charting behaviours, checking off behaviours on lists, and using styles needing inference in their recording, your background understanding of child development will also expand. Your learning will accelerate if you study theories of child development at the same time as improving your observations. Each will benefit the other.

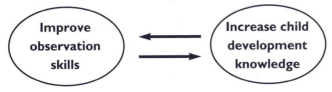

♦ ♦ ♦ ♦ # Observation as Part of an Assessment Procedure

Early childhood specialists focus more on the process of the child's learning than on its products. Observation of the process can tell us much about the child that would not be revealed by viewing only such products as the child's art work and writing. It is important, however, not to disregard the significance of such products. If you can gather information about the child from various sources, and in a variety of ways, you are going to be in a better position to make evaluations.

Formal **assessment** tools may require "**tests.**" (These are dealt with in Chapter 8.) The best of these have an observation component. Even in a structured play situation, the child is in a better position to be evaluated more fairly than in a testing situation. A restrictive "testing environment" can create stress. The child can demonstrate her skills more readily in a situation that resembles what she is used to. Members of an assessment team are wise to get their data through a variety of methods to ensure that they include naturalistic observations.

The portfolio technique combines the best of the evaluation styles. A portfolio can contain observations, charts, products of the child's efforts, test results, parental contributions, medical notes and any other pertinent information. It forms a record that can be added to at any time. The portfolio forms long-term documentation of the child's education, health, and experience to which those involved with the child may refer. As the child grows, she may choose items for inclusion to her own portfolio that form a personal record of achievement. Looking back at the child's life experience can stir the emotions and can supply significant information about her patterns of behaviour. (A full explanation of the portfolio method is given in Chapter 7.)

Focus on emerging skills

Observation is not necessarily an exercise to identify "strengths" and "weaknesses" in children's behaviour. Such value judgments are usually inappropriate in naturalistic observation. What you can do is to look at the skills that are present – rather than focus on what the child cannot do. Programs are more positive and more likely to be effective if they are planned on the basis of enabling the child to build skills from "where he is" rather than from what he has failed to do. A more developmentally appropriate curriculum plan should result from focussing on emerging skills.

Summarizing information

Often confused with analysis, the observation summary is a recap or overview of the essential parts of the observation. In many open-ended observations, the summary may try to collect information to identify or list behaviours seen. Here there is no interpretation but a look at the "totality" of objectively recorded behaviours. Developmental domains might be used as categories in the summary.

In a more structured observation that looks for particular identified behaviours, the summary might contain information such as the number, frequency, duration, or triggers for those behaviours. The summary is intended to be a brief outline of significant observed behaviour.

Understanding Development through Observation

You may wish that you could open up a door to see what is going on in a child's mind. You can certainly open the windows of your eyes to observe behaviours that can give you insight into a child's thinking.

Physical skills are the most easily understood aspect of development. A gross or fine motor skill is either present or absent; its quality is relatively easy to measure. Narrative recordings usually concentrate on the child's "activity," which is analyzed on the basis of the acknowledgment of what "physical skills" were demonstrated.

Communications and language are a little more challenging to observe because they can happen so quickly, and require accurate recording and somewhat more interpretation. Making deductions about the way in which a child is feeling is even more subjective. Observations frequently contain inappropriate **judgments** and assumptions about these emotions. Frequently deductions are made on the basis of facial expressions and body language, but these can lead to incorrect assessments.

Social interactions may be observed relatively easily. "Connections" between individuals can be recorded fairly objectively but you will tend to project your own biases when you record. Observers can be unaware that a belief that being sociable is desirable may colour what they actually see. Recordings need to be examined for these subtle biases. Some structured observations, such as those by Mildred B. Parten in the 1930s, were successful in overcoming such biases.

One of the most difficult areas of the child's development to observe is that of **cognition**. Any statement about mental activity can only be considered an inference. Piaget frequently focussed on the mistakes that children made rather than their "correct" answers or responses. He did, however, look at many kinds of children's behaviour to determine his theoretical explanations of development. You can observe with the help of these and other models; they can help you to know what to look for and appreciate what you see.

Only through a combination of practice in observation skill, increase in knowledge of developmental "**norms**," and a continued growth in the understanding of theoretical explanations can you begin to use observation as an effective tool for evaluation.

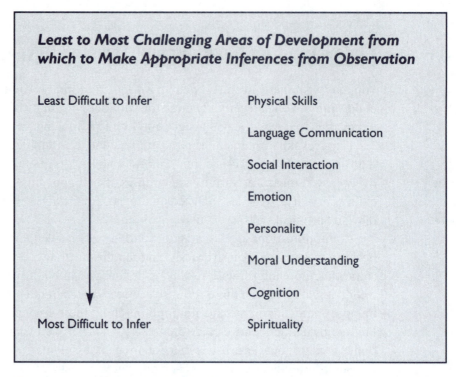

Least to Most Challenging Areas of Development from which to Make Appropriate Inferences from Observation

Least Difficult to Infer   Physical Skills

Language Communication

Social Interaction

Emotion

Personality

Moral Understanding

Cognition

Most Difficult to Infer   Spirituality

This sequence is offered to highlight the challenge to the observer in making sense of observational information. It is based on the idea that behaviours that are clearly observable are easier to interpret. The sequence focusses on the evaluation of the child's progression through developmental stages. (It is not intended to be a hierarchy of difficulty in attributing theoretical explanations as to why the behaviour is demonstrated.)

Analyzing the content of an observation

There are a few basic rules of analysis:

1. Focus on what was observed and recorded, not on other less accurate "bits of information."
2. Always separate the observation from its **analysis**.

3. Do not make inferences unless you can support them; that is:

    a. identify the specific behaviour(s) that gives you the cause to make such a deduction.

    b. support your **inference** with reason(s).

    c. **validate** each statement with the use of at least one (preferably all) of the following:

        (i)   observations made by others with similar inferences

        (ii) use of theoretical explanations

        (iii) comparison with recognized "norm"

    d. state the source of validation – professional input or book reference.

    e. use inferential language carefully:

    "it appears that … on the basis of … I think that … demonstrates behaviours in excess of … norm for his age."

    f. avoid judgments, assumptions, and generalizations that cannot be substantiated regarding background, social, or contextual information. For example, do **not** say "this is because he is an only child" or "he is much smarter than his brother" or "her English is poor because her parents don't communicate with her."

4. Put on paper only what you consider to be professional and could be challenged about.

5. Keep the analysis as well as the observation confidential. Students and teachers may find the word "analysis" quite off-putting or coldly scientific.

To make the "analysis" a more easily understood concept you may find it useful to think of this part of the observation process as the "making sense of what I saw" section. The easiest way to go about an analysis is to ask oneself, and then answer, a series of questions about what was observed. If the observation is set up to seek particular information, then that needs to be addressed first. Unless citing the source of "extra" information, it is best to stick to analyzing only what was in the observation just completed.

Structuring the analysis in a way that considers each of the developmental areas is helpful. Any section where there is no significant information can be left out. In practice you might find the following suggested plan a good idea. Adapt it to fit your needs. Write it up according to the required style, either in an essay or in notes under the organized headings. Note that it is by no means a complete list.

Plan to Assist the Analysis

BACKGROUND

What was the reason for observing? (Was I seeking specific information?)
Did the observation occur spontaneously; was the child aware of being observed?
What is my role as observer? (non-participant...)
Did I have any preconceived ideas about what I was going to see?
What contextual information might be helpful?
Who gave permission for or input into the process?

METHOD

Why did I choose this method of observing?
Were there any concerns regarding the procedure?
Did the method reveal what I wanted? What was it?

CONTENT

Physical development

What gross motor skills were demonstrated?
What fine motor or manipulative skills were seen?
What activity was the child observed doing?
What responses did the child make to any sensory experience (sight, hearing, touch, smell, or taste)?

Social development

What evidence was there of the child's sense of self?
What kinds of connection was the child making with
a.   adults?
b.   other children?
What adult interaction did I observe?
Describe the quality of the interactions.
What kind of self-help skills were seen?
Were there any examples of independence or dependence?
What can I see that indicates understanding of social roles and behaviour?

Emotional development

What demonstrations of feelings did I observe:
a.   in language?
b.   in posture and body language?
c.   in gestures?

Was there indication of control of feelings?
What attachments were evident?
What moods did I see?

Play
Did I see the child in onlooker, solitary, parallel associative, or cooperative activity?
What type of play (if any) was observed (e.g., one or more of imaginative, imitative, pretend, fantasy, sociodramatic, superhero, social constructional, functional, physical, or other)?
How long and involved were these sequences?
Was the play self-initiated and self-supported?
What props were used?

Language and communication
What utterances were made (in what language)?
What indications of non-verbal communication did I observe?
What kind of structure has the language?
How extensive was the child's vocabulary?
How effective was the communication?
What was the child's interpersonal style?

Moral and spiritual development
Do any of the observed behaviours indicate an understanding of "rights" or "social justice"? If so, how?
Are any of the behaviours pro-social in nature (empathetic, altruistic, sharing, taking turns, helping others)?
Is there evidence of beliefs about any philosophical issues, such as creation of things, in the child's world?
Do I see the child's curiosity and sense of wonder?
Does the child demonstrate respect for the dignity of others?
What indication is there of the child's categorizing himself into a subculture (racially, in belief system, family make up, dialect, etc.)?
What demonstration is there of an understanding, compliance, or rejection of any kind of rules or guidelines?

Personality
Did I observe any behaviours that indicate temperamental type (e.g., slow to warm, extrovert, orderly, etc.)?
What reactions to stimuli did I see?

Cognition

What draws the child's attention? How long was the span of concentration?
What behaviours indicated thought process?
Did I notice any "mistakes" the child made?
Did the demonstrated language or behaviour show understanding of any of the basic concepts (e.g., colour, shape, time, space, classification, relativity, seriation, conservation)? If so, what?
Does the child "experiment" with materials?
Is there evidence of conditioned responses?
Did I see any trial and error strategies?
What evidence might there be of an understanding of symbolism in language or behaviour?
Is there evidence of use of memory?
Is any of her art representational?
What behaviours indicate to me how the child perceives her world?
Did the child use concrete objects to help her perform tasks? Can she use any forms of abstraction?
What humour did she initiate or respond to?

The whole child

What outside influences affected what I observed?
In what ways did I see aspects of the child's development interact?

Each of the above questions needs responses incorporating deductions that cite the section of the observation to which they are related and are validated appropriately. For practice you might like to use the following chart. People who like to tabulate information may use this format in answer to each of the questions given above.

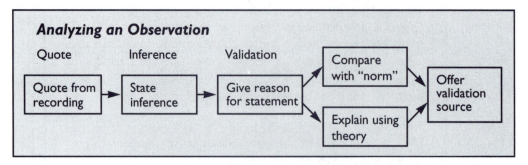

Analyzing an Observation

Quote → Inference → Validation → Compare with "norm" / Explain using theory → Offer validation source

Quote from recording → State inference → Give reason for statement → Compare with "norm" → Offer validation source

Give reason for statement → Explain using theory → Offer validation source

In each of the areas you will explore, ensure that all deductions and inferences can be supported. If such inferences are "checked" using this model they can be evaluated for their objectivity and likelihood of being accurate.

How to Support Your Inferences

Section of observation	Inference(s)	My reasoning	Validation by others	by theory	Reference to "norm"	Resources used
When Tom was playing with the other boys at the construction activity.	a. Tom played cooperatively.	He initiated directions to others and followed their lead.	Assistant teacher has noticed increased cooperation this week.	Clear example of cooperative play.	Typical of five-year-old.	Parten
	b. Tom used brief three and four word phrases to convey his ideas – he appeared not to need more complex language.	The children understood him but Tom's language was very simple because he didn't have to explain himself.	Mom says Tom can speak more fluently but frequently plays quite quietly for long periods with his friend.	Tom has good receptive skills but his expressive language is less evident – frequently demonstrated imbalance.	Five-year-olds can usually speak in complex sentences, but frequently choose not to.	Sheridan
Jamilia says, "There are more here" as she points to counters that have been rearranged (but both groups contain the same number).	Jamilia has not yet conserved the constancy of "six" and is fooled by what looks like more.	She can count to six but doesn't understand that six remains six even if the pile looks different.	Not observed by others.	Feature of pre-operational thinking that number may not yet be conserved.	Four-year-olds typically will not have gained this concept.	Piaget
When Tarmattie left her mom quickly on her first day at the centre.	Tarmattie seems confident, extroverted, and quick to respond to new situations.	I had not expected a two-year-old to separate so easily. Her temperament enabled her to leave mom and explore her new environment.	Mom observed and was also surprised.	Tarmattie's sense of self is clearly defined. She is securely attached, and comfortable with leaving mom for brief periods.	Securely attached children may separate more comfortably that others at this age/stage.	Thomas & Cross
					Her extroverted style may be relatively unchanging but is seen in well-attached toddlers.	Ainsworth

If your inferences cannot be validated then they should not be stated. With practice in going through the sequence of validation you will be able to discuss in writing what you are being forced to consider by fitting in the chart

Development of the Whole Child

THE CHILD'S EXPERIENCE

perceived culture	education, school/care programs	dwelling place
subcultural membership		gender
ethnicity	**THE WHOLE CHILD**	media influences
economics	physical development	exposure to political ideologies
acceptance/ encouragement	genetic inheritance cognition	
	language, communication	geographical location
employment/ occupation	moral/spiritual development self/social	
moral beliefs	personality	citizenship
family composition	emotion	language/ dialect
	religious practices	

The child is at the centre. Each interacting aspect of her development is affected by all of the environmental factors that contribute to her experience of the world. You observe the behaviours that help you to make inferences about the whole child's development.

◆ ◆ ◆ ◆ Using Observational Data to Plan

Those who teach teachers often say that students need to learn how to set goals and objectives for children. They sometimes go on to say that, after they have learned how, they won't always have to state such goals for their planning when they become practising teachers. Such a philosophy makes people believe that achievement is only possible with goal setting. It disregards the idea that children will, given appropriate open-ended experiences and support that enable them to operate at their own level, progress through the developmental stages. Learning and skill development are not only dependent upon our overt intervention. There is a difference between making appropriate curriculum provision based on observation of the child's developmental needs and goal setting that is presumptuous in assuming that you know what is the child's "next stage." However knowledgeable you are about patterns of development, it is rarely useful to set specific goals for children who are in the mainstream of our education and care agencies.

Children who have special needs that are identified and diagnosed may benefit from a more structured goal setting approach because objectives may need to be set to break down skills into component parts. These objectives can be addressed separately.

Interpretation of observational information is essential for all planning and curriculum design activities. Many inappropriate assessments have resulted in poor provision; the teacher's focus should be on supplying appropriate experiences and guidance to support the child in his own efforts to struggle with new skills.

Whether or not you set goals in the process of your program planning may be inconsequential to how appropriate the plan may be. If you choose to set goals you might be more focussed on the child's specific needs; thoughtful programming must always have some deliberate intention.

Individual program plans

IPPs and IEPs (**Individual Program Plans** and **Individual Education Plans**) are commonly devised to respond to the needs of children with identified special needs. All children have individual needs that should be met. The IPP helps you in that task. This is a way of formalizing the process of converting observational and other assessment information into an action plan.

An IPP needs to have a team approach to piece together all available information about a child and come up with an appropriate response to the child's individual needs. At its best it is a dynamic ongoing process that changes and is adapted in the light of new information.

Informal IPPs are devised regularly with parents and teachers working cooperatively in the effort to observe, evaluate, assess needs, and respond to them. In this case it might not be a recorded plan.

In situations in which there is a specific need to address concerns about the child's development it can be a much more thorough, written teamwork process that has clearly defined intentions and practical suggestions or objectives designed for implementation.

Individual Program Plan

Child's name: _____   D.O.B.: _____   Teacher: _____

Date: _____   Persons participating: _____

Reason for program development:

Developmental area	Observation summary (skills present)	Needs	Intentions	Practical supports	Person responsible

Individual Program Plan Review

Child's name: _____   D.O.B.: _____   Teacher: _____

Date: _____   Persons participating: _____

Reasons for review:

Developmental domains	Previous intentions	Observed skills	Progress made	Newly devised supports	Person responsible

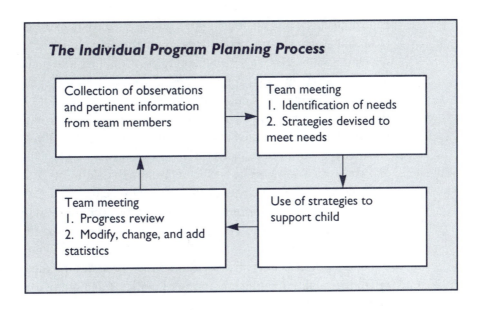

The Individual Program Planning Process

Collection of observations and pertinent information from team members

→

Team meeting
1. Identification of needs
2. Strategies devised to meet needs

↓

Team meeting
1. Progress review
2. Modify, change, and add statistics

←

Use of strategies to support child

↑

Observation as part of curriculum planning

The child's **curriculum** is her whole experience of life. What you may have thought of as "the program" or even "planned activities" are only a small element of that whole experience. When you take care to observe children in every aspect of their day, from waking, through all kinds of family inter-actions and domestic scenarios as well as more carefully designed daycare or school experiences, you can appreciate the child's style, indi-viduality, and social context, and how these affect her responsiveness and developing skills. As a trained observer you may make useful inferences from observation in an agency or school setting. Those observations will be much more revealing if you have some previously acquired informa-tion that tells you something about the child's family and background.

Making efforts to appreciate more about a child from observing her as widely as possible pay off because we can put together a picture of the "whole" rather than have only unconnected bits of information about some specific area of development.

The great challenge for the teacher is to take time to observe the indi-vidual within the group while acknowledging the dynamics of that group and endeavouring to provide for the needs of each of the children. These can come closer if the teacher appreciates that her skill in observing needs to be acute, that she understands what are the more "**normal" patterns** of development and evolves a philosophy of curriculum that includes the idea that everything that she provides, including herself, is part of the curriculum provision. If children are enabled to operate at their own level the variation of development within the group can be addressed, and that in providing changing environments the child is able to build his own knowledge.

These are attainable but difficult and time-consuming skills for the teacher to achieve. The teacher struggles with the notion that much of the time she is making compromises. These will be acceptable to the teacher if she realizes that some compromise is necessary in the most effective curriculum design.

Observation as part of curriculum design provides the means for ongoing evaluation of the environment of the development of each of the children in the group. By observing, the teacher can know if her intentions are being fulfilled in terms of the children's learning. How the children respond to the experiences helps her to see how the environment might be changed or modified to facilitate learning.

Teachers and caregivers may use observation as a means of assessing the achievement of previously set goals and objectives. While this may work for some teachers, it may not work for others, particularly if their educational philosophy is not one of goal setting.

Process of curriculum design:
Observe ⟶ Record ⟶ Interpret ⟶ Plan ⟶ Implement

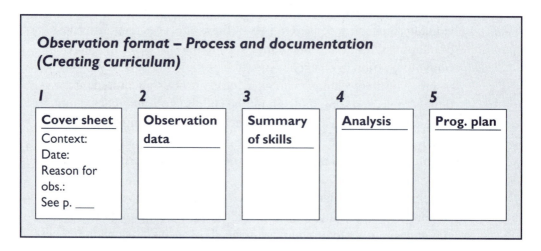

Observation format – Process and documentation
(Creating curriculum)

1	2	3	4	5
Cover sheet Context: Date: Reason for obs.: See p. ___	**Observation data**	**Summary of skills**	**Analysis**	**Prog. plan**

◆ ◆ ◆ ◆ Assignment options

Individual tasks

a. Think of reasons why human beings tend to watch each other. Write down a list of your ideas.

b. Watch a videotaped segment of children involved in any kind of activity. Watch it again, looking only at the child's fine motor skills. What did you see differently?

c. Research information about Montessori, Pestalozzi, Froebel, or Piaget. Find out what their approach was to observing children.

d. Compare the participant and non-participant observer roles. Identify the advantages and disadvantages of each role.

e. Ask practising teachers how they observe and record information about children. Request information about how these teachers plan the curriculum on the basis of what they observe.

Group tasks

a. On flip chart paper, brainstorm ideas about the conditions that could cause an observer to be biased.

b. Arrange to watch a play sequence with a small group of children. With everyone observing the same child, write down *everything* that child says and does for 10 minutes. Afterwards, compare your results in pairs. Did you see and record the same information? Explain.

c. With everyone in pairs, take turns in observing each other. Can you record all the behaviours? Is the one observed affected by being observed? How?

d. Observe and record everything a child says and does for five minutes. Have a partner act out what is recorded. Reverse roles. What happened? Did you get down sufficient information so that it could be re-enacted?

e. Show any five-minute videotaped segment of children at play. Members of the group write down any inferences that they can make. The group evaluates the inferences using the model on p. 26.

f. On the floor, mark with chalk or masking tape a "life-size" version of the flow chart on p. 26. Having shared a recorded observation, proceed through the process with the inferences that are made by the individual. Group members check to see if the inference can be validated step by step. Who can go through the *whole* process?

g. Brainstorm ideas on flip chart paper about why observation is important. Discuss the answers and prioritize them according to their importance in supporting the child's needs.

h. Role play a scene in which you try to explain to a parent why you want to observe his or her child and have a psychologist come to see how she is progressing with her social skills.

◆ ◆ ◆ ◆ Answers to focus questions

1. Educators believe that they can make a difference to the experience of the child. Observing children will help them to learn more about the needs and developmental patterns of children. Individual children can be observed so that their style, characteristics, skills, and needs can be identified and understood.

2. Spontaneous activity can tell adults much about the children's interests, motivation, concentration span, play patterns, emotional well being, physical skills, social interactions, moral understanding, and cognitive functioning. Operating without direction, children are more likely to show their true competence than they might in testing situations.

3. Observational information can be written down as narrative descriptions, or charted, sampled, rated, checked off on lists, photographed, audiotaped, videotaped, or stored in computer systems.

4. Awareness of biases is essential to objective recording. Practice in observing may help the recorder avoid judgments and assumptions, but it depends on the observer's commitment to strive for objectivity and evaluate the statements that he makes. Validating all inferences through a process of ensuring that they hold true and can be supported helps the observer to be objective and accurate.

5. The human being perceives information according to his previous experience and the attitudes and beliefs that have evolved from that experience. The observer must wish to be open-minded. Awareness of personal biases can only be achieved if the observer acknowledges his own philosophy and belief system and willingly submits to some uncomfortable experiences that alter his world view. Cross-checking with experienced professionals and evaluating recorded observations for their bias is a necessary and on-going process.

6. The validity of interpretations must always be checked before they are relied upon. The objectivity of the observation itself is the primary source of concern; inaccuracy in recording will inevitably lead to inappropriate conclusions being drawn. Frequently interpretations are made on the basis of too little information. Significant comments will likely be based on observation of more than one occurrence of a behaviour. The observations must be evaluated, in an effort to avoid an invalid conclusion. Valid interpretations can usually hold up against the inferences of others and be found to be consistent. (Of course, it is possible that both parties made the wrong conclusion.) The statement should be supported with reasons as to why it has been made and a reference to the specific behaviours from which the observer has made the conclusion. Further validation of an inference will lie in the use of theoretical models which are used to explain a behaviour. Comparison with an accepted norm-referenced schedule may also assist in the validation process. If the interpretation cannot be validated it should not be stated.

◆ ◆ ◆ ◆ Key Terms

observation
preformationism
kindergarten
maturation
child-centred
behaviourism
progression
developmental psychology
naturalistic
developmentally appropriate
   assessment
language
portfolios
scaffolding
regression
zone of proximal development
professionalism

confidentiality
objective
subjective
bias
assessment
tests
physical skill
judgments
cognition
norms
analysis
inferences
IPP – Individual Program Plan
IEP – Individual Education Plan
validate
curriculum
normal patterns

2 Narratives

The diary shares with the specimen record the advantage of providing rich, detailed description of behaviour, breadth of coverage, and the permanency of the written record.
Warren Bentzen (1993)

Observing young children at play, one is struck by the length of time that a child can spend blowing bubbles and learning about their characteristics, dressing up in adult or super hero clothes and trying on various roles, exercising creative talent while making a collage of found materials, figuring out how to build a snow creature or listening attentively to a story.
Ada Schermann (1990)

Narrative observations help us to notice what the child is doing in a more objective, detailed way. It is much easier to identify his fine motor skills than his thinking.

Focus Questions

1. How can you record a child's behaviour to capture every detail of action, reaction, posture, gesture, and communication without using a video camera?

2. What can you discover by describing in detail a randomly selected sequence of a child's play activity?

3. How can you avoid interpreting your observations according to your own biases?

4. For people whose writing skill is not very strong, what are some creative ways to record detailed descriptions of behaviour?

5. Anybody can write down what they see – what difference does it make to observe children with a trained eye?

6. Writing down particular incidents a child is involved with may be amusing, but how can you choose to record really significant episodes?

History Notes

Accounts of children's development were not always derived from observation. Early theorists, such as John Locke (1632–1704), arrived at their notions about children from philosophical speculation rather than observational material.

Jean-Jacques Rousseau (1712–1778) took much more interest in real children. He was intrigued with the observations of children made by Captain James Cook (1728–1779) in Tahiti. Using these recordings he compared the Tahitian children's behaviours with those of their European counterparts. Possibly the earliest forms of human observations, called "Baby Biographies," were made by Johan Pestalozzi (1740–1827). These were day-to-day recordings of the development of young children and infants. Pestalozzi studied the behaviour of his two-and-a-half-year-old son for a short period and made significant **inferences** about the importance of the mother's role in the child's life.

Early educators, philosophers, and **psychologists** frequently studied their own offspring. Charles Darwin (1809–1882) wrote anecdotal accounts of his son's behaviour in an attempt to explore his development. Sigmund Freud (1856–1939) used narrative accounts of early childhood experiences to formulate his theories of infantile sexuality.

Specimen descriptions of behaviour were first used by Dresslar in 1901 in *A Morning's Observation of a Baby*. These descriptions recorded behaviour "intensively and continuously." A succession of observers helped to validate narrative recordings as an acceptable method of study.

The school of **behaviourism** was founded by John Watson (1878–1958). The behaviourists focussed on the **objective** measurement of behavioural reactions. Their research centred on experiments with animals, which were carefully set up and meticulously recorded. While the experiments gave an opportunity for narrative recording, it was not the naturalistic type of observation with which narratives are usually associated.

The behaviourists looked at the total response of an organism and relied on objectively observed behaviours to make inferences. The developmental psychologists had different views, which involved making inferences about the causes of behaviour and the patterns of development by making detailed narrative accounts of children in naturalistic settings. The most significant developmental psychologist was Jean Piaget (1896–1980). His background as a biologist and observer of natural science led him to observe and record the behaviours of his own children. These observations form the most important series of **anecdotal records** yet written. From them, he drew far-reaching conclusions about the sequences of a child's development.

Narrative observations: Definition

Narrative observations are those in which a written sequential account of what is perceived is recorded.

Running record

A method of recording an observation that involves a written description of the behaviour of the child. This requires the observer to be separate from the child to be observed and to be without immediate responsibility for the child or for other chidren in the area (non-participant). The method involves recording exactly what the child says and does in sequence as it happens. The observer can attempt this method with little previous observation skill, but increased practice enables the observer to record more detail, to describe more accurately, to avoid assumptions, to be aware of his/her own biases, and also to make better use of the **data** that are collected.

Anecdotal record

This method of recording information requires the observer, usually a practising teacher or student teacher, to write a brief account of a selected incident or behaviour soon after if occurs. Anecdotal records are frequently used because they can be written up at the end of the working day and are an appropriate method of recording developmental stages. They require some expertise on the part of the recorder to chose significant sequences of behaviour.

Diary recording

The recording of a diary, or a day-by-day written account of the child's behaviour which is dated and timed, may incorporate features of the running record or anecdotal record as the observer thinks appropriate. This record can offer some of the contextual information which could help explain the behaviours. It may be used as a vehicle for an on-going dialogue between caregiver and parents. Particularly useful for infant caregivers or for those working with children with special needs, this method enables rigorous record keeping.

Specimen record

A method of recording the precise detail of the play or other behaviour of one child with such description and clarity that a mental image can be invoked when re-reading the account. This method may be carried out for a particular reason and therefore be undertaken at a pre-designated time, e.g., to determine the child's attempts to communicate or, perhaps, the child's efforts to use a particular limb. More often it is an intensive recording method used by a psychologist or teacher not working directly with the child. Alternatively the observation may have no specific focus but offer an opportunity for thorough observation of the child in **spontaneous play** to investigate his interests, choices, or **play patterns**.

This type of recording cannot be undertaken while the observer has responsibilities for the child or children. It requires skill on the part of the observer to record all the behaviours of the child. All possible detail, including all **gross** and **fine motor** movement, **actions** and **reactions**, description of **posture**, **gesture**, facial expression, and all utterance including the exact reporting of language expressed, should be recorded.

Field Unit Analysis (Barker and Wright) divides the stream of narrative into consecutive units and gives an immediate coding of the material. Used in research, this method enables the observer to record more detailed information than a pure narrative might allow. Specimen records can use a variety of coding systems which help the observer to capture detail.

◆ ◆ ◆ ◆ Features of Narrative Observations

The recording of a child's behaviour in a narrative description is a direct non-interpretive method, in most cases. Where the observer is skilled, an accurate recording of the behaviour can be made; for the less well practised, the method can lend itself to accidental inferences being drawn and assumptions made. The running record can be undertaken by a trained teacher or untrained person. The specimen record is not used by unskilled observers. Both of these methods can be non-selective in what is recorded, in that the observer can decide on a time and place and watch to see what the child is doing at that time.

The anecdotal record, although also a narrative, is written after the event has occurred and has been chosen by the observer to be a significant behaviour.

Describing behaviour

The greatest challenge of all narrative recording is to ensure that you have included as much detail as necessary to describe what happens, and the way in which it happens, that the reader of your recording can get an accurate "visual" impression. The goal will be to strive to record very much like a video camera.

The use of an actual video camera is covered in Chapter 6. Narrative recording goes further, though, because by looking for the minute detail of behaviour, you will perceive it more closely than if you were to record it on tape. The process of making a narrative recording enables you to be a better observer. There is a place for videotaping but this methodology allows for further learning on your part.

"But I can't write down everything," many students say – and they are correct! It is impossible to ensure that you have a description of every muscle movement, blink of the eye, and breath the child makes. What you do is to describe as much as you can of what is going on – this means there is a degree of selection even if it is inadvertent or because of the limitation of our use of language. By recording, you learn to see more clearly.

Even with the intention of recording all nuances of behaviour, the practicalities mean that you use whatever skill you have to write as quickly as possible everything which seems significant. Your early observations will most likely contain a lot of information involving gross motor movement and language. Later, you may add some detail of fine manipulative skills. As you practise the method, you will probably be able to add descriptions of posture, eye contact, and more detail regarding the subtleties of communication. The skill building on your part is valuable in enabling you to write narrative recordings but it will also help in your emerging ability to "see" with new eyes.

Finding the right words can be difficult when describing behaviour and indicating the quality of actions. A review of some of the components of narrative may help you.

a. **Adjectives:** These are the describing words, used to qualify or define. Use them to signify how something is being done, e.g., a *loud* noise made the *sleeping* infant startle.

b. **Verbs:** These are the action words – they tell what is being done. These are the most significant words used in a narrative as they indicate the type of behaviour observed, e.g., she *skipped*, he *ran*, she *jumped*, he *sorted* the counters.

c. **Adverbs:** These words describe the quality of an action or modify a verb, e.g., he rose *quietly* from the chair, not saying anything, straightening his knees *slowly* as he twisted his ankles *sharply* to pass the book to the teacher.

d. **Sequencing:** The sequencing of what occurs can also be a hurdle to those people who are not good at telling stories in the order in which they happen. Some cultural groups find this a particular challenge as their language or tradition may emphasize different elements of a story line. Writing down what happens, as it happens, can help with sequencing difficulties.

e. **Tense:** Purists would have us write what is happening in the present tense, e.g., he squats down and picks up the book.

Others are mainly concerned that the tense be consistent, e.g., he squatted down and picked up the book.

Unless otherwise directed, use the one which you find the most comfortable.

f. **Observer Bias:** The direct recordings of behaviour in narrative styles have less scope for bias than the interpretive methodologies like sampling.

There are risks, however, that the observer sees from a biased perspective. Descriptive words may themselves seem biased, e.g., to describe a child as smiling may suggest happiness whereas the word *grin* may have broader connotations.

The observer may have a subjective feeling towards the child observed and consequently records, as fact, something that might be a negative interpretation, e.g., the description of a child "whining" might be a subjective description.

The selection of one anecdote rather than another may in itself contain further bias, e.g., the anecdote you select is one in which you recorded a pre-schooler being uncooperative when more often than not she is observed to cooperate and share.

Biased data presented for analysis results in inadequate invalidated **subjective** inference with little usefulness. See Chapter 1 for a more detailed explanation of observer bias.

The use of running records

The writing of descriptive sequences of children's activity is particularly useful to the teacher or caregiver whose philosophy incorporates a **child-centred** approach to planning the curriculum. Open recordings enable the observer to record whatever behaviours are demonstrated rather than looking for specific behaviour categories. The nature of a child's play is unstructured and directed by herself. If we can observe the child in action in her natural setting,what we see is the child being herself.

The lack of specific behaviours which are looked for may be a challenge to the observer because you will have to record whatever you happen to see. Skills of description and an ability to record a number of behaviours in quick succession is another concern. An untrained individual may, however, attempt the running record, which is the method of choice for students starting an observation course because it is not dependent on high levels of child development knowledge.

When looking for some behaviour in particular you may well see it because you are expecting to. If you are looking for nothing in particular, you may run the risk of not interpreting correctly what you do see – but you are more likely to be more objective.

Running records frequently contain unexpected happenings because they include anything that occurs. Here an ECE student administers first aid and support after a minor accident.

Depending on the time you undertake your running record, you are likely to see a variety of behaviours. As you write down what you see, you must not include any inferences. Leave them for your analysis when you will have to validate your comments.

In your efforts to write what you see, you might find yourself writing "he played" or possibly "she went." These are examples of phrases that do not describe with sufficient accuracy what actually happened. If you need to say what the child is doing, write down specifically how he moves and what he does rather than vague interpretive terms.

Running records are useful when planning parent interviews. Having some substantial information to share with parents helps the caregiver and parent work together. At this time the teacher may request the informal observations of a parent and add them to his collection of information about the child.

Regular **assessments** may involve the running record along with other assessment or observational tools. These may be presented at a case conference with the parents at which a multi-disciplinary or co-worker team may plan the required curriculum.

The running record is the most frequently used method for learning about children in every aspect of their development. Teachers, students, and parents gain; the process benefits everyone.

The use of the anecdotal record

Although open to greater subjectivity because of the choice made by the observer to record particular behaviours, the anecdotal record is a technique often used by psychologists, teachers, caregivers, parents, and students.

The most basic forms are those recorded by parents in a baby book or logbook of development. As the child gets older, caregivers and parents can use this method for formal record keeping for meetings with parents or, most effectively, as a log of developmental or behavioural changes. Students may learn from recording anecdotes while working with children or during observational opportunities when not engaged with the children.

Piaget recorded anecdotal observations of his own children in the 1920s. Later his observations were more systematic and focussed on asking children questions, but his early observations enabled him to formulate his cognitive theory. Here recording what seemed noteworthy enabled Piaget to study the behaviour of the child; in this case by noticing the child's mistakes or misunderstandings.

The choice of event to record can be challenging for the untrained or inexperienced. Parents may be able to identify a significant behaviour worthy of recording because of the change it indicates to previous behaviour patterns. A new strategy may be demonstrated or an **emerging skill** be seen. These would be opportune moments to record.

The degree of description required is dictated only by the necessity to detail the essential elements of the anecdote. This can be tested by the reading of the anecdote by another individual to see if they can appreciate its significance. In a similar way there is no set length of narrative for an anecdotal record. Usually a paragraph, or even two, is adequate as the context and behaviour can be captured in that time.

Anecdotal records can be kept by researchers or psychologists and classified under behavioural types, social play categories, temperamental styles, cognitive activities, child's age, etc. In this way, they can be resourced or cross-referenced so that key elements can be drawn together as required.

The practising teacher may have a card index system, record information on tapes for each child, or keep a daily log book which can be completed by parent or child. Infant caregivers may find this a particularly easy and effective way to pass information back and forth from home to agency.

Caregiving in a private home environment is particularly challenging because there is little time to write up observations. The anecdotal record enables the caregiver to make a few written notes while remaining a participant.

Time constraints are difficult for all those who work with young children. Toddlers' teachers may find the anecdotal record convenient and efficient. Fragmented bits and pieces of activity typical of the toddler can be written up as anecdotal records. They could be recorded at nap time, if the caregiver is lucky.

Accidents, potential child abuse, or serious incident reports may be written in an anecdotal form. Dated anecdotal records of a child's behavioural changes and health observations may be required and used as evidence in a court situation and considered to be important documentation.

The use of the diary recording

This may be the oldest of all narrative recording methods. Involving little technology or expertise, the diarist chooses what is significant to record. Diaries usually involve a series of anecdotal recordings. More detailed in some or all of its parts, the diary may be an open communication or a private record of events.

You can use the same diary technique for keeping an up-to-date account of the development of an individual child, or group of children. You select the significant area of development to record and write it up on a frequent, usually daily, basis. The style is often anecdotal, but other forms of recording can be included.

A parent may initiate this activity, as the daily process of recording results in a valuable document. Teachers and others may also desire an open diary to be kept as a dialogue between themselves and parents; it may encourage parental involvement where little had previously been demonstrated.

The use of specimen records

The most detailed narrative recording was described by Goodwin and Driscoll as "a comprehensive, descriptive, objective and permanent record of behaviour as it occurs." It is the most challenging of the narrative methodologies because of its comprehensive and open-ended nature.

Usually undertaken by research psychologists because of their developed skill in observing and recording, the specimen record may incorporate some coding or script writing so that maximum information is recorded. The first term used for these recordings was "specimen descriptions" and was coined by Barker and Wright in *Midwest and its Children* (1955). Their work reads like a play script rather than a full narrative description in paragraphs. Coding systems can be harder to read but form a more detailed picture of the behaviour. They may be written by re-running a video recorded sequence – particularly in a detailed movement study. Rarely, if ever, does the practising teacher have the time or reason to do this kind of observation.

Running Record

Advantages	Disadvantages
Can be used by untrained observer.	Successful recording requires fluent use of language.
Observation less likely to be affected by bias when written at the time behaviour occurs.	Bias of observer may not be obvious where **assumptions** made.
A description of child's behaviour can be used for a variety of purposes, e.g., developmental assessment, parent meetings, program planning, or learning about child development.	Observer needs to be away from responsiblities with children.
	Can be a long and laborious task to write.
Observation data can be used by team of professionals for objective analysis.	Inferences may be difficult to draw from a bulk of data.
Provides opportunity to record all behaviour, including the unexpected.	Can only be undertaken with one child at a time.
May indicate the need for further observation/assessment using other methods.	
Information accessible for analysis by others.	

Anecdotal Record

Advantages	Disadvantages
A brief account of what happened is easy to record.	Observer needs to decide what behaviour is pertinent to record.
Short anecdotes are easy to write.	Time delay can involve observer bias.
Observer can record behaviour soon after it occurs.	Relies on observer's memory.
	Selective recording can be biased.
Useful means of recording behaviour for record keeping/communication with parents.	May offer insufficient contextual information.
Data can form useful selection of significant behaviours.	Requires observer skill to record most significant behaviours.
Method can be used by almost anybody.	
Observer can concentrate on more than one child.	
Observer can remain as a participant in the program.	
May form basis of documentation used for legal purposes.	
Can be used as a learning tool for students.	

Diary Record

Advantages	Disadvantages
Easy to record.	Might be subjective in choice of content.
Useful way of keeping daily record of behaviour.	Requires persistence to keep record going daily.
Valuable tool for communicating between parents and caregivers.	Easy to overlook need to interpret data.
Provides valuable record or "keep-sake" for parents and/or agency.	Usually situation requires further observation. This alone may be insufficient.
May be used alongside other methods of observation.	Inferences may be subjective.
Can be used as a learning tool for students as part of a child study.	Selection of information may be influenced by observer bias.
Useful in determining behavioural changes and revealing patterns of behaviour.	
May be written about one or more children at a time.	
Frequently helpful to teachers in reviewing previous months/years' program or children's progress.	

Specimen Record

Advantages	Disadvantages
Gives a rich, detailed narrative description of all behaviour.	Requires refined observer skill to record.
Data collected can be analyzed by one or more professionals.	Needs observer to be non-participant in children's program.
Useful for case conferences, may be used in research work. Less likely to be affected by observer bias.	Heavily dependent on written language skill of observer.
May be focussed on one behaviour category or entirely open-ended.	Observer can observe only one child at a time.
Provides opportunity to observe unstructured play activity.	May incorporate complex coding to enable recorder to include sufficient detail.
May establish causes of behaviour.	Frequently used by professional without full contextual information and may not involve appreciation of the "whole" child.
May indicate development in one or more domain and show necessity to observe using other methods.	

How to Record a Narrative Observation

1. Decide on your reason for using the narrative method.

2. Choose one of the narrative styles that fits your reason for recording.

3. Check that you have parental permission.

4. Prepare a method chart to meet your needs.

5. Write observation as it happens in a rich, descriptive narrative or as you select behaviours to record after they occurred.

6. Write up your "neat version" of the observation as soon as possible, making only additions that you are certain help your description but do not change the content.

7. Review your data and make objective inferences as clear statements – but support your statements. (Refer to Chapter 1.)

8. Use your inference statements to learn about the child's development and devise an action plan or learning prescription. (Refer to Chapter 1.) You can share your findings with the child's parents and ask for their informal observations and input to have a cooperative plan of action.

Ways to Make Narrative Recording Easier

If your writing is a problem
Try using a tape recorder. Speak your observation into it, using verbally rich, descriptive language. Write up the observation as soon as possible before any of the detail is lost.

If English is your second language
You could try writing your observation in your own first language using the method as described. Translation may be necessary if your work is for an assignment or for record keeping. Be aware of translation affecting objectivity.
or
Tape record your observation in your first language to capture the detail and then translate as you put it down on paper.

If you cannot write fast enough
Try using a map indicating movement to accompany the observation.
or
Videotape the observation and take your time writing your version on paper, using the "pause" button and "replay" frequently until you have the descriptive narrative written down.
or
Observe the child with another observer recording simultaneously. Afterwards, sit down together and discuss your perceptions. If possible, write a narrative between you.
or
Use a form of shorthand. If you do not know standard abbreviations, you can study them. Try using R. instead of Richard, chdn. instead of children, etc.

If your language lacks sufficient descriptive powers
Write your observation in point form and add the adjectives, adverbs, or whatever is missing afterwards with the help of a teacher or colleague who observed at the same time or with whom you can get language support.
or
Prepare lists of adjectives, adverbs, and even verbs to help you write up your observation.

Each of the above strategies may help a student or teacher who has particular difficulties in writing. These are skill-building ideas which can help but must always be mentioned in the observation. Clearly they may affect the accuracy of a recording and should not be considered as desirable in the long term.

Method Chart: Running Record

1. Split page format

Name: _____   Observer: _____

Age/D.O.B.: _____   Date: _____

Reason for observation: _____

_____

Context: _____

_____

_____

_____

Time	Observation	Comment/explanation

This chart enables the observer to log the time of events as described. The "Observation" column is most heavily used, and hence is wider. In this column the detailed description of the behaviour is recorded as it occurs. The right-hand column allows for comments that clarify or explain what is happening (this section is not to make inferences).

Method Chart: Running Record

2. Full page format

Name: _____   Observer: _____

Age/D.O.B.: _____   Date: _____

Reason for observation: _____

_____

Context: _____

_____

_____

_____

Time	Observation

Although a running record can be written on any paper, an organized chart can be helpful. The left-hand margin keeps track of the time.

Method Chart: Running Record

3. Categorizing format

Name: _____   Observer: _____

Age/D.O.B.: _____   Date: _____

Reason for observation: _____

_____

Context: _____

_____

Category of behaviours: _____

_____

Time	Observation	Classification of social play

This chart offers the possibility of writing a running record (it could be in note form or in detailed narrative). Time is recorded as behaviours occur. After the recording, the observer categorizes each play or behaviour sequence according to the required classification (in this case, Onlooker, Solitary Parallel, Associative, or Cooperative).

Method Chart: Anecdotal Record

1. Basic recording system

Name: _____   Observer: _____

Age/D.O.B.: _____   Date: _____

Reason for observation: _____

_____

Time/date: _____

Context: _____

Observation anecdote: _____

_____

Time/date: _____

Context: _____

Observation anecdote: _____

_____

These anecdotal forms can be used on a card index system or to form a log for each child.

Method Chart: Anecdotal Record

2. Accident/serious occurrence

Date	Time	Name of child	Incident	Tchrs present	Action	Parent informed (sign)

This chart is useful when spread over the open pages of an accident book. The incident should be described as fully as possible – a drawing might be included.

Method Chart: Diary Record

1. Daily log

Date: _____

Caregiver observation: _____

_____

Caregiver signature: _____

Parent signature/comment: _____

Date: _____

Caregiver observation: _____

_____

Caregiver signature: _____

Parent signature/comment: _____

Date: _____

Caregiver observation: _____

_____

Caregiver signature: _____

Parent signature/comment: _____

This systems allows for a daily anecdote to be recorded and shared with the parent. Another style could include equal space for parent observations. The caregiver can be given an updating of what occurred at home, which may help the caregiver.

Method Chart: Daily Recording

Infant observation log

Child's name: _____   Date of birth: _____

Date: _____   Caregiver's name(s): _____

Feeding: _____

Diapering: _____

Sleeping: _____

Played with: _____

New interests/achievements: _____

Caregiver signature: _____

Read by parent (sig): _____

These sheets can be copied and left on a clipboard for each infant each day. After a week, they can be kept in a binder, for each child, which the parent may want to keep. The new interests/achievements category may be completed as an anecdotal record.

Parents and other adults in the child's life may wish to write down what they judge to be significant. An anecdotal record can capture the essence of the moment.

♦ ♦ ♦ ♦ *Assignment options*

I. Skill building

Individual tasks

1. Watch and write down everything you see as you observe a child for five minutes. Review your notes to check for the following:
   a. Did you write down everything the child did?
   b. Did you record exactly what the child said or uttered?
   c. Were you able to get down on paper every action you saw?
   d. Did you manage to avoid making inferences or assumptions that might have been incorrect?
2. Using an observation you have just recorded, choose three or four phrases of description you have written and see if you can improve them so that they are more detailed, more accurate, or less subjective.
3. Review your narrative recordings to assess your writing ability. Acknowledge the challenges you are experiencing that are due to your lack of writing technique. Seek help from an English teacher or other appropriate resource.
4. Write a list of the ways narrative observations can be useful to you. Your answers will depend on your skill and role.
5. Review the focus questions at the beginning of the chapter. If necessary check the answer notes at the end of the chapter.

Group activities

1. Carry out a narrative recording of a child's activity at the same time as another student or colleague. Compare your notes.
2. Use a short video-recorded segment of a child playing alone as a base for narrative recording practice. A group of people can compare recordings to learn descriptive techniques from each other, to contrast perspectives in observation, and to focus on common assumptions.
3. Try to record all the action and communication of one of your peers as they go about their normal activity. (You may wish to tell them what you are doing or they may question your seemingly strange behaviour!) You may wish to discuss this with the chosen individual – he or she may comment on the accuracy or objectivity of your report. This

activity can be done in pairs with the partners changing roles between being observed and being the observer. Being watched might alter an individual's behaviour, but in this case, the exercise is designed to build your observation skill – not to make inferences from the behaviour.

4. Share written recordings of sequences of a child's activity. Using only what is recorded, let the group make some summarizing comments. As the comments are made, group members will need to challenge the validity of the statements until all can agree.

5. After 1/2 hour to one hour of a class, it can be suggested that class members recall, as an anecdotal record, the first few minutes of the class. Comparison afterwards usually indicates a personal view of what actually happened.

6. Review the following list of words that are frequently included in narrative recordings. Each of them makes some kind of assumption, is inaccurate, or lacks precision. What other words or phrases could be used instead?
   a. plays
   b. went
   c. likes
   d. remembered
   e. happy
   f. shares
   g. reacts
   h. knew
   i. lost interest
   j. thought

II. Practising narrative methods

1. Observe and record a child using a running record method for 15 minutes. Evaluate the observation for:
   a. accuracy (recording exactly all actions and utterances)
   b. completeness (recording in detail without selection)
   c. objectivity and lack of assumptions

2. Write at least two inference statements from a narrative recording. Validate each comment by ensuring your statement is objective, supported by reason, and underpinned with the use of an accepted reference.

3. Write a series of brief anecdotal records during, or at the end, of your day, which focus on one of the following:
    a. children's activity and interest in a particular curriculum area
    b. one child's significant communications
    c. examples of pro-social behaviour
4. Review the examples of narrative recordings which follow.
    Take note of the strengths and weaknesses of each example which has already been evaluated. Use the further examples for your own evaluation and learning.

Examples to critique

The following points might be helpful for evaluating narrative recordings:

◆ contextual information offered
◆ rich description of what the child says and does
◆ information sequenced accurately
◆ observation free from judgments and assumptions

For the anecdotals:

◆ incident cited is significant
◆ information recorded offers sufficient detail

For running records:

◆ narrative flows in detail of spontaneous activity
◆ use of descriptive language

For specimen records:

◆ key to coding offered
◆ recording offers significant information

Final points to check:

◆ summary gives overview of each developmental domain as the data allows
◆ analysis makes objective inferences
◆ inferences supported by reason and evidence
◆ inferences supported by reference to theory or accepted norms or other criteria
◆ suggestions for program planning are included

The following examples are offered as observational samples to critique. They are not intended to represent "ideal" examples of the technique.

Example to Critique #1

Running Record

Child: *Sharita*

Date: *April 12*

Place: *School yard*

Age: *7 years 4 months*

Time: *5:00 p.m.*

Observer: *Daniel R.*

Playing Hopscotch

Length of observation – *2 minutes*

Jumps on both feet
Lands on right foot
Hops on right foot 3 times
Hops on left foot
Hops 6 times on left foot
Jumps
Lands on both feet spread apart
Bends down and picks up pebble
Hand walks back up into standing position
Jumps
Lands on right foot
Hops 4 times on right foot
Jumps and lands on both feet spread apart
Hops on left foot
Turns body around to face opposite end
Hops on left foot 10 times
Switches leg to right foot
Hops twice
Hops
Lands with both feet spread apart at same time
Turns around and jumps
Lands with both feet on floor
Turns around and jumps
Lands with both feet on floor
Hops on one leg – right leg
Hops 4 times
Jumps
Lands on left foot
Hops 5 times
Spreads arms out
Sways from right side to left side
Sways from left side to right side
Jumps
Lands on right foot
Hops 2 times
Jumps
Hops on left foot twice
Jumps
Lands on two feet
Turns around by standing on tip-toes

Example to Critique #2

Running Record

Name of child: *Bronwen*   Age: *28 months*

D.O.B.: *Nov. 10, 1990*

Date observed/time observed: *March 14, 1993*

Physical characteristics: *small build*

light brown hair

25 pounds, approximately 2 1/2 feet tall

brown eyes

Observer: *C.D.*

Observation:

Bronwen is eating a peeled Granny Smith apple with one hand. She is sitting on a bench watching the other children play. Bronwen then finishes most of the large apple and gives it to her mom to put in the garbage. Quickly, Bronwen runs to a hoop and jumps into it using both her feet. After jumping in and out of the hoop several times, she walks over to the gym bars and begins to climb the first and second step (which were approximately one foot apart). Unable to reach the third step (two feet higher than the second), Bronwen stands on the second step for a moment and then climbs back down. Once back on the gym floor, Bronwen appears to wander around aimlessly for a few minutes – putting her hands on and off her head. Spotting a daycare staff member, Bronwen walks over and smiles. She stops and pauses – making noises with her voice. The staff member then picks her up and plays with her in her arms: doing aerobics with her arms and legs. Bronwen laughs and giggles and continues to move her legs in the air. When the staff member puts her down, her mother picks her up and Bronwen attempts to bite her. "Don't bite, Bronwen." Bronwen grins and laughs dryly. "Don't bite. We talked about this yesterday," says her mother. Bronwen then stops biting and gives her mother a great big kiss. The two of them begin to play. Bronwen is lying on her back, in her mother's lap. Her mom is tickling her and Bronwen shows enjoyment by laughing. Sitting up in her mother's lap, Bronwen says, "Are you happy?" Her mother replies, "Yes. Are you happy?" "No", Bronwen states. Then she climbs off her mother and goes over to hug Ryan. After they hug for a moment, Ryan runs off and is followed by Bronwen. She chases him all around the gym, stopping at Yusef to give him a hug, and then chasing him. Once Bronwen is tired of chasing after the two boys, she comes and sits down on the bench and watches the other children.

Comments
Appears to have good control over large muscle skills and seems quite courageous at climbing those bars (that makes me very nervous).
After observing Bronwen for a couple of months now, she seems to enjoy the company of both staff members and peers.
Bronwen likes to spend time with her mother and can often be heard asking, "Where is Mommy?"
One of the wonderful characteristics I have noticed about Bronwen is that she is very affectionate with her classmates.
Seems to enjoy observing other children.

Example to Critique #3

Anecdotal Record

Age/stage/period: *Preschooler*
Name of child: *Mark*   Age: *2 years, 10 months*
D.O.B.: *June 12, 1988*
Date observed/time observed: *March 28, 1991 2:00 p.m.*
Observer: *V.R.*

Physical characteristics:
- *wearing jeans*   – *blond hair*
- *sweater*   – *blue eyes*
- *running shoes*   – *all teeth*
- *good vocabulary*

Setting:
Child Care Centre. Children have just woken up from nap.

Reason for choice of methodology:
I wanted to observe a preschooler in different situations to compare different actions and reactions.

Incident:

Mark is putting together a puzzle, after his nap. "I need help," says Mark in a distressed voice. He picks up two alphabet cards and puts them on the puzzle board. He hands the boards to Troy and picks up two more. Troy takes them away from him. "Go away, Troy," replies Mark in a possessive voice. Mark gives one board to Alex. He watches the other children playing while holding the cards. Mark walks over to the teacher and says "How 'bout this one?" and holds out the card to her. "Just a minute," the teacher answers him and takes the card. Mark goes and takes a giraffe puzzle (seriation). He takes the pieces out one by one. "Look, a big one!" he says excitedly, taking out the big giraffe. "A little one, too. A big one and a little one!" he says, showing each one. He takes the two giraffes and pretends they are having a conversation with each other. "Hi, daddy." "What are you doing, son?" "Trying to put my puzzle away." He uses the big giraffe as the daddy, and the little one as the son. Mark puts the puzzle pieces away correctly. "I did it Maria!" he exclaims and shows his puzzle. He puts the puzzle away and takes a different one. He takes the pieces out of the new puzzle one by one. He is speaking to himself, "All different colours." He then puts all of the pieces back in the puzzle correctly one by one. "I did it" he says, smiling and showing the teacher. Mark repeats this same procedure three more times, but doesn't say anything until he's finished. He says that he did it, after each puzzle, and shows the teacher.

Summary:

Mark appeared to be a very active child during the day, but possibly the reason he chose to do a quiet activity was because he had just woken up from the afternoon nap. During free play in the class Mark seemed to be more interested in playing with the blocks and building towers, houses, and windows, as opposed to playing with the puzzles. Mark would appear to have very good fine and gross motor skills because he uses both the blocks and puzzles with good control. He seemed to be very proud of his own accomplishments. He was eager to show off his doings. He was not playing with any other children at this time. He seemed quite content in being by himself, perhaps his own quiet time, or space, after a sleep. He did offer one alphabet board to Alex, and it seems that he doesn't mind sharing, when he initiates the act first.

Example to Critique #4

Running Record

Child's name: *Mona*

Child's age: *8 months*

Date: *February 5*

Place: *Sue's observation skills class. Three infants are being observed in front of 40 students.*

Mona folds her fingers, and bends her body and opens her mouth. She scrunches up some paper perhaps to see what reaction might occur. She then bends to get a book that was out of her reach. She proceeds to get the small book and put it into her mouth with both of her hands. She looks at the faces in the room and the expression on her face looks as though she is perhaps trying to communicate with us.

Mona then looks at a toy that is close to her. She reaches out with her hand and touches the toy, then she puts it into her mouth after squeezing it with her hand first.

When she is given a bottle, she is put on her back although she does help to put herself on her back. She puts her hand up to steady the bottle, it looks like. Her mouth is sucking and she seems to be enjoying the bottle. It appears that perhaps she is hungry. She then chews on the bottle with her two lower teeth on the bottom gum. She seems to be rooting.

Mona looks at her mother, who is talking while she is eating. It appears that Mona likes the sound of her mother's voice, and perhaps the fact that she looked at her mother means that she could distinguish the voice of her mother. Perhaps Mona also feels some security having her mother right there while she eats.

Mona then finishes the bottle and reaches for a toy. She drops the toy and then reaches again to pick it up with her hands, grasping it this time. She then sees something different. It is a book this time and not a toy. Her fingers are all bent as she tries to get the book. She succeeds in attaining the book. She bends her arm at the elbow and brings the book closer to her face. It appears that perhaps she likes books because when she brought it close she also made sounds as though perhaps she was reading. This could also show that perhaps she is read to a lot. Then she looks around the room. She pulls her knees up and bends them so that she can almost touch them. Her head seems to stay on the table where she is lying. She turns her head to look at her mother (to the right) and then she smiles.

The class makes a sound and Mona smiles as though perhaps she likes the attentions she is getting. Perhaps she likes people. She then sits up, pushing with her hands.

She turns her upper body and spreads her hands out, and then leans back as if perhaps for balance, to keep herself from falling, and hurting herself. She then moves her arms back and forth. The class laughs and she responds by smiling. She seems to enjoy the attention.

There is a toy on the table which, since she is sitting up, she reaches for. She stretches her whole arm to get it. She pulls the lever down with three fingers. She then changes her hands as if perhaps she is testing out what she can do.

Mona looks around the room again. She tries to get onto her back; she rolls a little (as if perhaps by wriggling she is learning different ways to move).

She sees a different toy and reaches for it as if contemplating how to open or close the toy. She decides to push the toy away from her with her whole hand.

She doesn't appear to like being on her tummy too much. She isn't really able to go from sitting to crawling, however, I think that will come when she is ready to do it and there is no need for concern.

Mona is given a piece of paper in her hand. She puts the paper into her mouth and has both hands outstretched to the fullest.

Mona is able to stand with help. She waves her hands up and down. She has some sounds which she demonstrates when it looks as though she is reading (un, ah).

Mona appears to like an audience, as she smiles when the audience reacts to her. She is able to follow instructions a little with a toy. She is able to blow on it to create a sound that her mother desires her to do.

Mona seems to have a good understanding of what is happening around her at the time.

◆ ◆ ◆ ◆ Answers to Focus Questions

1. Only a rich, full narrative description of the child's behaviour will offer sufficient detail, that, when read, provides a "picture" of what was observed.

2. An open-ended, non-focussed observation will record any behaviour which happened to occur at the time the recording was made. If the activity observed was a spontaneous play sequence it may be possible that any of the following may become evident:

a. interests/motivation
b. concentration span
c. play patterns
d. social interactions (child-adult or child-child)
e. language abilities
f. gross/fine motor skills
g. expression of feelings
h. cognitive activity
i. response to materials
j. creativity or use of imagination

3. Awareness of your own biases is essential. These may be concerned with professed attitudes or be more subtle. Writing down only what you see as you observe it will help you to separate objective "facts" from interpretations. Sensitive evaluation of what you record is essential in the process of limiting observer bias.

4. Many observers can run into difficulty in recording their observations because their use of language is limited in some ways. A tape recorder can help. The observer can sometimes describe behaviour orally when their handwriting cannot keep up. The tape recorder can also be used to record a spoken narrative in a language other than English. Tapes can be transcribed or translated as necessary. Although these methods are a step away from direct observation, they can offer a means of enabling the observer to record more accurately than they would otherwise manage. Videotaped recordings can be transcribed using a replay technique to ensure objective recording. Shorthand techniques can be used to aid faster recording; coding can also be devised to assist in including sufficient detail. Recordings can be written in note form and then revised to include remembered descriptions. Although helpful, these techniques should be evaluated for their accuracy and objectivity. They may help the observer but decisions on the basis of these "second-hand" observations should be made with caution.

5. Narrative recordings can be made by anyone who has an adequate use of descriptive language. Skilled observers may, however, record their observations somewhat differently because of their background knowledge that affects their perception. The more an observer observes and studies child development, the more their understanding of what they see is shaped. The language used by professional observers is somewhat different from that of the casual observer because they can describe behaviours using more appropriate terms. Narratives will be written differently by two people "seeing" the same thing because each will categorize behaviours according to their own perspective.

6. Anecdotal recordings involve the selection, by the observer, of particular incidents which are significant. The observer needs to have sufficient understanding of child development to know what to choose as being relevant. Some observers have selected for inclusion mistakes made by a child, examples of behaviour which are typical or atypical in terms of developmental norms, anecdotes which offer an insight into the child's humour or individuality, or scenarios that demonstrate a newly acquired skill or evolution in the child's understanding.

◆ ◆ ◆ ◆ Key Terms

inference	diary recording	gesture
assessments	specimen record	sequencing
behaviourism	spontaneous play	subjective
objective	play patterns	child-centred
bias	gross motor	assessments
anecdotal record	fine motor	emerging skill
narrative observation	actions	assumptions
running record	reactions	
data	posture	

3 Samplings

In order to be able to observe in a focussed way, staff need to organize their nursery to enable children to operate as independently as possible.

Above all, however, staff need to really believe that observation is important. The most committed teachers and nursery nurses manage to find plenty of time for observation.

M. Lally and V. Hurst (1992)

This method (event sampling) proves to be very efficient in reducing observation time and has the added bonus of providing data that could be summarized easily and subjected to statistical analysis.

D. Michelle Irwin and M. Margaret Bushnell (1980)

Cooperative play can be encouraged if time, space, opportunity, and materials are available. Sampling this type of activity can help in understanding the children's social skills and assist in programming.

Focus Questions

1. How could you label a behaviour so that it could be charted as a separate entity from the general flow of a child's action?

2. We all have differing perceptions and biases – how could you avoid making assumptions about what are "good" behaviours and what are "negative"?

3. In what ways could you use observational information that indicates the frequency of a behaviour?

4. If you could identify a trigger or cause of a behaviour, what use could you make of the information?

5. When you reveal a pattern in a child's behaviour, what might it tell you?

6. In recording information about the seriousness of a behaviour, how could you rate severity in the form of a code?

History Notes

To get around the problem of the amount of time it took to carry out narrative recordings, new ways of collecting information were devised in the 1920s. **Samplings** enabled pre-selected behaviours to be charted and quantified more efficiently and enabled researchers to observe a wider number of children and make more significant inferences.

Irwin and Bushnell cite Willard C. Olson at the Institute of Child Development at the University of Minnesota as being the first to use time sampling as a technique, in 1926-27. This study focussed on the nervous habits of children. At about the same time, Mary Cover Jones used a form of event sampling when recording observations of pre-school children's emotions. This was a more scientific testing situation than the forms of event sampling that are used today. Studies of children in the 1930s and 40s used these techniques in a variety of forms. Some used samplings to analyze the content of narrative recordings, others to measure behaviour in a more scientific manner. Further work concentrated on recording behaviours in a naturalistic way, focussing on spontaneous activity. Possibly the best known work of this period was Mildred B. Parten's study of children's play, which valued the spontaneous play of young children. She categorized social behaviour using the terms that are commonly understood today – unoccupied, onlooker, solitary, parallel associative, and cooperative. The use of clear behaviour categories is shown in Parten's work. Today you need to imitate this by using well-stated definitions of the behaviour that you are seeking to record.

The use of both time sampling and event sampling in research work has increased over the last fifty years. Much of the data that have been collected and analyzed form the basis of our current knowledge of the sequences and patterns of child development.

Sampling observations: Definition

Sampling observations are those in which examples of categories of behaviour are recorded as they occur or at previously decided intervals.

Event sampling

A method of observation recording occurrences of behaviours called "**events**," which are examples of a previously selected category of behaviour. Event sampling is most frequently focussed on one child at a time but may be constructed to record behaviours of a number of children simultaneously. Varying formats enable the frequency, duration, causality, or severity of the behaviour to be highlighted.

- ◆ frequency: how often the behaviour occurs
- ◆ duration: how long the behaviour continues
- ◆ causality: what triggered the behaviour
- ◆ severity: the degree to which the behaviour can be considered to be serious or a cause for concern

Time sampling

A method of observation and recording selected behaviours during previously set regular time periods. These observations can be used for recording information about one or more children simultaneously. Time samplings are usually structured to record behaviours at regular intervals but may also be done at randomly chosen times.

◆ ◆ ◆ ◆ Features of Sampling Observations

The sampling of behaviours or events is an indirect or interpretative style of observing children. Practising teachers may choose to record them frequently because of their very specific nature and the speed at which results can be produced. Recording information while involved in activity with the children can be challenging; some samplings can be done without disengaging from them for any significant length of time.

Causes of behaviours

The ABC format is possibly the most useful of the event sampling methods. The "ABC" part indicates

A: the **Antecedent** behaviour or event – the "happening" just prior to the behaviour example cited
B: the **Behaviour** – the example of the behaviour category you are looking for.
C: the **Consequent** event – the effect, consequence, or event that occurs after the example given.

Event samplings can give clear indications of the causality of the behaviours recorded. In using the ABC format the trigger or cause for the behaviour may become apparent. Viewing the antecedent enables us to see if there is an identifiable pattern involved in which responses are elicited by particular stimuli. The stimulus-response pattern may be initiated by the child herself but could also come from the teacher's behaviour, a routine occurrence, or an environmental factor.

This style enables the observer to see possible effects as well as causes of the behavioural example.

Segments of behaviour

When you go about recording specific behaviours you may think you know what you are looking for. As a result, you frequently make value judgments about the positive or negative connotations of the behaviours.

The "event" or behaviour you are looking to record must be defined. An **operational definition** needs to be more than a list of behaviours that fall within a broad category. The definition must offer a clear explanation of what will be recorded.

Choosing, then defining, the behaviour category can be troublesome. As behaviour is a continuous flow of activity, it is hard to compartmentalize. Teachers need to make categories of behaviour to make sense of what the child is doing.

Use of event sampling

The nature, duration, severity, or cause of a behaviour can be highlighted with sampling techniques. Frequently this method is used for analyzing behaviours that present a challenge, but this is only one of the uses from the teacher's perspective.

Greg (4y11m) and his brother Dan (3y8m) had both attended a child care centre near their home since they were a few months old. In the family grouping environment they had been in a room together for some months and had mostly got on well together, Greg frequently showing concern for his brother. The teacher was presented with a situation requiring observation and analysis. Both boys started to play in a more aggressive way than usual; Dan frequently tried to bite Greg when they got into an argument. Greg began to bite back. In charting the boys' aggressive behaviour the teacher found there was a pattern to the behaviour in that the severity of the aggression was related to only one factor that was obvious. The boys were much more challenging when their father brought them in the morning. Speaking to both parents, the teacher couldn't find out any further useful information. In this case the reasons were never obvious but the caregiver acted on observations she made, encouraging the children to "use their words" to articulate their frustrations and reward positive attempts to find resolution while providing each boy with strategies to solve their problems.

The category of the behaviour recorded is for the observer to decide. You may wish to chart a particular, recurring behaviour you have already observed.

EXAMPLE

Shana (21m) was at home with her mother for most of the day; occasionally her father, working a night shift, would be at home to share the caregiving. Mealtimes had always been happy, jovial occasions and, when possible, the family ate together. Noticing that Shana was sometimes quite disagreeable about eating what was provided, Shana's parents decided to see if they could find out the reason by recording incidents of difficulty. A clear pattern was not evident but Shana's dad was the first to notice that Shana was particularly challenging on the days he had been responsible for her care even if both he and his partner were sharing a meal with Shana. They speculated that this difficulty might be a form of protest regarding the absence of Shana's mother. A further charting of the behaviour validated their conclusion.

Alternatively, you might need to look for behaviours in a general category because you have not observed them by chance and think you might have missed something.

Time might be a significant element in the event sampling, either the time at which particular behaviours are evident or the duration or length of time that the behaviour is exhibited.

Recording samples of the occurrences of behaviour can reveal the severity of intensity of a behaviour. An initial reaction to a child's behaviour may be emotional in its inference. It can feel like, "Mary is screeching all the time." When you actually record her crying/screaming you might find it is less frequent than you thought but it is, nevertheless, intense. Recording information about the severity may be less objective than you might desire but you may manage to develop an intensity rating scale to accompany your chart – this helps to get around the concern. Working towards **objectivity** is necessary but it is not an absolute science.

that some of the children demonstrated a foot-stamping refusal to cooperate and tears of rage more frequently and more severely than others. She decided to do a series of sampling recordings to get to know the patterns of frustration experienced by her toddlers. Devising a rating scale to accompany her sampling chart, she recorded examples of frustration and the severity of such events. She was surprised by the results because all of the children demonstrated frequent frustrations. The severity of the behaviours had not previously been clear to her because it became apparent that the children had varying degrees of verbalizing their frustration. The teacher inferred that her earlier informal observations had been influenced by her high sensitivity to crying and shouting.

Inferences from patterns of behaviour

Patterns of behaviour encourage you to believe that your **inferences** are more likely to be objective. If a three-month-old infant, Lindy, cries before she is fed you must be careful to avoid the **assumption** that when Lindy cries she is always in need of a feed. You can get many useful clues, however, from the sequences of behaviour you observe. Event samplings can give quite clear causes for the behaviours you have recorded. These inferences need to be substantiated particularly if you are to act on the results. (See also Chapter 1 on on making inferences and analyzing data.)

Time intervals for samplings

Time sampling observations need to be even more rigorously set up than event samples because the interval at which the behaviours are to be sampled must be structured so that you get the information you need. A sampling made across several days at 15 minute intervals may give information about an infant's pattern of sleep and wakefulness but it may not give such useful insights into a seven-year-old's concentration.

Such difficulties tend to influence the observer in deciding on a methodology; if the technique is not fully understood and practised the results will be affected. Coding behaviours is particularly hazardous if you don't know what you are looking for in your categories. You may find that choices made from your own experience are good enough but they are better when carried out using a researched system.

EXAMPLE

The differences between the social skills observed in a grade one class were very wide ranging. Probable reasons were related to the children's development and level of social experience. The teacher showed concern because he did not know if his expectations for cooperative activity were reasonable — he wanted to evaluate the program by looking at each child's demonstration of social skills. He set up a time sampling chart using 10 minute intervals and recorded observations each morning for a week during the free play period. He devised a behaviour category system to record the levels of social skill:

S – Solitary

O – Onlooker

P – Parallel

A – Associative

C – Cooperative

This was a method evolved from Parten's categories of social play and proved useful to the teacher who had understanding of the developmental sequences of social activity.

Evaluation of the data collected enabled the teacher to confirm that there were variations in the children's skill level. He altered some activities to enable children to participate according to their developing skill level.

Within a group, some children may take on the role of "leader" or "follower." Careful observation can help a teacher guide behaviour to empower the less assertive.

Behaviour Categories

Operational definitions of behaviour

Sampling techniques involve the categorizing of sets of behaviours. An operational definition of the behaviour to be observed is essential for the success of the observational recordings; without it the observation will be built on quicksand.

Categories can be broad or specific according to needs but they must be precise. A useful way of clarifying your thinking is to ask yourself the question, What range of behaviours am I expecting to see? The commonality of the set of behaviours should become apparent.

Example 1 If you expect to see examples of hitting, biting, and shouting, you will see that the commonality is anger or aggression.

Consider the following definition of the words "anger" and "aggression":
Anger: This is a behaviour in which the individual demonstrates rage and passionate resentment.
Aggression: This is a behaviour in which the individual demonstrates acts of violence or verbal anger.

Creating your own definition of aggression might be more useful because you could include all action and communication. Your definition could be more open-ended and therefore be likely to cover other examples of the behaviours you might see.

Example 2 Your pre-school child demonstrates a variety of attention-seeking behaviours but you are interested in recording all types of attention seeking.

Narrower categories can be useful if you are looking for a specific behaviour. In this case you might choose a precise category. Instead of choosing a category like social behaviours you might need to be more exact because you are seeking examples of altruism or empathy.

Example 3 When explaining to a new assistant teacher the particular behaviours of individuals in your class, you realize you want to highlight those children with an obvious habit because you want the assistant to help you analyze the causes.

Observing all repeated behaviours does not give you information that you want about nervous tics, nail biting, etc.... The term habitual behaviour is more useful to you.

Defining the behaviour to be observed limits the parameters of the observation while supporting its objectivity. The examples of behaviour that fall into a category may be more than you anticipated – the operational definition will allow for that.

Some frequently used categories of behaviour:

aggression	habitual	assertive	imitative
attention seeking	independent	cooperative	regressive
dependent	solitary	empathetic	uncooperative

"Positive" and "negative" behaviours

When first using an event sampling technique, there is a tendency to choose the more "**negative**" **behaviours** and only use the methodologies for calculating the number of times the behaviour occurs. While this can be useful to some observers, there is much to be learned about the more socially acceptable or developmentally influenced behaviours. The presence or absence of such behaviours can help us to understand a child's personality, social adjustment, and developmental progress. Avoidance of classifying behaviours into "**positive**" or "negative" ("good" or "bad") leads to greater objectivity.

> **Example** *An assumption that numerous examples of assertive action in play can be inferred as a positive and beneficial personality trait is a mistake. Only after careful analysis should such a* **judgment** *be made.*

Coding behaviours

Closer detail of behaviour sampling involves the use of coding categories of events. You can write these of your own accord depending on your need but a coding system evolved from research in child development and observation might be more accurate.

Observable behaviours

All actions and most communications can be recorded because they are observable. Actions can be observed, but thoughts can only be inferred from actions; it requires considerable skill and knowledge to make objective inferences about cognitive activity or an individual's feelings or morals.

Samplings of behaviour may include events that draw from examples such as problem-solving activities, pre-operational thinking levels, or emotions. These behaviours require more interpretation than, for example, a physical skill. Where evaluative deductions need to be made for each behavioural example there is a significant hurdle in maintaining objectivity of recording. Observation methods other than samplings depend on this kind of inference-making in the analysis of the data; samplings use interpretation in the actual recording of the observation. Be aware of the possible inaccuracy of the examples you cite if the behaviour category you choose is too abstract or dependent on interpretation.

Deciding What Sampling Methodology to Use

1. Become aware of the various techniques, know their advantages and disadvantages and what information they could give you.

2. Assess your need for a sampling: What do you need it for? These are some of the most obvious uses:

    a. To help you learn about sequences of development.

    b. To support the understanding of an individual child's behaviour.

    c. To look at the behaviours demonstrated by a group of children.

    d. For formal record keeping.

    e. To support communications with parents, colleagues, and for other professionals.

    f. To help evaluate the program offered to an individual or group.

    g. To provide information for behaviour modification plans or for learning prescriptions.

3. Choose the method of preference, use it, and evaluate its usefulness for the purpose required.

4. Practise use of sampling techniques and build skills in the component parts of objectivity, clarity, and accuracy of recording, checking with others on their perceptions as to the validity of your work.

Event Sampling

Advantages	Disadvantages
A quick and efficient method of recording. Behaviour can be charted in convenient units.	Lacks the detail of narrative recordings. High degree of selectivity and inference required in categorizing observed behaviour.
Provides opportunity for recording information more quickly than narrative observations.	Breaks up the natural continuity of behaviour into separate units.
Enables both "positive" and "negative" behaviours to be charted.	May encourage judgmental inferences.
Sampling may be blended with other methods, i.e. with a detailed narrative account, rating scale, etc...	
Method may reveal: – behavioural patterns – frequency of behaviour – cause and effect of behaviour/event.	Relies on repetition of behaviour – not useful for infrequently observed behaviours.
It is possible to observe and record more than one child at a time.	
The results easily interpreted into appropriate program planning/behaviour modification strategies.	
Observation can be recorded at the time or soon after its occurrence.	Any observation not recorded immediately is more likely to be affected by **observer bias**.
Enables teacher involved with children to record as he/she interacts in the program.	
Sampling may offer information about duration/length of behaviour.	
May indicate severity of recorded behaviour.	
Some basic formats can be selected by consulted professionals and with only a little instruction can be carried out by parents and caregivers.	Relies on the skill of the observer: 1. to choose appropriate methodology, 2. to define behaviour category, and 3. to evaluate the child's behaviour patterns .

Time Sampling

Advantages	Disadvantages
Provides frequency data about behaviours.	Lacks qualitative information.
Information can be recorded quickly.	Event recorded may be misunderstood
More like to allow for representative sample of behaviour appropriate for students and researchers.	because of lack of contextual information.
Results tend to be **reliable** over time.	Behaviour observed infrequently may not be recorded effectively.
Provides overview of wide range of behaviours.	Relies on skill of observer to structure observation appropriately to elicit significant information.

Time Sampling vs Event Sampling

Event Sampling	Time Sampling
Can be used to study any event or behaviour.	Limited to regularly recurring behaviours.
A little less likely to give information about frequency of behaviour over longer periods of time.	
More likely to give qualitative information.	May be easier to quantify behaviour.
May indicate causes of behaviour.	
Used more often by practitioners.	Used more often by researchers.
Every natural occurrence of focus behaviour is a sample.	
May offer information about duration of behaviour.	
May indicate severity of behaviour/event.	
Can be user-friendly and easily carried out by parents and para-professionals.	May require professional background in child development to structure behaviour coding systems.

How to Record a Time or Event Sample Observation

1. Decide on your reason to observe sampling of behaviour.
2. Select the behaviour category and time frequency that applies.
3. Prepare a method chart to meet specific requirements.
4. Write your operational definition of the behaviour category.
5. Record as soon as possible the precise details of the examples of behaviour observed.
6. When sufficient examples are recorded for your purpose, take time to analyze your findings.
7. Write your objective inferences as clear statements – but support your statements.
8. Use the inference statements to devise an action plan or learning prescription.

Method Chart: Event Sampling

1. "ABC" format

Name: _____ Observer: _____

Age/D.O.B.: _____ Date/s: _____

Behaviour: (This is a behaviour in which) _____

_____

Reason for observation: _____

_____

Time	Antecedent	Behaviour	Consequence

*This chart enables the observer to chart the chosen behaviour as it occurs, giving information about what was observed immediately prior to the sample behaviour and also what happened afterwards. Detailing the surrounding events lets the observer have some clues to the possible causes or triggers for the behaviour, gives a **tally** of occurrences, and can give a more detailed set of information which may be helpful in understanding the child's behaviour.*

Method Chart: Event Sampling

2. Frequency count

Name: _____   Observer: _____

Age/D.O.B.: _____   Date/s: _____

Behaviour: (This is a behaviour in which) _____

_____

Reason for observation: _____

_____

Day/date	Tally count	Total

Here the observer records the occurrences of the selected behaviour as they happen. This can be useful for a practising teacher because it can be done efficiently without a break from the responsibilities with the children. No detail about the behaviours can be recorded.

Method Chart: Event Sampling

3. Duration chart

Name: _____   Observer: _____

Age/D.O.B.: _____   Date/s: _____

Behaviour: (This is a behaviour in which) _____

_____

Reason for observation: _____

_____

Day/date	Time (from–to)	Total in minutes

Allowing the observer to get a sense of the duration of the selected behaviour can be useful, although with this chart no other explanation of the occurrences of behaviour can be offered. The observer might find it advantageous to calculate average duration as well as analyze the pattern of behaviour examples.

Method Chart: Event Sampling

4. Group samples

Names: _____   Ages/D.O.B.: _____
_____   _____
_____   _____
_____   _____
_____

Observer: _____   Date: _____
Context: _____
Behaviour: (This is a behaviour in which) _____
_____

Reason for observation: _____
_____

Time	Name	Antecedent	Behaviour

Recording information about more than one child at a time has its limitations for practical reasons. Here the observer can record a set of examples of a pre-selected category of behaviour. It is wise to limit the breadth of categories in this method or there may be too many examples. Further variants can involve simple frequency counts, duration, recordings, or for the observer without direct involvement, a full ABC format.

Method Chart: Event Sampling

5. Severity recording

Name: _____ Observer: _____

Age/D.O.B.: _____ Date/s: _____

Behaviour: (This is a behaviour in which) _____

Reason for observation: _____

Inference Coding Rating Scale

I		3		5		7		9
Mild				Moderate				Severe

Date	Time	Behaviour	Rating	Comments

This is a combination of an event sample technique and a rating scale. Charting the severity of behaviour is more interpretative than some other sampling methods because the observer is required to evaluate the behaviour's severity as it is recorded.

Method Chart: Event Sampling

6. Complex behaviour sampling

Name: _____ Observer: _____

Age/D.O.B.: _____ Date/s: _____

Behaviour: (This is a behaviour in which) _____

Reason for observation: _____

Inference Coding Rating Scale

I		3		5		7		9
Mild				Moderate				Severe

Date	Antecedent event	Behaviour example	Consequent event	Duration	Severity	Comments

*This chart can be too demanding for the caregiver of a moderate or large group of children. Parents, student observers, and psychologists whose focus is on only one child at a time find this an appropriate method of recording detailed information. It is particularly useful with behaviours presenting a challenge; where guidance strategies need to be developed for **behaviour modification**, cognitive therapy, or other management or therapy technique.*

Method Chart: Time Sampling

1. Interval Recording

Name: _____ Observer: _____

Age/D.O.B.: _____ Date/s: _____

Context: _____

Behaviour: (This is a behaviour in which) _____

_____

Reason for observation: _____

_____

Date	Time/interval	Behaviour	Comments

This chart presents a standard format, which can be adapted to various uses by altering the time interval designation as required. Here the behaviour category could be open-ended or be quite specific if necessary. An observer may wish to see the general pattern of activity during the course of the day or look for types of behaviour to see if they are present or absent in the sample period.

Method Chart: Time Sampling

2. Group interval recording

Names: _____ Ages/D.O.B.: _____

_____ _____

Observer: _____ Date: _____

Context: _____

Behaviour category: _____

Reason for observation: _____

#	Child	Behaviours (Time/units/intervals)	Comment (Total)
1.			
2.			

A group of children can be observed in this time sampling. The detail of activity that can be recorded is quite limited.

Method Chart: Time Sampling

3. Group coded chart

Names: _____ Ages/D.O.B.: _____

_____ _____

Observer: _____ Date: _____

Context: _____

Behaviour category codes: A. _____ B. _____

(complete as required) C. _____ D. _____

Reason for observation: _____

Please use a (✔) to complete.

Child	Time intervals											
	A	B	C	D	A	B	C	D	A	B	C	D

Pre-selected coded behaviours can be used here to observe the complex behavioural activity of a number of children.

◆ ◆ ◆ ◆ # The Analysis or Summary: Interpreting Data Collected from Samplings

Remember that your inferences rely heavily on the objectivity of your recording.

You will need to review the effectiveness of the sampling before you proceed to analyze the content. Some samplings require you to select specific behaviours. The decision to observe a particular behaviour may be found to be ineffective because you didn't see the behaviour you expected. The operational definition of the behaviour category can also be a source of difficulty – you could perhaps have selected a suitable category but not defined it well to cover the samples you include.

Interpretation of observational data relies on the success of the recording.

Look at the objectives of the observation before drawing inferences. Only when you start to ponder the reason for doing the sampling observation can you begin to make appropriate inferences.

EXAMPLE

In an observation regarding attention-seeking behaviours you have, over several days, recorded some examples of Joshua's attempts at gaining the teacher's attention in kindergarten. Some of them seem to be quite appropriate, others, like drawing attention by making grotesque faces, you think are less desirable. The reason to record this observation was to increase awareness of Joshua's attention seeking and to help gain an objective perspective on the behaviour of what feels like a demanding five-year-old. Your record shows that Joshua has put his hand up, asked questions, has jumped up and down when others are talking and has also shouted, "Miss...Miss...," tapped you on the shoulder and made grotesque faces. The answer to your question might be as simple as to recognize the frequency and severity of Joshua's attention seeking and acknowledge that it is within the bounds of the expected for a five-year-old with a relatively vibrant personality.

Sampling techniques will often give information regarding the frequency with which a behaviour occurs. Analyzing the sequence may help reveal something of the child's personal style. Identifying patterns does not necessarily indicate the reason for them. It is essential to remain non-judgmental and to validate the statements you do make.

The duration of a particular behaviour can be indicative of its significance but a series of occurences would need to be observed before a conclusion could be drawn. Noting the severity of behaviour may be a **subjective** way of looking at a child's actions but if the child is to be encouraged to behave in a particular manner then it is reasonable to evaluate the gravity of the behaviour. It is necessary to be as objective as possible in assessing severity. Tabulating behaviours in sampling techniques tends to encourage this objectivity.

The ABC format of the typical event sample will enable you to answer the most obvious questions about the cause and the effects of the sampled behaviour. Clearly you mustn't jump to hasty conclusions about triggers for behaviours, but you may well see a pattern of behaviour which gives you possible clues.

EXAMPLE

If you were to see each example of the dependent behaviour that you have focussed on in a spontaneous play situation, you might infer that the child was being dependent because she could not cope with the choices presented to her in free play. This might be true but you need more than a few examples to be able to substantiate your point. In fact your conclusion might be entirely incorrect because you have missed another part of the behaviour pattern – that, in this case, free play times were always at the start and end of the day for this six-year-old and it was at this time that she found separations challenging.

When evaluating the sample of behaviours you have recorded you will need to consider your observation with a view to understanding the development of the child in each interacting domain. The behaviours you will have recorded may be typical of the group of children you teach; however, avoid making inferences by comparing children in your care. While you will build up a wealth of information over the years of working with children, you need to remember that your current group do not really represent a statistically significant sample from which any appropriate comparisons can be drawn. Your experience will help you to observe more closely, record more carefully, and give clues to areas where you can start seeking a more objective analysis. Consulting prepared developmental charts depicting a "norm" of behaviour might help you to make some valid statements regarding stages of development but be careful about the biases of the norms.

It is a useful habit to ask yourself questions about the observation material you have collected. Initial questions might be as simple as "What does this behaviour tell me about...the child's physical skill, social awareness, intellectual understanding..." and so on. Frequently what we see combines these developmental areas.

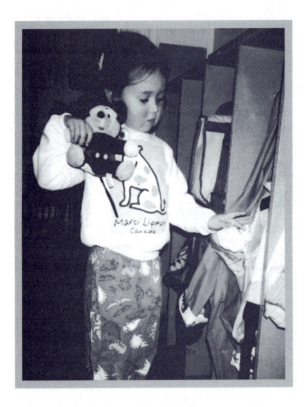

The frequency with which a behaviour is observed can be charted. Event samplings may offer clues as to the cause of a behaviour. Mickey offers some comfort at a time of insecurity.

The use of inferences drawn from the analysis of the sampling observations

Other than for purposes of dry record keeping there is little point in recording copious numbers of observations without putting them to some use. There is a wide range of reasons to record samplings, and often there is more than one reason for each observation.

Having checked the inferences made for their validity, reliability, general objectivity, and supporting argument and reference, you will be ready to make use of your analysis.

The inferences can be used in a similar way to those drawn from other methods of observation (see Chapter 1). Samplings are, however, frequently used as a forerunner to devising a learning prescription or individualized program plan for children. The way in which the methodology reveals causality of behaviour means that it easily lends itself to specific teacher action. Here is an example of how samplings prompted program changes to accommodate to the needs of the child.

Seemingly happy as he eats his lunch, this boy, who has Down's Syndrome, suddenly burst into tears a moment after the photograph was taken. An event sampling of these occurrences revealed a significant behaviour pattern.

◆ ◆ ◆ ◆ *Assignment options*

I. Skill building

Individual tasks

1. Observe any child known to you and decide
   a. What two behaviours he/she demonstrates, that you can sample.
   b. Categorize the behaviours.
   c. Define the behaviours.
2. Read the list of frequently used categories of behaviour listed in this chapter. Add to the list by suggesting other broad categories of behaviour that could be sampled.

Group activities

1. Practise writing operational definitions on the categories of behaviour given in this chapter. Present your definitions to the group and see if they can guess the behaviour category.
2. Discuss the following behaviour category descriptions and decide which are insufficiently objective to be useful in sampling observations.
   a. self-initiated activity   b. temper tantrums
   c. laziness   d. child-centred learning
   e. playing   f. generosity
3. After discussion, write a list of potential uses for both event and time sampling methods of observing children
   a. for a student learning about child development.
   b. for a parent involved in the daily management of young children.
   c. for a caregiver of a small group of under-three-year-olds.
   d. for a kindergarten teacher with a large group of four-and five-year-olds.
   e. for a consultant psychologist.

II. Practising sampling methods

1. Undertake a time sampling observation using the Method Chart 1, Interval Recording. Focus on one child's behaviour, recording any play activity during a free play/spontaneous activity period in the child's day. Use five-minute intervals, recording for a few seconds.

2. Evaluate your observation for its objectivity and lack of judgments and assumptions. What did the sample tell you about the child? What inferences did you have to make to record the information?

3. Choosing a toddler or pre-schooler with whom you have had previous contact, carry out an Event Sampling using the ABC format. Decide what behaviour category you are going to use, ensuring you write an operational definition of it. Record four or more examples of the behaviour with the Antecedent and Consequent events charted.

4. Evaluate your observation for its objectivity and lack of judgments and assumptions.

5. Write at least two inference statements that you can draw from your data. Underpin the statement's objectivity with reasoned argument and where possible supporting references to validate your points.

6. Agree with another student or teacher to observe a pre-schooler simultaneously. Record the frequency of a chosen behaviour of a pre-school child using the method chart Event Sampling #2 Frequency Count. Compare results with your partner.

7. Devise a rating scale that could accompany an event sample as if you were preparing to do an Event Sample Method Chart #5 Severity Recording. (You do not need to do the observation itself.) Choose one of the following behaviours or decide on another appropriate category:
   a. cooperation
   b. hitting
   c. food rejection
   d. illness
   e. culture shock

8. Evaluate the sampling observations that follow (Examples to Critique 1 to 4). Consider these criteria as you assess them:
   a. structure and layout
   b. effectiveness
   c. observer bias and assumptions
   d. appropriateness of operational definition
   e. the objectivity of inferences

9. Re-read the sampling observations Examples to Critique 5–8. Choose two that you think are relatively objective and reliable. Do not read the summaries. Attempt to make objective supported inferences from the data provided. Try to validate every statement you make with reason and reference to appropriate resources. Now, critique the analyses that were offered, with reference to your own inferences.

Example to Critique # 1

Event Sample

Name: *Hansen*   Age/D.O.B.: *Turned 4 March 5*

Date: *April 4, 199—.*

Centre: *A kindergarten class*

Behaviour: *This is a behaviour in which the child is getting attention through negative actions or verbally negative things to say.*

Date	Time	Antecedent event	Behaviour	Consequent event
Apr 4	3:10 p.m.	Hansen is out on the climber and is ready to play on the slide.	Yells at some of the bigger children, "Ha ha, the big fat jerk."	Hansen gets no reaction and slides down the slide.
Apr 4	3:18 p.m.	Hansen goes halfway down the slide.	He stops halfway down presumably to get a reaction from some of the children.	Children get annoyed and some are saying, "Hansen, get out of the way."
Apr 4	3:19 p.m.	Hansen immediately tries to go to the slide again.	He walks up the slide blocking the children's way.	This provokes the teacher to approach Hansen. She says, "Hansen, the slide is for going down not up!"
Apr 4	3:28 p.m.	Hansen is playing on the cement with some of the other children who are with bikes and skipping ropes etc...	Hansen approaches Akeyla, a classmate, and attempts to grab her toy gardening tool away from her. He manages to grab it from her and she grabs it back. At that point Hansen hits her.	At this point I intervened.
Apr 5	3:13 p.m.	Hansen is on his bike with gardening tool in hand.	Hansen is yelling, "Shut up, Akeyla, shut up!"	Akeyla walks off – no reaction and the teacher tells Hansen that he is either to play on his bike or in the sand box.
Apr 5	4:10 p.m.	Hansen is in the sand box playing with Denver.	Suddenly Hansen gets up and shouts at the other children, "Na na na na boo boo." (I don't know why.)	No reaction, so he sits down and continues to play in the sand box with Denver.

Example to Critique # 2

Event Sample

Name: *Andrew*   Age: *2 1/2 Years*   D.O.B.: *September 16, 1989*

Date & time observed: *March 7, 19— from 9:00 a.m.–11:00 a.m*

Physical characteristics: *– slightly over average weight and somewhat shorter than average*
– appears to have retained much "baby fat"

Setting: *– in the playroom and playground of the day care*
– the events took place during clean-up time, washroom time, snack time, dressing-up
time as well as during the outdoor activities

Method of observation/recording: *event sampling*

Reason for choice of methodology: *– I was interested in observing a preselected*
behaviour to determine its frequency, duration, and severity.

Behaviour: Defiant behaviour   *– to resist or confront*

                                      – bold opposition

                                      – disposition to oppose or resist

                                      – may include physical or verbal resistance

Time	Antecedent	Behaviour	Consequence
9:00 a.m.	*During clean up time one of the teachers tells Andrew that he needs to be tidying up if he wants snack.*	*Andrew dumps the blocks out of the basket and yells "NO!" while remaining sitting by the mess of blocks.*	*Teacher comes over and physically assists him to clean up the dumped blocks while Andrew resists and continues to say "NO!"*
9:10 a.m.	*The teacher asks Andrew to come and line up with the other children to go to the washroom.*	*Andrew runs into the dolly house and begins to play peek-a-boo through its window.*	*The teacher asks him again to come line up which results in no response, therefore she goes over and takes him by the arm to lead him to the line.*
9:15 a.m.	*The children are seated to have snack. The teacher asks Andrew to sit down. When he does not comply with the request the teacher physically places him on his seat.*	*Andrew pushes himself away from the table and getting out of his seat says "NO! ME HELP!, ME HELP!"*	*The teacher tells him it is not his turn to help and asks him to sit down anew. Andrew does not comply with her request immediately, but as soon as he sees the others eating he joins the table.*

Time	Antecedent	Behaviour	Consequence
9:30 a.m.	Most of the children have finished their snacks. The teacher tells Andrew, who is still eating, to hurry up because it is time to go outside.	Andrew quickly eats his remaining toast and throws his plate on the floor. He remains sitting and refuses to move by saying "NO!"	The teacher physically removes him from the table and helps him pick up his plate to take to the garbage. Andrew continues to say "NO!" and tries to squirm away.

Example to Critique # 3

Event Sample

Name: *Malar*　　　　　　　　Observer: *John*

Age/D.O.B.: *5 yrs, 2 mths*　　　Date/s: *August 9–24*

Context: *Pre-school room of child care centre*

Behaviour: *Frustration – This is a behaviour in which the child shows difficulty in keeping his equilibrium and demonstrates annoyance.*

Reason for observation: *Malar is finding many tasks in the room challenging and appears angry and unhappy.*

Day/date	Tally count	Total
August 9	++++ ++++	10
August 10	/ / /	3
August 13	++++ ++++ ++++ / /	17
August 14	++++ /	6
August 15	++++ / /	7
August 16	++++	5
August 17	++++	5
August 20	++++ ++++ / / /	13
August 21	++++ ++++	10
August 22	++++ /	6
August 23	++++	5
August 24	++++ /	6

Example to Critique # 4

Event Sample

Name: *Patrick*   Observer:

Age/D.O.B.: *6 yrs, 1 mth*   Date/s: *April 19*

Place: *Catholic School, grade one classroom*   Time: *2:10 p.m. – 2:47 p.m.*

Operation behaviour: *short attention span – showing interest in an activity for a short period of time, doing specific things and then moving on to another activity.*

Time	Antecedent	Behaviour	Consequence
2:10	*Was playing with another child with a car port.*	*Another child came over and showed him a boomerang he had made out of popsicle sticks.*	*Patrick moved to creative table and made a boomerang out of popsicle sticks.*
2:15	*Went back to carpet to play with cars.*	*Child came over and asked Patrick to play with him in a fort which was under a table (like a jail).*	*Patrick was lying down and he reached up on top of the table and knocked a plant over. He fixed it and went back to play.*
2:18	*Teacher announces it is time to clean up.*	*Patrick was cleaning up but another child gave him a piece of pencil sharpener.*	*Teacher came and asked him to clean up again.*
2:20	*Teacher asks Patrick to clean up again and put things away in his cubby.*	*Went to cubby but was fooling around with boomerang with another child.*	*Teacher came over and Patrick hid sticks in his shirt and left the area.*
2:45	*Patrick was sitting in circle. Teacher told other children to put their garbage away.*	*Patrick watched them. Children came back.*	*Patrick sat waiting for instructions from teacher.*
2:47	*Teacher told children they were going outside and to go over to cubbies to get ready.*	*Patrick ran over to cubby and put coat on. He took his pinwheel out of cubby and went to the line. Patrick was swinging his pinwheel around.*	*Patrick did not get in trouble but was asked to go outside so he followed the line outside.*

Analysis: *Patrick should have a longer attention span. It may be because he's a boy that he finds it difficult to concentrate. The teacher needs to be more strict with him and make a quieter classroom so that he can concentrate.*

Example to Critique # 5

Event Sample

Name: *Zac*   Observer: *R.D.*

Age/D.O.B.: *8 1/2 months*   Date/s: *February 7*

Setting: *Infant Centre*

Behaviour: *Crying – In this behaviour the individual puckers the face, shows distress in sound, and may shed tears.*

Reason for observation: *Zac was crying frequently in the infant centre. We found his voice piercing.*

Objective: *To determine if Zac cries more frequently than other infants.*

Day	Time	Comment	Total
February 7	8:31–8:35	– separation from mom	4 min.
	8:52–8:55	– fretting? reason	3 min.
	10:03–10:08	– cried after waking	5 min.
	11:09–11:23	– sobbing and crying? attention	14 min.
	11:40–11:43	– saw food and wanted it	3 min.
	12:03–12:04	– ? wind	1 min.
	12:44–12:45	– angry screams and cry – wants toy	1 min.
	1:08–1:14	– cries to be picked up	6 min.
	2:12–2:19	– frustrated with activity	7 min.
	4:20–4:31	– fretful after waking	11 min.
	4:35–4:39	– cries until diaper change	4 min.
	5:01–5:03	– squeaks and cries for attention?	2 min.
	5:08–5:13	– cries - wants food?	5 min.
	5:15–5:18	– cries and throws food on floor	3 min.
	5:30–5:42	– cries while rubbing reddened cheek?	12 min.

Analysis *We did not achieve our objective because we could not time the other infants' crying! We realized that making a comparison was not a statistically significant way of arriving at useful information. It is clear that Zac cries easily. Now we have charted the cries it is obvious that we will have to observe Zac more closely. This observation will be followed up with an ABC sampling so that we can look at possible causes. Narrative recordings might give us some more understanding of Zac's emotions. I have called an informal meeting with Zac's mom. In the back of my mind I am concerned but I cannot put my finger on the problem. I may need to call for some professional support. I am finding that Zac's crying is getting to me and I am not sure if I am objective.*

Example to Critique #6

Event Sampling

Name: *Laura*   Age: *2 years, 2 months*

Date of observation: *March 4, 19—*

Time of observation: *8:30 a.m. – 1:45 p.m.*   Behaviour: *Aggression*

Operational definition: *This is a behaviour in which the child purposely expresses him/herself through undesirable actions or words. These actions and words usually appear as a result of anger or frustration on the child's part. Most of these actions/reactions are hostile actions that can cause harm to the recipient.*

Examples of behaviour: *biting, kicking, slapping, pushing, pulling, spitting, pinching, hitting, name calling, throwing things, physically forcing someone to do something, restraining someone, destroying property, and/or forcefully taking something from another individual.*

Time	Antecedent event	Behaviour	Consequent event
9:32 a.m.	*Inside classroom during freeplay children playing with playdough. Mira took a piece that Laura was playing with.*	*Laura grabbed Mira with both hands pushing her backward.*	*Laura took playdough. Mira picked up car on the floor and began to play with it.*
10:02 a.m.	*At circle time a child sat beside Laura edging closer trying to see the book. Teacher looking at Laura.*	*Laura hit the child with left hand.*	*Teacher said, "I don't like that!"*
		Hit teacher with right hand.	*Teacher grabbed Laura's arm and said, "Oww. I don't like that when you hit me, it hurts me."*
	Laura turned around to shelves behind her.	*Grabbed basket full of people and dumped it on the floor and dropped the basket.*	*Teacher –"Laura you need to pick those up now, we're reading a story now."*
10:06 a.m.	*Asked to pick up the toys.*	*"NO!", pushed basket and people away with hands.*	*Teacher physically removed Laura from circle and talked with her as other teacher read the story.*

Time	Antecedent event	Behaviour	Consequent event
	Came back to circle and began picking up people.	Grabbed man out of another child's hand who appeared to be trying to help. Threw man in basket.	Teacher said, "Laura" while watching what she was doing.
	Finished putting men away (standing).	Sitting back down in original spot in circle, pushed and squirmed her way back into her spot between the other children.	Other children seemed to make discomforting noises and looked towards the teacher.
10:10 a.m. 10:17 a.m.	After circle children all taking off their shoes and putting them in shoe box.	Dumped shoe box upside down and tugged back and forth with it with another child.	Teacher grabbed Laura with both hands and sat her in her lap. Laura squirmed a little but soon appeared to settle.
10:23 a.m.	Children getting ready to go outside, putting snow-suits on. Child whose coat got pulled to the floor stood close to his cubbie looking at Laura.		"Laura and Kimm, the shoes go in the basket." Kimm looked at teacher and began putting shoes back in. Laura walked off towards cubbie. Another teacher grabbed Laura's arm and said, "Kelly asked you to put the shoes back" and walked Laura back to the shoe box and watched as she put the shoes back. Teacher appeared not to notice.
10:30 a.m.	Children putting on their snowsuits and teachers assisting.	Laura grabbed everything in her cubbie and pulled and dumped it on the floor. Went to cubbie to the right of her and pulled out bag – went to next cubbie and pulled out coat. Laura pushed him. Screaming loudly and moving arms and legs around.	Teacher appeared not to notice. Child fell to the ground. Teacher approached Laura and said, "I think you need to leave the other children alone" and removed her and sat her on a chair separate from the other children. Teachers continued to assist children. Teacher sits next to Laura and talks to her alone, then tells Laura to go outside and join the other children (still crying).

Time	Antecedent event	Behaviour	Consequent event
10:45 a.m.	Outside in the playground, Laura climbed up the climber.	Pushed Sophie, who accidentally tripped on her.	Sophie pushed back. Teacher stepped in saying it was an accident.
11:02 a.m.	Playing beside Danny with sand toys.	Danny put down the shovel he was using. Laura picked it up then Danny grabbed it again and they began to tug and scream. Laura eventually got the shovel and then hit Danny on the arm with it. Laura then hit Danny again.	Danny screamed. Teacher came up behind Laura, touched her shoulder, said, "Laura I don't like it when you hit the other children. It hurts." Laura got up and went back to the climber.
	3 children were in washroom getting diaper changed. Laura and Kimm ready to sit on potty. Kimm gets there first and sits down, semi-pushed by Laura. Waiting to use potty.	Laura grabbed Kimm's hair and began to pull. Grabbed Kimm's face with one hand and began to pinch it. "NO!" pulling her arm from and freeing herself from teacher.	Kimm screamed and teacher said, "Laura!" She let go of Kimm's hair and stood in front of the potty looking at Kimm. Kimm screamed and pushed Laura back. Laura stumbled. Teacher said,"Enough you two", then lifted child down from change table and approached Laura. Helped her up and said, "Laura, Kimm is sitting on the potty right now, you can use this one," guiding her over to other potty. You will have to wait until Kimm is finished then." Laura stood back as teacher watched on.
11:53 a.m.	Children lining up after everyone used washroom.	Laura pushed child in front of her. (Seemed to have no reason to do so.) With both hands, squeezed the child in fronts of arms.	Child bumped into next child which caused other children to be bumped. More pushing occurred. Child screamed out. Teacher removed Laura from other children. Children moved to sit in their seats for lunch.
11:57 a.m.	Teacher talking to Laura about pinching and pushing other children.		
12:01 p.m.	Teacher then releases Laura letting her join other children.	Gets to seat at table, pushes chair hard against table.	"Laura, you need to sit down in your chair to have lunch with us." Laura sat down and began to eat her lunch slowly.

Observation Summary

I chose to observe the aggressive behaviours of Laura because of previous observations and encouragement from one of Laura's caregivers. I hoped to discover under what conditions (if any) Laura exhibited aggressive behaviours and the frequency and severity of their occurrences.

I discovered that Laura did in fact exert aggressive acts that usually got a reaction from her caregivers. Her aggressive acts on this particular day resulted in her being removed from the other children on three separate occasions. The circumstances under which Laura was removed, however, were different. She was first removed for appearing to be disruptive and aggressive during circle time and next for pushing a child to the ground and then finally for pushing and pinching a child while lining up for lunch. After each removal the caregiver spoke with Laura about her actions. Laura screamed and cried during the second and longest removal but did not exhibit an aggressive act until approximately 15 minutes later. On the other, shorter removal periods, Laura exhibited an aggressive act almost immediately after returning to the group. Although the severity of these subsequent acts was not very high, it appeared that removing Laura for a longer period of time was more beneficial.

It appears that Laura used physical aggression more often than verbal aggression. She seemed to use her upper body (arms and hands) as a means to commit aggressive acts, (i.e., pushing, hitting, pinching, throwing things, etc...) as opposed to her lower body (legs – kicking or stepping on). It appears that her gross and fine motor skills are more developed than her language/verbal skills. I wonder if Laura's means of expressing anger or frustration will change as she grows and her language development is enhanced?

It seems that although Laura did commit aggressive acts throughout the morning program I was observing, these aggressive acts were not as frequent as I had originally thought. On this particular day the period during and after circle time seemed to cause the highest frequency of aggressive behaviours (11 out of 21 aggressive acts occurred within this time period). It appears that Laura may need a little more individual attention during this time or to be given more appropriate activities to curb her frustrations or anger.

It seems like group activities (circle time, lining up, etc...) are situations which bring about aggressive acts in Laura. In both situations the group's needs were being focussed on by the caregivers more than the individual needs of the children. Because of the toddler's egocentric and solitary style of play it seems that activities like these should occupy the least amount of time possible. I wonder if having the children more involved in the reading of the story or having the children do something while waiting in line could have led to less aggressive behaviours in Laura and the other children.

It seemed like when another child demonstrated an aggressive act on Laura she reacted with an aggressive act (i.e. when pushed, she pushed back). This type of behaviour certainly seems to be the most appropriate type of aggression, however, it still is not a desired reaction. But at this age/stage it certainly should be allowable and not punishable.

I noticed that Laura's aggressive behaviours usually were severe enough to cause harm to other individuals but fortunately did not on this occasion. It seemed like the severest of the aggressive acts Laura exhibited occurred when Laura appeared to want to do or have something and some other child prevented her from having or getting it, (i.e. hitting Danny with the shovel and pinching and pulling Kimm's hair). Again these types of behaviours are undesirable but possibly having more materials (potty's in the washroom, etc...) would decrease the frequency of these undesired behaviours.

From this one written observation I could not distinguish any real patterns in Laura's aggressive acts. She appeared however to be more aggressive towards the other girls in her class on this particular day, but again this was only one observation.

Although Laura's behaviours are not unusual for her particular age/stage it is interesting to wonder why Laura appears to be the most aggressive child in the toddler room. I wonder how her aggressive acts are dealt with in her home environment and how severe they are there and how much of an influence her home environment is on Laura at the daycare. I also wonder if these aggressive acts will in any way help or hinder her future development.

It will be interesting to note the changes (if any) in Laura's aggressive behaviour during the next observation. Of course that will be another day and a whole new set of circumstances and events.

Example to Critique #7

Event Sample

Name: *Crysta*   Age/D.O.B: *5 years, 7 months/August 1, 1985*

Date: *April 8, 19—*

Behaviour: *Pro-social Behaviour – This is a behaviour in which the ability to show generosity, empathy, and be able to take turns is displayed.*

Time	Antecedent event	Behaviour	Consequent event
8:10 a.m.	She is sitting at a table colouring. Another child comes over and says his eye hurts, as he rubs it.	She says to the other child, "Maybe you got sand in it." She looks at him carefully. Then she says, "The more you rub it, the more it will hurt."	The other child stops rubbing his eye for a while.
8:30 a.m.	Five children are sitting around a table colouring. One child is talking.	She looks directly at the child who is speaking and listens actively to the child.	The other children are finished talking. She nods and goes back to drawing.
9:05 a.m.	The teacher says for everyone to stand for 'O' Canada.'	She stands very straight with her hands behind her back throughout the entire song.	She then sits back down when the song is over.
9:15 a.m.	She finds a picture on the floor and she asks whose it is. Another girl says that the picture is hers.	Crysta says, "I don't think it is" and she does not give it to the other child. Then she says, "OK, here," and hands her the picture.	The other girl says, "Thank you" and gives her another picture.

Observation Summary

Pro-social behaviour is usually learned through the modelling of parents and caregivers. At the age of five a child is beginning to interact with others and is becoming less egocentric and therefore is learning to understand other's feelings, thoughts, and ideas. The environment into which a child is placed often affects her behaviour. The centre to which Crysta goes models pro-social behaviour and encourages the children to share and take turns. She seems to show the cognitive abilities to understand how another feels as was seen in the first event. She also seems able to help other children complete a task such as in the last event where she showed another child how to do something. All of these behaviours that are classed as pro-social actions are still in their immature form at this age and stage but the beginnings of these behaviours seem to be present.

Example to Critique # 8

Time Sample

Name: *Perry*   Age/D.O.B: *5 1/2 years*   Date: *January 8–January 15*
Behaviour: *Play – any spontaneous experimental activity.*
Reason for observation: *To see what types of play Perry was involved in during free play.*

Date	Time	Behaviour
January 8	*9:00 a.m.*	*– construction play – associative*
	9:10 a.m.	*– onlooker to book corner*
	9:20 a.m.	*– construction play – cooperative*
	9:30 a.m.	*– construction play – cooperative*
	9:40 a.m.	*– puzzles - solitary*
	9:50 a.m.	*– sand and water – associative*
January 9	*9:00 a.m.*	*– construction play – parallel*
	9:10 a.m.	*– construction play – cooperative*
	9:20 a.m.	*– explaining science table – parallel*
	9:30 a.m.	*– onlooker to book corner*
	9:40 a.m.	*– onlooker to puzzles*
	9:50 a.m.	*– construction play*
January 15	*9:00 a.m.*	*– construction play – associative*
	9:10 a.m.	*– transportation set-up – associative*
	9:20 a.m.	*– transportation set-up – cooperative*
	9:30 a.m.	*– transportation set-up – cooperative*
	9:40 a.m.	*– onlooker to puzzles*
	9:50 a.m.	*– transportation set-up – associative*

◆ ◆ ◆ ◆ Answers to Focus Questions

1. Categorizing behaviours so that they can be charted relies on an understanding of what constitutes a "significant" behaviour. These might be positive, negative, or neutral categories; the observer needs to decide on an objective label for what they are looking for. Observers with a trained eye will select and label categories of behaviour which are developmentally significant.

   Deciding on what you are seeking is the first step but it is essential that you define the label. If, for example, you are looking for samples of cooperative behaviour you need to state what you mean by cooperation; each of the examples must fall within that definition.

2. When labelling and categorizing behaviours observers need to be aware of their own biases and evaluate their actions and recordings. Samplings often imply that a behaviour is "good" or "bad," "positive," or "negative." When writing down the reason for the sampling observation, the observer should check that there is no inappropriately subjective categorizing. Subtle beliefs do influence the way we see; for example, many teachers believe "independence" to be entirely desirable and "dependence" to be avoided. To some, "assertiveness" is similar to "aggression." More subjective still can be the teacher's reaction to different personality types. Charting behaviours, if well categorized, can limit subjectivity.

3. The frequency with which a behaviour occurs can give the observer some clues as to seriousness. Patterns of behaviour can be seen from sampling charts that indicate causes of behaviour and the way in which the child responds to guidance from the teacher. Appreciating the frequency of the demonstration of a behaviour may indicate the necessity for further observation, program changes, or intervention on the part of other professionals.

4. Where patterns of behaviour become apparent there may be an indication of what brought about the behaviour. A sampling may suggest a trigger or cause of a behaviour but this should not be decided on from a single observation. Where a trigger is identified the adult would need to consider removing that trigger, making attempts to de-sensitize the child to whatever precipitated the behaviour, or allow the situation to continue. Where the observation highlighted a cause

of a behaviour the teacher or caregiver might want to evaluate the situation and consider possible changes to the program or guidance strategies. The cause of a behaviour may be outside the adult's influence; where this is the case the adult will need to consider how to help the child to accommodate. The variety of possible causes is wide so that the response would have to be appropriate to the situation. It is necessary to have parental input at all times so that the needs of the child can be met sensitively and so that home and agency work effectively together.

5. Patterns of behaviour can reveal a wide range of information to the observer. A pattern may be determined by any of the following: developmental stage of the child; individual, personal or learning style; previous or other experiences; reaction to the program, staff, or peers; or the state of health and well being. Frequently patterns will be observable which are the result of two or more of these factors.

6. A rating scale could be attached to a sampling chart so that the severity of a behaviour can be evaluated. This tends to be done in situations that are considered to be "negative,"although "positive" behaviour could also be charted. A numerical scale or semantic differential could be used which attempts to make the rating more objective. (See Chapter 5 for further help in using rating scales.)

◆ ◆ ◆ ◆ Key Terms

samplings	inferences
events	assumption
frequency	negative behaviours
duration	positive behaviours
causality	judgment
severity	observer bias
time sample	reliable
antecedent event	tally
behaviour	behaviour modification
consequent	subjective
operational definition	
objectivity	

4 Checklists

Contemporary assessment approaches ask teachers to use checklists to enhance the process of observation and make it more reliable.

Samuel J. Miesels (1993)

Checklists are closed, because they reduce raw data to a tally that indicates the presence or absence of a specified behaviour.

W.R. Bentzen (1985)

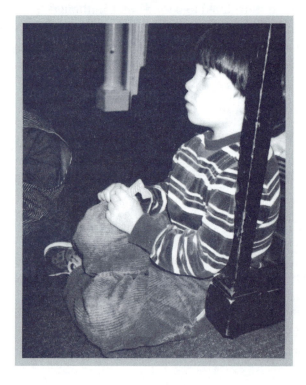

Without appreciating the context of a situation you may jump to the wrong conclusions. This young boy was not being shy, withdrawn, sad, or unco-operative. He sat listening carefully to an adult telling a story.

Focus Questions

1. How could you record behaviours quickly when you are looking to see whether the child exhibits a particular skill?

2. If you listed some behaviours, how could you determine if they were in an appropriate developmental order?

3. Using the list of behaviours you have written and checking them off when you see them might be a good idea, but what could it tell you?

4. If you had to observe and record using a ready-made checklist comprising gross motor and fine motor skills, how would you know if the checklist was any good?

5. If checklist results are not what you expected, what might be the problem?

6. Would you have any concerns about comparing one child's behaviour with what other children can do?

History Notes

Checklists, in their simplest form, allow you to check off items, on a pre-determined list, as they are observed. The testing of children became common in the 1920s. Many testing procedures have been modified over the years to enable the untrained to use them. Items were identified as checklist criteria from the sequences of skills which formed the basis of the earlier tests.

After World War II, a more scientific approach to child rearing focussed on the new post war "baby boom." This approach fostered a need to measure and quantify children's **behaviours** whenever possible. Risking questionable methodologies, teachers, psychologists, and parents sought systems to evaluate children. Checklists easily fulfilled the need; both **norm-referenced** and **criterion-referenced** systems were made easily accessible and usable.

During the 1960s and 70s a less competitive approach to child rearing and a gradually more child-centred focus in learning developed. Some parents and teachers moved away from the more obviously measurable forms of observation and those that they considered to be too subjective or reliant on appropriate inferences. Checklists were, and are, still used but you should be aware of their limitations as well as their uses.

Checklists: Definition

Checklists record the presence or absence of particular pre-determined behaviours such as skills, attributes, competencies, traits, reactions, achievements, or stages of development.

The items on a checklist may be chosen by the observer for a certain purpose, may be from a prepared checklist by a well-known authority or may be written by a group of individuals who have a common reason for observing.

In this interpretative style of observing, the observer records a behaviour demonstrated by checking off the item on the checklist. This may be done at the time it was demonstrated or a short time afterwards.

The home-made checklist

This is a useful tool for the teacher or student to record developmental information about one or more children in a quick and efficient manner. The teacher may want information about the children's **skills** in a particular areas such as language, **fine** or **gross motor skills**, or shape recognition. A list of such skills, if developmentally appropriate and complete, will give the observer some insights into the child's **skill acquisition**. This may be used as part of a program planning change if it is thought that new activities or experiences might be desirable to enable the child to gain the skill.

A parent might desire to keep a record of the sequence in which or dates by which their child achieved particular milestones. In this case a checklist can be prepared which indicates key achievements; not only can these be checked off when they occur, they can also be dated.

A knowledge of the **patterns of development** is essential for either of these types of checklists. This recording can only be as useful as the items in it are sound; reference to recognized authorities on child development will support the writing of the checklist criteria.

The items in the checklist must be **developmentally appropriate** and designed to give you the information you want.

The prepared checklist

Many well-designed checklists are available for use with young children. When choosing ready-made observational tools, the same criteria for appropriate categories apply. If the items are not developmentally appropriate or fit the job you need done, then they will not give useful information.

A teacher, psychologist, caregiver, student, or parent may wish to carry out checklist observations for different reasons, but find that a part of a prepared checklist might be sufficient for the purposes; the whole schedule does not have to be used.

In addition to a specifically prepared checklist, it can be useful to look for sources of checklist criteria from a variety of resources. (See end of chapter for an annotated list of prepared checklists and sources of checklist items. Developmental profiles or schedules could be used for this purpose.)

Features of a Checklist

A checklist can give you worthwhile information if the items it indicates are appropriate. To work out the usefulness of a checklist you will need to assess its appropriateness, validity, and reliability.

Appropriateness

To judge the suitability of a prepared checklist you will need to determine the following:

1. That the checklist covers the areas of behaviour you wish to record.

2. That the items included cover a suitable developmental span of behaviours in the selected domain.
3. That there will be a sufficient blend of behaviours demonstrated to show a pattern, rather than simply whether a behaviour is absent or present.
4. That the checklist will fit your purpose; e.g., for reports, record keeping, program planning, identification of a concern, etc.

Validity

Checklist items must be effective in measuring the behaviours that they intend to assess. You may at first look at a checklist's broad categories and consider how they will provide information in those areas. There need to be sufficient sub-categories which are graduated in their level of difficulty. Without these there will be little chance that the criteria will, in fact, measure what you desire.

Behaviours itemized in a checklist need to be validated by assessing their theoretical basis and underlying foundation of accepted sequences of development. (Refer also to the Introduction and the Screenings and Assessment chapters to examine the notion of validity).

Reliability

Prepared checklists have usually been tested for reliability but you should not assume this. These standardized measures may be used in many situations and be found to be useful, but the reliability may be affected by in-built bias not easily seen. Most significant, but least easily detected, is a cultural bias that can lead an observer to believe that a child is either more advanced or less skilled than he or she is. Even supposedly "standardized" measures may not have eliminated these biases.

To be reliable, a checklist should evaluate a child's behaviour in a way that does not fluctuate from one observation situation to the next. There should be some short-term consistency between outcomes of the checklist recordings. Results should be consistent among observers recording information about a child.

Recording

The observer needs to interpret the checklist criteria and match the observed behaviour to the item. The checklist requires you to mark the presence or absence of the behaviour; often, only check marks are used when the item has been demonstrated. This recording may not be done all at one time, but over a period of a few days, if a wide variety of behaviours is sought.

Most usually the items are checked off as a result of the child's spontaneous activity. On occasions, some desired behaviours will not have been demonstrated, so that an observer may decide to set up a situation in which the behaviour may occur or organize a more formal "testing" situation to elicit the desired response. In any situation, the observer should record the contextual information that might have impacted the behaviour example.

Checklists are frequently used to evaluate information gathered from informal observations, but they may be compiled from a narrative recording or from other documentation. The direct method is more likely to give accurate results.

The analysis or summary: Interpreting the data collected from the checklist

Inferences should not be drawn from the information unless the checklist has been assessed for its suitability and the recording has been made in an objective manner. A typical analysis might cover the following areas:

1. Deductions drawn from the pattern of skills present or absent from the checklist. Statements can be made that highlight the strengths demonstrated.
2. Inferences about the child's skill level can be made by making comparisons with expected performance. This "norm referencing" needs to make clear supporting statements that have thorough validity.
3. Depending on the reason for the observation, you may need to evaluate the effectiveness of the checklist and examine its outcome.
    a. look at the supposed "lack" of skill development; ask yourself

whether the skill has not been acquired or perhaps is present but was not demonstrated

b. verify the checklist with information from others

c. follow up with a variety of other observation methods and attempt to match the outcomes

d. develop an individual program plan that devises activities and experiences to enhance skills

e. ask the parents/school or other interested party to offer insights or other informal observations to help explain the behaviour pattern

f. if the child demonstrates all the criteria little information about the stage of development can be elicited. Use another checklist which is more developmentally appropriate.

How to record a checklist observation

1. Decide on the purpose for using a checklist method.
2. Choose a prepared checklist or devise a list of behaviours that fits your purpose.
3. Assess the checklist for its developmental appropriateness, validity, and reliability.
4. Prepare the checklist and place it where you can record the behaviours as they occur or soon afterwards.
5. Check off the items you see demonstrated and about which you are certain.
6. Make note of any areas about which you are uncertain because of difficulty in interpreting the criteria or when the behaviour is just emerging.
7. When behaviours are not demonstrated, set up experiences so they may be seen. Document this with the results.
8. Make appropriate, validated inferences, remembering that the absence of a behaviour does not necessarily indicate that the child is incapable of performing the behaviour.

Prepared checklists and sources of checklist items

K.E. Allen and L. Marotz, *Developmental Profiles – birth to six.* New York: Delmar, 1989.

Six, one-page developmental checklists charts for children at 12 months, 2 yrs, 3 yrs, 4 yrs, 5 yrs, and 6 yrs. Each contains broad categories of behaviours – good for an overview but not very refined. Emphasizes easily observable skills rather than cognitive activity that requires more interpretation. Text of book covers more detailed profiles of growth and development in each developmental domain, offering age/stage divisions. These could be adapted for use as checklists.

J. Herr. *Working with Young Children : The Observation Guide.* Illinois : Goodheart – Will Cox, 1990.

Several prepared age-related (birth to five yrs) or developmental-domain-itemized checklists designed for college students learning about children's development. Could also be used by practising teachers, caregivers, and parents.

J. Beaty. *Observing Development of the Young Child.* 2nd Ed. Ohio: Merrill,1990.

Textbook written around a developmental checklist called "Child Skills Checklist," appropriate for three- to five-year-olds in any setting. Each developmental area is included (12 categories) with eight items in each category. Broad categories may not reveal specific information but useful for any observer. Book identifies how each skill may be developed by appropriate **curriculum** planning.

D. Norris and J. Boucher. *Observing Children.* Toronto Observation Project, The Board of Education for the City of Toronto '80.

A guide to observing children in the age ranges 2 – 5 yrs, 5 -7 yrs, 7 – 9 yrs, 9 – 11 yrs, and 11 – 13 yrs. Categories of skill development are identified. The school age profiles are particularly useful and could be used as checklist items.

M. Sheridan. *The Developmental Progress of Infants and Young Children .* HMSO, 1968.

M. Sheridan. *Children's Developmental Progress from birth to five: the Stycar sequences.* NFER, 1974.
A detailed listing of emerging behaviours identified in closely defined age ranges. Intended for developmental paediatric use, the book lends itself to formulating theoretically sound checklists which might be used by any caregiver, teacher, or informed parent.

G.J. Schirmer, ed. *Performance Objectives for Pre-school Children.* Sioux Falls, SD: Adapt Press, 1974.
A developmental checklist covering a wide range of developmental domains. Each age category and domain has several identified categorized skills.

S. Furuno, K. O'Reilly, *et al. Hawaii Early Learning Profile (Birth to three years).* HELP Checklist '88 VORT Corporation. *Help for Special Preschoolers Assessment Checklist. Ages 3 -6.* VORT Corporation, 1987.

Two detailed checklists covering hundreds of behaviours. Supporting resources include *HELP Activity guide* and *Help... at home*, which give those working with children practical suggestions for supporting skill development. HELP charts enable checklist information to be presented in an easy-to-interpret format. Both checklists are intended for the majority of children who fall within the age ranges – not necessarily those with developmental concerns.

A mom brings her young son to the college for ECE students to observe. Observations are more likely to be successful if the child feels emotionally supported. The students record their observations and compare their findings after the visit.

Checklists

Advantages	Disadvantages
Quick, efficient.	Recording so simple, errors not easily seen.
Can be used in a variety of settings.	It loses the detail and context of the observed
All details need not be recorded.	behaviour.
Records clear picture of the presence or	May require a degree of inference or interpre-
absence of behaviour.	tation in recording.
	Criteria can easily be inappropriate, invalid, or
Observer can choose criteria to observe.	unreliable.
Observer can record observation while	
responsible for children's care.	Interpretation typically focusses on what the
Observer can choose to record information	child cannot do rather than the skills she has
about more than one child at a time.	mastered.
Coverage of a range of developmental aspects	Checklist requires prior evaluation and prepa-
may offer overview of whole child.	ration.
Information can be used for program planning.	Tends to represent a selection of isolated frag-
	ments of behaviour.
Prepared checklists may be available which are	Information about child's skill development
valid and reliable.	does not necessarily translate into appropriate
Method can identify concerns where individual	goal setting/planning.
is not performing as per the "norm."	
	Checklist criteria may be difficult to validate for
Method records only presence or absence of	developmental appropriateness.
behaviour. Most formats do not allow for	Typically relies on "norm referencing," which is
"evidence" to be stated.	considered a dubious tool by some educators.
	Recorded behaviours may require a qualitative
	description in addition to stating presence or
	absence.
	The absence of a behaviour does not neces-
	sarily indicate an inability to perform the
	behaviour.
	Recording might be affected by emotional
	conditions or illness which might not be
	evident.
	Teachers and parents tend to "remember"
	behaviours and record them as present from
	previous occasions – these may be expecta-
	tions rather than objectively recorded exam-
	ples.

◆ ◆ ◆ ◆ *Assignment options*

I. Skill building

Individual tasks

1. From the data of a narrative observation, transfer information to a checklist. You will need to select a checklist that encompasses the skills identified.
2. Evaluate any available checklists to determine their
   a. usefulness
   b. age/stage appropriateness
   c. validity/reliability
3. List your reasons for using checklists. Prioritize your list. If speed is the first criterion, evaluate your use of checklists to ensure that you avoid using them for speed rather than accuracy.

Group tasks

1. Choose a checklist, distribute it to the group, have each member record the presence or absence of behaviours of skills demonstrated by a child. Compare results.
2. Find any ready-made checklist and see if you can find any significant behaviours that might be missing.
3. Write a list of caregiver skills and score each member of the group using your checklist.
4. Using the child development knowledge you have gained from Piaget's work, write a sequenced list of behaviours that would be in accordance with his theories. Is this a valid or reliable tool?
5. From an already scored checklist, work in groups to formulate objective inferences. You might wish to start by making some summary statements in each of the developmental domains. Critique each other's statements; record only what the group agrees to be objective.
6. From the inferences stated (in #5), work in your group to determine an individual program plan for the child.

II. Practising checklist methods

1. Instead of checking only the presence or absence of skills on a checklist, write down, in brief, the specific evidence for each criterion.

2. Select a checklist to fit the purpose you require – state the purpose and why your choice of checklist is appropriate.

3. Scan a checklist's items to see if you expect the presence of some behaviours and absence of others. (A checklist which has each item checked off will tell you as little as if none is checked. What proportion of items should be considered "present" for the checklist to be considered valuable?)

4. For each cluster of developmental criteria, ensure that behaviours not identified are not missed. What behaviours might you add to the checklist?

5. Attempt to write your own checklist based on what you want to reveal. State its limitations.

6. Critique the checklist examples that follow, according to the following criteria:
   ◆ appropriateness of methodology chosen
   ◆ contextual information offered
   ◆ checklist substantially completed
   ◆ objectivity of recording
   ◆ summary of information in each developmental area
   ◆ analysis makes objective inferences
   ◆ inferences supported by reason and validation
   ◆ inferences supported by reference to theory, accepted norms, or other criteria
   ◆ insight into the "whole" child – interaction between areas of development
   ◆ suggestions for program planning
   ◆ parental input
   ◆ further need to observe identified

Examples to critique

The following checklist examples are offered as observational samples to critique. They are not intended to represent "ideal" examples of the technique.

Activities may be set up so that a teacher can evaluate particular skills. Three girls chose threading beads. Their fine motor skills are evident and can be recorded on checklists.

Example to Critique #1

Infant References Checklist (A checklist designed by a caregiver)

Name: *Alyson*   Age: *3 weeks (20 days)*

D.O.B. : *Jan 15, 1991*   Date observed/time observed: *Feb 5, 1991 at 9:30 a.m.*

Physical characteristics: *Alyson has a little brown hair, brown eyes, and a dark complexion. She weighs 10 lb 1 oz.*

Setting: *Alyson was brought into development class for the students to have an opportunity to observe a newborn infant. Alyson sat on her mother's knee in front of the class with the students facing her.*

Method of observation/recording : *Checklist – self-selected list of infant reflexes*

Reason for choice of methodology: *This was the best way to identify and record the many reflexes that are said to be present in a newborn infant.*

What I intended the observation to reveal: *In observation class we've read and discussed the importance of an infant's inborn reflexes. This observation gave me the chance to observe for myself and get a better understanding of the different reflexes present in the newborn.*

Observer: *Student Early Childhood Educator P.R.*

Checklist of Major Reflexes in the Neonate

Reflex	Present (Yes/No)	Comment
Rooting	Yes	At first it didn't appear to be present, but after her mother stopped rubbing her cheek, Alyson turned toward her.
Sucking	Yes	Alyson appeared to suck on her mother's finger when it was placed near her mouth. This shows that an infant may suck on anything placed near its mouth.
Swallowing	?	Although this reflex could not be seen we know that in order for an infant to be able to live they must be able to swallow. Therefore it is assumed that Alyson has this reflex.
Moro	No	At this time the moro reflex was not able to be seen. A book, which made a loud noise, was dropped to the side of Alyson. Alyson made no movement that I could see. This, however, would have to be tested more to really tell.
Babinsky	Yes	This reflex could be seen quite well when the bottom of her foot was rubbed. Alyson splayed out her toes and then tucked them back in.
Grasp	Yes	Alyson grasped her mother's finger when it was placed in her palm – the palmer grasp.
Stepping	?	It appeared that Alyson has passed the time to demonstrate this reflex -when she was held up in a standing position she didn't make any movement at first and when she did move it was only a slight movement with her legs. This reflex is usually seen in the first days of an infant's life and then it disappears – it appears that it is now disappearing with Alyson.

Summary

By watching Alyson it was apparent that many of the newborn reflexes were present in her. The reflexes that I have recorded are the major reflexes and there are many more, but these are the most important ones and easily recorded. The only reflex that appeared to be disappearing was the stepping reflex, which could only be seen slightly. The moro reflex could not be seen when a book was dropped, but this is not sufficient testing to make a clear statement.

This was the first time I had an opportunity to observe a neonate. At 20 days she was not demonstrating the reflexes as would a completely newborn infant, as some of the reflexes disappear soon after birth.

Example to Critique #2

Name: *Jahar*

Age: *17 m*

Observer: *(R.S.) – home daycare provider*

Observation checklist: *– motor development list for 18 month child*

Source of items: *F. Caplan,* The Second Twelve Months of Life

Setting: *Private home daycare*

Background info: *Jahar has been in my home during the weekdays for 5 months. He has gotten used to my other children, Thomas, 14 months and James, 2 yrs 2 months. Jahar lives with his mom and his 7 yr old sister in an apartment near my house.*

Why observe: *Jahar's mother and I are concerned that he is not yet walking.*

Gross motor

Onset of creeping backward downstairs	*– creeps by shuffling on bottom*
Picks up toy from floor without falling	*– only when holding on to stable furniture*
Moves chair to cabinet and tries to climb	*– No*
Tries to climb out of crib	*– No*
Walks fast; seldom falls	*– No*
Runs stiffly; falls	*– No*
Can run into adult chair and seat self	*– No*
Uses whole arm movements in ball play	*– hold out arms as ball comes to him when seated*
Walks with one foot on walking board	*– ?*
Jumps off floor with both feet	*– ?*
Walks into ball; not yet able to make definite imitative kicking motion	*– No*

Summary

This checklist gives the idea that at 18 months Jahar should be walking. Jahar has an unusual way of moving himself – he slides along the floor in a seated position with his left leg always tucked under him. I wondered if he has a leg problem but when he pulls himself up, he balances OK on both legs. I've suggested to Mom to take Jahar to her family doctor to check this out. Some children don't walk until 18 months or so. I don't know if this is a problem but I've never met a child of this age who can't walk.

Example to Critique #3

Name: *Mark*
Age: *8 yrs 8 months*
Date: *November 16 1992*
Observation: *Checklist*
Source: *"Observing Children" Toronto Observation Project, 1980*
"values, attitudes, and decision making" 7-9 yrs.
Setting: *After-school program at Metro Toronto Child Care Centre*
Method: *Observation assisted by child's answers to questions.*
Reason for observation: *Mark appeared to be lacking in social skills and did not mix easily within the group. He was willing to talk about himself to the adults. We felt that some self revelation would be positive for his self esteem.*
Observer: *(M.R.) Early Childhood Educator*
     Recreation Leader

Values, attitudes, and decision-making

1. Is child developing confidence and a feeling of self-worth? Note: independence and motivation; growing awareness and acceptance of own strengths and short comings.
2. How does child show sensitivity to others? Does the child respect rights and property? assume responsibility? become more interested in others? accept individual differences?
3. How would you describe child's working style? e.g., thorough, superficial, quick, slow.
4. Does child prefer to work independently? with small/large groups?
5. What role does child take in group? e.g., prefers to lead, follow.
6. How does child share? e.g., willingly, with assistance, with difficulty.
7. How long does child work at a task? e.g., tries more than one way of doing the same thing.
8. Is child able to change easily from one task to another?
9. Are plans made, started, left unfinished, changed, completed, compared with plans of others?
10. How are plans described?
11. How does child react to conflict? e.g., banters, argues, tattles.

12. Is child able to make decisions? Can child make choices? How much assistance is required? Can child support own decisions? Can child assume responsibility for them?

13. How does child "deal with" own /group problems? e.g., becomes frustrated, perseveres, changes, adapts, asks questions, seeks help, shares, and cooperates with others.

14. How does child accept and respond to limits, rules, and routines?

15. How does child describe, evaluate, and share own achievements? e.g., suggests way to improve, shows willingness to accept opinion of others.

1. *Obs – appears quiet and introverted*
   Mark – "I know I'm not good at some of the games but the other kids leave me out – I should be friendlier."

2. *Obs – seems to be helpful with younger children but has little contact with his own age group*
   Mark – "I like the little ones and they look up to me, I think everyone's different – but they don't accept me – or I don't think so."

3. *Obs – slow, thoughtful*
   Mark – "I do better at school where I know what I've got to do."

4. *Obs – solitary or with younger children*
   Mark – "I like my own company and I don't want to force myself on no one."

5. *Obs – prefers to be leader with younger children*
   Mark – "I'd like to be a leader – wouldn't everyone – but they have to follow – the kids follow, so to them I am a leader."

6. *Obs – shares with anyone if asked – gives away own candy, shares toys.*
   Mark – "I have a big family, we have to share – but Alan – my big brother – he takes everything if I don't hide it."

7. *Obs – about average*
   Mark – "Once I've gotten into something I stay at it."

8. *Obs – changes direction easily to please*
   Mark – "My concentration is not always good but I get along with what people want me to do."

9. *Obs – doesn't always finish what he starts*
   Mark – " I haven't really done much since I got here."

10. *Obs – none described*
    Mark – "I haven't really got any."
11. *Obs – avoids conflict – tells tales*
    Mark – "I don't see the point in a fight – they think I'm a nerd."
12. *Obs – makes choices as a "soft option"*
    Mark – "What decisions do I have to make?"
13. *Obs – avoids group problems – they are not "his"*
    Mark – "I leave people alone to get over it. I don't like people getting upset – my mom does sometimes – I like people to get along."
14. *Obs – accepts rules, doesn't argue*
    Mark – "I wish everyone obeyed the rules, why don't they, it's a lot easier."
15. *Obs – Mark doesn't think he has achieved much*
    Mark – "I don't like people telling me I'm not doing it right -it's better not to bother."

Summary

We will need to continue to assess Mark's self-esteem. At the group meeting we may think of ways of getting Mark to be more positive and to be successful at something.

Example to Critique #4

Name: *Taylor*
Age: *4 yrs 10 m*
Observation: Checklist: *Source Q 29 – 35 "Protecting Children – A Guide for Social Workers"*
Setting: *child's home/ nursery school*
Observers: *Nursey School Teacher and Teacher's Assistant within the child's home*

Reason for observation: *an incidence of child abuse has been detected involving an older female sibling. The abuser has not been identified. Taylor needs to be assessed; nursery school teacher reports regression in social-emotional areas.*

Background information: *Taylor has been an active young child appearing to be developing normally. Recent concern about changing family arrangements, potential abuse of an older sibling, and her mother's depression has brought social work involvement.*
Observer *(R.L.) Social worker*

Does the child:	Yes/no
◆ use speech appropriately?	*yes*
◆ explore the environment in a normal way?	*yes*
◆ respond to parent(s)?	*yes*
◆ keep himself or herself occupied in a positive way?	*no*
◆ seem relaxed and happy?	*?*
◆ have the ability to express emotions?	*?*
◆ to react to pain and pleasure?	*yes*
◆ express frustration?	*yes*
◆ respond to parental limit setting?	*?*
◆ exhibit observable fears?	*yes*
◆ react positively to physical closeness?	*yes*
◆ exhibit body rigidity or relaxation?	*relaxation*

Summary

The checklist items indicate areas of behaviour which could, if supported by other evidence, lead to questions being raised as to their cause. This is highly speculative observation. Each indicator lends itself to interpretation and perhaps examples being given. Many of the behaviours are not to be considered as constant; a brief observation is insufficient to make any significant inferences.

Taylor does appear to be behaving as expected and is not demonstrating any behaviours that lead us to believe that she is at risk.

Further observations, and interviews with the parents and with Taylor's teacher will need to be tracked. The summary is drawn more from intuition than recorded data.

Answers to focus questions

1. The fastest, but not always the most accurate, way of recording developmental information is to check off items on a checklist. The checklist items should be developmentally appropriate and cover the areas that the observer was seeking.

2. Listing behaviours and using that list as a checklist is an acceptable way of gaining developmental information. But the list might not cover behaviours in an appropriate developmental sequence. If you wrote the list without reference to a well-researched authority you might find stages missing or wrongly sequenced. There are several recognized authors of developmental charts which are carefully norm referenced. These might be useful resources to check your own listing or to be used as the basis of checklist items. Gesell, Allen, and Marotz, Sheridan, or Norris and Boucher might be good sources to look for.

3. Checklists will give you a quick overview of the presence or absence of the demonstration of particular skills. Where they cover a range of developmental domains you might find that they can offer a profile of an individual's development. They may raise concerns, indicate areas of need, point to necessary curriculum changes or the need for further observation and evaluation. It is essential that the user of a checklist understands their limitations as well as their apparent efficiency.

4. It is important to examine the underlying philosophy and theory of development on which a checklist is based. This will help the observer to evaluate its usefulness and consider its match to their own philosophy. Standardized checklists will have been tested for their validity and reliability; the data showing this can be checked out. You would have to determine whether or not the checklist fitted your needs and covered the developmental stages required. When you have done these things you will know if it is of any use to you.

5. Results from any systematic observation may be at variance with what you expected for reasons attached to the checklist's effectiveness, the observer's recording, and the child's performance. Check out the checklist itself to ensure that it measures what you need to be evaluated (see previous question). The way in which items are scored will affect the outcome; the observer will need to double-check this, ensuring that the items have been understood and interpreted correctly. If the child's performance differs from what was expected there may be some reasons for that. The observer might have been

unduly influenced by subjectivity in making incorrect assumptions about the child's ability when observing in a naturalistic manner. Systematic observation can be more objective. Against that, it is highly probable that the child might feel watched for the testing purposes and behave in a more subdued or anxious way. The time when the checklist was recorded may not have been one where a representative sample of behaviour was being demonstrated; the child may have been sick or unhappy at the time. Because a checklist focusses on the presence or absence of a skill it is possible that an item is presumed "absent" when the child happened not to demonstrate it. These concerns highlight the importance of validating inferences by seeking information in a variety of ways.

6. Teachers tend to know what is typical behaviour in their age group. They learn this from observation. The information is quite valid and guides them to make appropriate programming. The group of children in the teacher's care is not, though, a statistically significant sample. A much larger group would need to be surveyed and measured for teachers to be able to make reliable comparative comments. Comparing two children is not appropriate and leads to subjective evaluation.

◆ ◆ ◆ ◆ *Key Terms*

checklists
behaviours
norm-referenced
criterion-referenced
skills
fine motor skills
gross motor skills
skill acquisition
patterns of development
developmentally appropriate
validity
reliability
curriculum

5 Charts, Scales, and Pictorial Representations

Mapping the children's movements on a floor plan of my room helped me to reorganize my space a bit better. The older children watched me watching them – they decided to record my movements so I gave them a copy of the floor plan.

ECE student (1993)

Plotting on the chart shows a steady upward curve for each child. When this ascent either slows down abnormally, dips or flattens out, it tells the caregiver something is happening to that particular child.

Veronica Rose (1985)

Menu plans need to be provided for parents to review. Although known allergies must be catered for, adults must also observe and record any significant behavioural changes.

◆ ◆ ◆ ◆ # History Notes

Visual depictions of observational information have derived from mathematical-style representations. Some of these forms have been used for hundreds of years. They usually rely on quantitative evaluation, which is presented as numerical **scales**, **graphs**, and scale diagrams.

The idea that social topics could be subjected to **quantitative analysis** acquired prominence in the first part of the 17th century. This analysis concerned demographic enumeration, rather than the types of quantification needed by teachers and psychologists today. In 1886, Meitzen, a professor at the University of Berlin, published a book on statistics which described the usefulness of collecting, tabulating, and interpreting demographic and social data. Although the book was published in the United States, the move towards data collection was occurring in Europe as well as in North America.

Family trees are a form of social data collection. Some date back before the 11th century. A renewed interest in tracing ancestry has re-established itself, perhaps because of the mobility of families and the need to search for roots. Family, cultural, religious, or ethnic attitudes and beliefs may be under threat when such moves occur. Appreciation of the importance of the child's background has led professionals and parents to seek this documentation.

Mappings and **trackings** pre-date the emphasis on the learning environment, which evolved from the theories of 1960s educationalists. But the 1960s and 1970s were times of change in educational and caregiving agencies. New understandings about how children learn led to different styles of construction of children's environments to allow for choices, self-direction, free movement, open planning, and, in some instances, mixed age groups. The environments needed to be planned and evaluated in use. Mappings and trackings came to be well-used ways of maximizing learning potential in space and activity planning.

Observation charts have evolved out of the need to find quick and efficient ways of recording information. Many have evolved from charts used by the medical and nursing profession, which date back more than a century. Growth, medical, and infant information can fit the chart methods most easily because they offer clear-cut, rather than qualitative, ways of recording.

The earliest rating scales were in use in the 1920s and 1930s. The *Twenty-Eighth Yearbook of the National Society for the Study of Education* (1929) cites types of personality and social rating scales. Further scales were published by other authors in 1930 (Irwin and Bushnell, 1981).

Educational planning is documented to have happened for centuries. Monks or other religious people formulated **syllabuses** for the students, which pre-dated the invention of the printing press. These often focussed on religion, were rigorous, and demanded a high level of skill acquisition. "Content" was the emphasis of syllabuses for several hundred years. The specific subjects, topics, or material to be learned was decided upon on the basis of necessary trade skills; the student's social class, and what was considered "essential" knowledge. Not until research psychologists offered insights into how children grow, learn, and develop was the focus moved from what should be taught, to the way in which children learn. Significant changes in the 1960s led to **integrative curriculum models**. Newer educational trends have led to developmentally appropriate planning models.

The newest thrust is towards accountability for the children's learning outcomes. The most up-to-date planning models evolve from a blend of developmental understanding and clearly stated learning outcomes which also contain elements of in-process evaluation.

Social relationships were not commonly represented in diagrammatic forms until the late 1960s and 1970s. **Sociometry** became popular in the 1970s because it offered a way of depicting the dynamics of relationships. At this time there was a rising awareness of the necessity for individuals to be evaluated in their naturalistic setting rather than in a test situation. Also, new insights encouraged both individual and group behaviour to be looked at; sociometry allowed for both simultaneously. For similar reasons, at much the same time, the **genogram** evolved from family systems theory. Murray Bowen's (1978) work provided the conceptual framework for analyzing genogram patterns.

The **ecomap** is a more recent model than other social mappings. Offering a simple diagrammatic representation of the ecological influences on the child's development it came into frequent use in the 1980s. Allowing for a clearer understanding of the influences on an individual, it has gained popularity with social workers and psychologists interested in the sociological and contextual aspects of the child's experience.

Charts, scales, and pictorial representations: Definitions

Charts

Observed information that is recorded onto a pre-written format or map according to specified criteria.

Scales

A form of measurement of information that uses lists of behaviours or other items and rates them according to pre-determined values.

Pictorial representations

Any form of recording or interpretation that uses visual presentations to demonstrate collected data.

Features of Charts, Scales, and Pictorial Representations

Charts, scales, and pictorial representations are all interpretative methods of recording observational data. They enable the recorder to write down information quickly and efficiently as the observer perceives it. These methods are heavily dependent on the objectivity of the recorder; frequently there is little way of validating the accuracy of the recording. Practising teachers may need to observe while engaged in activity with the children. These forms of recording may enable the teacher to collect information that might be impossible using more time-consuming methods. The caregiver may need to find ways of jotting down bits of information without leaving the activity of the group.

Some charts and many pictorial representations and scales are completed soon after the activity is over. Again, their easy use enables the teacher to record some of the essence of what was observed without writing all the details. This recording requires professional skill in deciding what is relevant and what is not significant. Almost any untrained person could complete a rating scale or chart; some of the information might be useful and accurate but it is difficult to know if it is reliable. What is most troubling is that the outcome may look fine but lack the objectivity of the professional's work. These observations should not be used alone to determine any individual's program plan. They can be used as an adjunct to other observation methods, in which case they may be helpful in providing a fuller picture.

Useful recording methods

Charts, scales, and pictorial representations are methods for recording observational data or ways in which information is presented after analysis. They have in common the use of visual representation of information. The following are the most useful categories for the observer.

Observation charts

These are prepared "blank" forms with labelled and sectioned categories to be used for charting behaviours, relationship dyads (connections/inter-actions between two individuals), routine events, and other significant information as it is observed.

Observation scales

Commonly called rating scales, these are listings of behaviours or traits prepared in advance for scoring at the time of or after observation. These can be open to subjective recording. They may include **forced choices**, semantic differentials, numerical scales, or **graphic scales**.

Social maps

Pictorial presentations of the family composition, history, social relation-ships, or life experiences are all helpful to the observer. These may include sociograms, ecomaps, genograms, family trees, and flow diagrams or pictorial profiles. Information is gained from an individual, involved family members, or those in other social relationships and is presented as a chart or diagram.

Mappings

Trackings or mappings are observations of a child's movement or activity within a specified room zone or space. By recording the path of movement on a prepared map of that space, the teacher has evidence of the child's mobility interests and attention span. Mappings may support a teacher's evaluation of the use of space.

Interpretive graphic representations

In analyzing quantities of observations the observer might wish to explain her findings in visual ways. Graphs, block charts, and pie charts are simple methods designed to make evaluative comparisons.

Planning/curriculum models

Visual presentations of planning approaches derived from observational information are easier to use than narrative forms. Various models have been designed to complement curriculum design theories.

Observation charts

Recording behaviour on a wide variety of charts has been an observation method of choice for many teachers because it can be quick, efficient, and be done while the teacher continues to participate in the children's program. Routines and sequences of the child's day may be recorded to help indicate the child's personal rhythms, their adaptation to a changing environment, and to assist a caregiver in being responsive to the child's needs. Using a prepared form or chart, the caregiver can check off when particular events have occurred. These may involve sleep, rest, feeding, periods of activity, diaper changing, or when bowel or bladder elimination has taken place. They can detail much more than the input/output charts used in nursing. The pattern of feeding, wakefulness, sleep, and toileting can give clues to the child's health and well being. These have often been used for infants but their use should not be underestimated with toddlers and older children in circumstances where identification of behaviour patterns could help the teacher/caregiver to appreciate the needs of the child in a holistic sense.

Effectiveness of charting observations relies on the underpinnings of the philosophy on which the chart is based, the appropriateness of the chart in its inclusion of a range of predictable categories, the accuracy of the recording of the adult as he interprets what he sees, and the consistency of interpretation between adults using the chart.

Obvious limitations of charts lie in their simplicity, which offers little opportunity for explanations of behaviour. It is tempting to make efficient use of a chart and to avoid analyzing the resulting patterns and identifying need for intervention. As forms of record keeping they need to be used, not just stored. While you must appreciate the need to observe indicators of individual needs, health, well being, and disease so that you can be responsive, it is also important to see this information within its familial and social context, and to understand its impact on the interrelated aspects of the child's growth and development.

Note: The inferences made on a chart may be helpful but should not stand alone in making evaluations of any child.

Participation charts can give teachers a good indication of the interests, motivation, and focus of individual children or groups. They frequently quantify involvements but their weakness can be that they offer little opportunity to describe the quality of activity. Some charts allow for recording the number of children involved in a specified activity, others count activity in pre-designated time slots or will enable the teacher to determine who has participated. Charts may be designed to increase the child's responsibility for her activity by having the child herself check off what she has "done."

Charts may be designed to increase parent – teacher communication or facilitate exchanges of information between caregivers. Separate charts for each child may be useful for focussing on an individual; adults may consider "group" charts helpful for program planning. If the latter is the case, caution should be taken in making assumptions about the "average" or "majority" responses, and planning curriculum on that basis. "Averages" may in fact apply to nobody; the groups of children may have levels of **competence** and participation above or below that average; your programming may not suit anybody. Similarly, focussing on the "majority" may leave out children who are in need.

Observations of health indicators and symptoms may be needed to be made by adults, caregivers, social workers, or teachers who may be able to offer information to health professionals. Charting symptoms can only be done where the non-health professional is trained in what to look for. Children with a variety of special medical conditions such as asthma, anaemia, cystic fibrosis, diabetes, eczema, epilepsy, or allergies may be in mainstream settings but need close observation and appropriate intervention when particular symptoms are demonstrated. Many of these children may have mild conditions, others much more severe; they all will need to have observational information passed from and to parents and caregivers and a further connection made with the assigned health professionals assigned.

Caregiver – Parent Information Chart for Infants

Infant's name:

Week of:

Age/D.O.B.:

Caregiver(s) names:

		Mon	Tues	Wed	Thurs	Fri
Liquid intake	a.m.					
	p.m.					
Solid intake	a.m.					
	p.m.					
Sleep	a.m.					
	p.m.					
Activity	a.m.					
	p.m.					
Urination	a.m.					
	p.m.					
Bowel movements (BMs)	a.m.					
	p.m.					
Behaviour notes	a.m.					
	p.m.					
Comments/ messages	a.m.					
	p.m.					

In this example the information chart offers essential information to parents. It may allow for a changeover of caregiver while sustaining the information flow. However brief, the notes can form the basis of a log, which over weeks can show developmental changes. The chart may be an aid to the caregiver's memory when he/she can offer some verbal anecdotal accounts to support the information. This is an example of an observational recording chart that the caregiver uses to keep an ongoing record of observations of the infant's day.

Daily Program Implementation Chart

Children's names:

Ages/D.O.B.:

Date:

Observer(s):

Activity area	Materials	Objectives	Observation
Creative			
Language			
Sensory			

This planning and observation chart underpins the notion of a dynamic, ongoing process of observation and activity planning. Although the activity area is mentioned first, it would always be as a response to the previous day's observations. The following day, these observations would be used to determine the new plan.

Activity Response Chart

Zone, activity, or room area	Children's names				
	Child 1	Child 2	Child 3	Child 4	Child 5

The activity response chart shares some features with event sampling, but the observer writes only a tally or check-mark to identify the individual child's involvement in a particular activity. An alternative is to have separate charts at the activity or learning centre. You can check off the child's name as he or she participates.

Pattern of the Day Chart

Name:

Age/D.O.B.:

Date:

Context:

Observer:

Time	Activity/routine	Y/N – Choice	Feeding	Personal care	Rest/sleep	Outdoor activity	Play	Other
6:00 a.m.								
6:30 a.m.								
7:00 a.m.								
7:30 a.m.								
8:00 a.m.								
8:30 a.m.								
9:00 a.m.								
9:30 a.m.								
10:00 a.m.								
10:30 a.m.								
11:00 a.m.								
11:30 a.m.								
12:00 p.m.								
12:30 p.m.								
1:00 p.m.								
1:30 p.m.								
2:00 p.m.								
2:30 p.m.								
3:00 p.m.								
3:30 p.m.								
4:00 p.m.								
4:30 p.m.								
5:00 p.m.								
5:30 p.m.								
6:00 p.m.								
6:30 p.m.								
7:00 p.m.								
7:30 p.m.								
8:00 p.m.								
8:30 p.m.								
9:00 p.m.								

The pattern or rhythm of the child's day needs to be considered with reference to her context and any routine which is imposed. Infant schedules may be structured or responsive; if flexible, the pattern will reveal the child's natural rhythm and may help indicate the child's personal style. Older children continue to have their own patterns; if accommodated, they may be happier and more able to maximize their learning opportunities.

Immunization Record

Immunization type	Date	Reaction	Given by

Parents may wish to keep an immunization record card for their own benefit to keep aware of immunization needs. Agencies may wish to see the record with verification of the information.

Patterns of Relationships Within a Group

Children's names:

Ages/D.O.B.:

Date/times:

Context:

Observer(s):

Child	A	B	C	D	E	F	G	H	I	J
A	■									
B		■								
C			■							
D				■						
E					■					
F						■				
G							■			
H								■		
I									■	
J										■

This chart is appropriate for use with pre-school and school-age children. Observe the children involved in various activities where they are free to choose their companions. Record interactions between children with a **tally mark** in the appropriate box. Where two children interact for longer than five minutes, put another check-mark. Patterns of interactions will enable you to identify isolated children and those who have made social relationships. It is possible to use the chart to classify (by means of a colour-coded tally) positive, negative, or neutral interactions which would add a further dimension. This does require further interpretation, which has to be recorded in-process.

Components of Participation Chart

Names:

Ages/D.O.B.:

Observer:

Activity:

Names	Physically involved	Follows instructions	Attempts to solve problems	Cooperates with others in action/ verbally	Constructive /creative	Keeps on task

This chart can be used by teachers/caregivers to record participatory information about a selected activity for a group of children. While providing ease and efficiency of recording, it should not be assumed that each of the components of participation is, of itself, always positive. Participation that is appropriate and valid may involve solitary activity, experimentation, and even destruction! The chart's results can be useful if analyzed with an avoidance of judgments and assumptions.

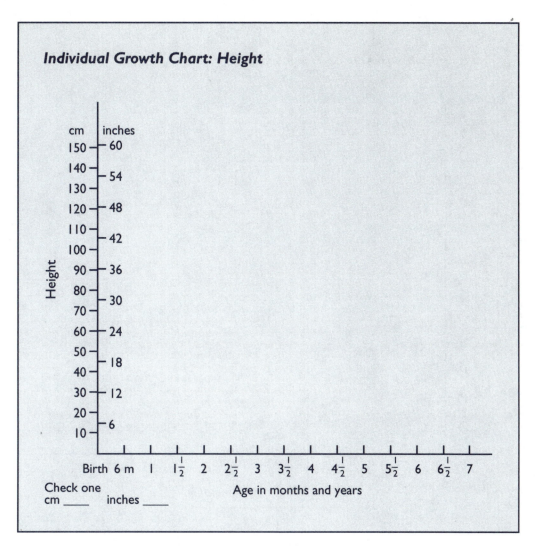

Individual Growth Chart: Height

cm	inches
150	60
140	54
130	
120	48
110	42
100	
90	36
80	30
70	
60	24
50	18
40	
30	12
20	
10	6

Height

Birth 6 m 1 1½ 2 2½ 3 3½ 4 4½ 5 5½ 6 6½ 7

Check one
cm _____   inches _____

Age in months and years

A child's height can be plotted on this chart. A pattern of growth is a useful consideration when evaluating aspects of gross motor skill development.

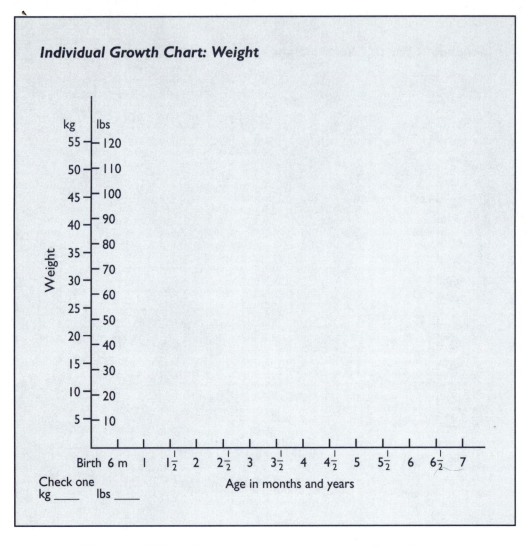

Individual Growth Chart: Weight

kg	lbs
55	120
50	110
45	100
40	90
35	80
30	70
25	60
20	50
15	40
10	30
5	20
	10

Weight

Birth 6 m   1   1½   2   2½   3   3½   4   4½   5   5½   6   6½   7

Check one

kg _____   lbs _____

Age in months and years

Plotting the child's weight gain can help the parents and professionals determine the pattern of change. Comparisons with norms can be helpful if there is an understanding of the range of what constitutes an average; undue emphasis should not be placed on slight variations from a norm.

Symptom Chart for Chronic or Special Medical Conditions

Name:

Age/D.O.B.:

Observer(s):

Diagnosed condition:

Date(s) from: to:

Reporting line:

Date	Behaviour symptom	Number of times observed	Severity	Comment

The parent or caregiver, teacher, or other professional may need to record their observations of a child's specific behaviours or symptoms as and when they occur. If a child with a special medical condition is integrated into a mainstream setting the caregivers need to be taught to identify the behaviours which are important to record for that child, and ensure that such information is reported appropriately.

Observation Charts

Advantages	Disadvantages
May enable behaviours to be recorded quickly and efficiently.	Requires prepared chart, which includes all predictable categories.
May be recorded during or after behaviour is observed.	Needs advance preparation.
May include routine information as well as behaviours, e.g., feeding, diapering.	Often requires inferences to be drawn at time of recording.
Pleasant, user-friendly.	May encourage observer to concentrate on domestic routines rather than on responses and learning.
Usually easy to interpret.	May be used for efficiency rather than depth.
May identify behaviour patterns.	
Useful format for information exchange between caregivers and parents.	Tends to offer only superficial information. Limited to observation categories that are expected.
Frequently offers health as well as developmental areas for observation.	May encourages simplification of developmental issues.
	Should not be relied on as sole source of observational information.

Observation scales

Rating observed information according to the degree to which a quality, trait, skill, or competence is demonstrated can take a variety of forms. The simplest may involve the use of a checklist-style inventory of items which is accompanied by a scale which is an elaboration of a yes/no response. The scale may contain opposites on a continuum, **numerical ratings**, choices of levels of behaviour or **pictorial or graphic representations**. More complex rating scales may have established criteria for grading a performance or demonstration of skill. Each type of scale is scored at, or soon after, the time of observation. Some require "evidence" to help validate the scoring. All rating scales require inferences to be made at the time of recording. The complex inferences required in identifying a behaviour, labelling it, and evaluating its quality of performance require considerable skill on the part of the user. The components of the inventory itself, coupled with the form of evaluation that goes with it, may mean the scale is insufficiently valid. It can be challenging to assess the validity and reliability of a rating scale; too often it is chosen because of its apparent ease of use rather than its technical merit or appropriateness. A scale can only be as good as the philosophy, theory, and research on which it is based. Allocating a grading or scale to a checklist may alter its intrinsic reliability if it was not designed to be used that way. Also be aware that evaluating skills based on a pre-set scale presumes that the performance will fall into the stated grading system.

Here is an outline of the range of observation scales.

A. Forced choice

Observers choose between pre-determined ranges of behaviour to identify levels of functioning.

e.g., handwriting
Range:
(Circle the category most applicable.)

messy,	— some —	some —	words —	phrases —	clear,
illegible most of the time	letters readable but untidy most of the time	words readable but quite untidy most of the time	legible, varying tidiness most of the time	legible, tidy most of the time	legible, sentences most of the time

B. Semantic differential

The observer's choice with a semantic differential scale is between two extremes or opposites or at one of 3, 5, 7, or 9 points between them. Typically 7 categories are used between the extremes. The categories may not be numbered or there may be an open continuum.

example

a.	cooperative	uncooperative
b.	sociable	unsociable
c.	honest	dishonest
d.	skilled	unskilled
e.	extrovert	introvert

C. Numerical scales

Rating the inventory items may take the form of a number system. The item is graded with reference to a predetermined set of criteria. Assigning a number to a skill can indicate the level at which it is performed. Pre-assigning the grading can help in ensuring objectivity in the structure of the scale but does not ensure objectivity in grading.

Examples:

a. How well does the child dress herself? (Choose one of the categories.)
   1. Competent in all respects, including doing up buttons, laces, zippers.
   2. Puts on clothes, tries to close fasteners, but lacks sufficient skill to complete task.
   3. Attempts to put on clothes, cannot do fasteners, and needs help.
   4. Does not attempt dressing.

b. Pre-school physical skills. (Circle the number as appropriate.)
   1 = poor skill ——————————— 5 = highly defined skill

runs	1	2	3	4	5
skips	1	2	3	4	5
hops	1	2	3	4	5
climbs stairs	1	2	3	4	5

c. Communicates wishes and needs verbally.
   1. Clear articulation in full sentences.
   2. Makes self understood with phrases and gestures.
   3. Attempts to make self understood with some success.
   4. Attempts infrequently to make self understood.
   5. Does not attempt to communicate wishes and needs.
   Circle one: 1   2   3   4   5

d. Obeys simple instructions
   Scoring
   5   Clear following of a series of instructions in order they are given.
   4   Follows instructions/does not keep to sequence requested.
   3   Attempts to follow instructions but makes some mistakes.
   2   Makes limited attempts to follow instructions but makes many mistakes.
   1   Makes erratic effort to obey instructions but follows them incorrectly.
   0   Does not attempt to obey instructions.

D. Graphic scale

Points along a line indicate the degree to which the item is applicable. This evaluation form is frequently seen as a scale between "always" and "never." Descriptions may also be used for clearer evaluation.

Examples:
a. Speech fluent and grammatically correct.
   Never   Usually   Always
   Asks meanings of abstract words
   Never   Usually   Always
b. Response to new activities:

positive, enquiring, and exploratory approach, long attention span	—	erratic, inconsistent, varying attention relatively easily distracted	—	negative, disinterested, does not respond to stimulation

Observation Scales

Advantages	Disadvantages
Can be used to record information about a wide range of behaviours.	Validity of items may be questionable..
Efficient in use.	Offers little contextual information.
	For effective choice and use, thorough training is necessary to evaluate behaviour.
Appears to require little training to use at basic level of implementation.	Rater needs to make qualitative judgments of behaviour.
Can be used to measure behaviours not easily measured in other ways.	Position of items on inventory may affect scoring.
May be used to record information at the time of observation or shortly afterwards and allow for continued participation of observer in program.	Requires inferences to be made rapidly and without full validation.
	Scale may have wording inconsistency or lead to assumptions about "positive" and "negative" behaviours.
May offer a large amount of information about children quickly.	Scoring may not be consistent over time.
	Scoring may depend on observer's interpretation of an item.
	Evaluation should not stand alone as sole information gathering technique.
	Observer bias not easily detected.
	Observer bias may take a variety of forms.
	Tendency to rate well-known, liked, or attractive children higher.
	Tendency to over-compensate for known and recognized biases.
	Tendency to avoid extreme scores.
	Tendency to cut subjective or irrelevant information bias results.
	Tendency to be affected by positioning of inventory items.

Social maps

The complexities of a child's social context can make professionals very wary of delving into the child's background. It is wise to acknowledge that quickly drawn conclusions can lead to quite inappropriate judgments and assumptions. Nothing can replace the sensitive observations and recording of the observer who has taken time to delve into the home life and social backdrop of a child. We will certainly benefit from understanding who the child is and appreciate the range of factors which affect the child's growth and development. Social maps can offer a backdrop against which you can increase your understanding of what you observe directly.

Representations of the child's social context can be made in various ways. These are not intended to replace a more detailed study; but they may help support an in-depth study. What they can do is to offer, in a diagrammatic form, key life experiences, family trees, social relationships, or factors impacting the child's world so that we can have a structure to help us make sense of the whole. In themselves they offer little detail of the child's life but they may provide some basic hooks on which to hang our observational information.

Family trees

Sentimental interest might be a prime motivator for an individual to research a family tree. More important, it may offer the possibility of understanding the child's genetic inheritance, life patterns, and history, which can help medical professionals, social workers, caregivers, and teachers, as well as the child herself. A family tree provides historical background information gained through interviews, diaries, and archives. Name searches can be part of the research. According to the Geneological Research Library, "Surnames – often called 'last names' or 'family names' – are that part of our names that stay basically the same from one generation to the next. In the eastern hemisphere, surnames began in China a few thousand years ago. In the Western hemisphere surnames began in France around the year 1100 AD." These surnames can help in the tracking of family members but should not be relied on in determining complete ancestry.

The mobility of families has increased considerably since the last century. Immigration has frequently complicated research but information recorded in relation to passenger ship lists and diaries has assisted the tracing of ancestors. Adoption, multiple partners and offspring, name changes, wars, changes of location, inadequate local record keeping, and translations, and individuals trying to cover up their ancestry are some of the common challenges in formulating a family tree. A typical family tree may look like this:

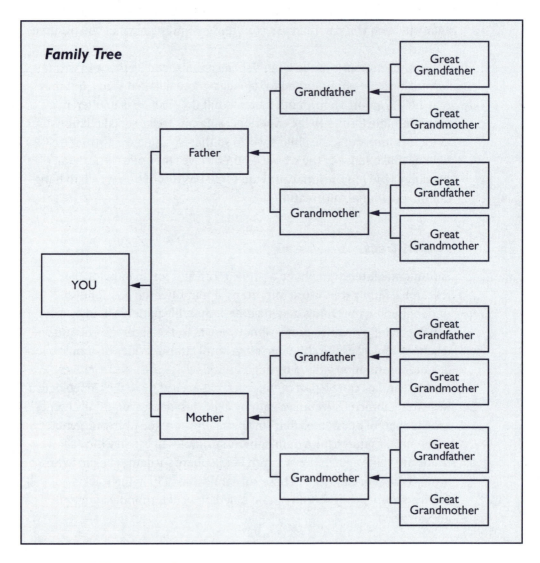

Ecomaps

An ecomap is a diagrammatic representation of the child's world, the significant people, activities, and organizations in that world and the relationships between the child and those elements of her environment. For social workers, it might help facilitate an understanding of "the balance between demands and resources of the family" (*Protecting Children*, 1988.) Teachers, caregivers, and parents might find the exploration of the child's ecosystem to be enlightening in the understanding of how the immediate social setting (the family) and the more remote social settings such as child care, school, media, clubs, and so on influence the child's development.

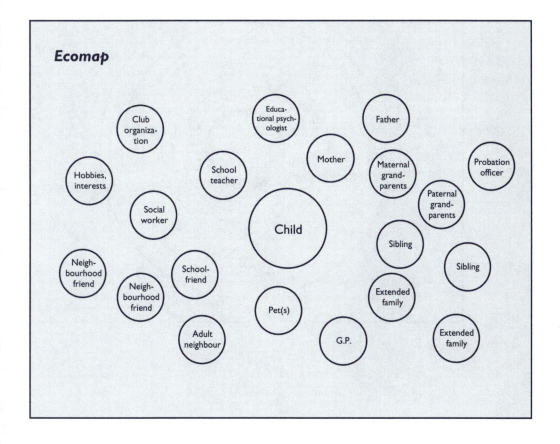

Ecomap

Urie Bronfenbrenner's (1986) **ecological model** of child development can help in determining the components of the child's environment. He describes four systems which impact the child's development. These can offer an ecological model on which to base a study of the child's environment. It is, perhaps, impossible to include all environmental components and to determine their effects on the child. The ecomap makes an attempt, but we need to acknowledge its limitations.

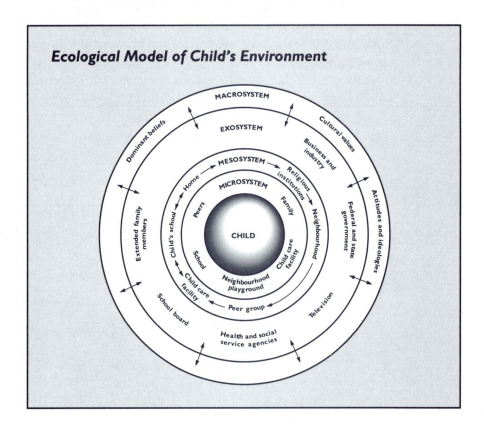

Ecological Model of Child's Environment

Beckey Myers.

Genogram

"A genogram is a format for drawing a family tree that records information about family members and their relationships over at least three generations." (McGoldrick and Gerson,1985). It is arrived at with the use of interviews, discussion, and research with family members. Family structure and composition may be depicted in a variety of forms, there being no "standard" way to do it. A genogram may include critical family events, dates of birth, marriages, adoptions, custody arrangements, partnerships, separations, divorces, deaths, and details of places of residence, occupations, and other significant information. It provides a clear view of complex family scenarios, family patterns, lifestyles. It is not intended to detail the day-to-day interactions or be a "snapshot" that evaluates the family's functioning. Social workers will find the genogram a valuable tool.

The process of collecting the data with family members may be as important as the product. Adults in the child's life may find the genogram enlightening as it enables them to look at the connectedness of the family members and identify possible stressors. Sensitivity to the privacy and range of styles and practice of families is essential when undertaking a genogram. Symbols for representing birth order, individuals, relationships, and living arrangements need to be agreed on before a genogram can be drawn.

Genograms in Family Assessment

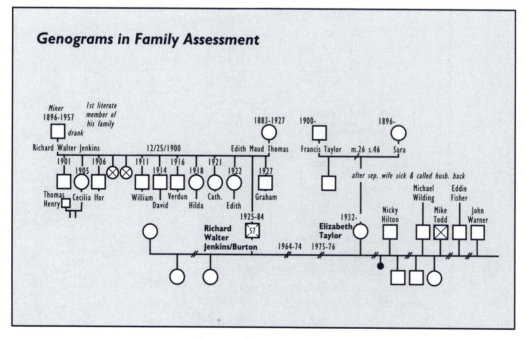

Sociogram

Sociometry is a research technique used to identify the acceptance of children among their peers and to explore their social status. A **sociogram** is the visual representation of the child's perceptions of acceptance within the group. Children in an organized setting may be asked to name the child who is their "best friend" or "person they do not especially like" or "like best" or "most admire." Results depend on the phrasing of the question and may be influenced by what the child thinks the adult wishes to hear. Information gathered from group members is pieced together and presented diagrammatically. "Popular" children and those who are solitary or isolated may be identified quickly; some unexpected connections may come to light which can lead the teacher to want to observe interactions more closely. Over a period of time the sociogram may change quite radically. It may be interesting to use a sociogram at designated times during the year and assess the dynamics of the group. Children must be old enough to understand the question posed, be able to give a clear answer, and be of sufficient maturity to have formed social relationships within the group. The interactions or "friendships" of younger children tend to be transitory because the children are not yet able to communicate, appreciate the perspectives of others, or form social attachments with peers. For these children a sociogram would reveal little.

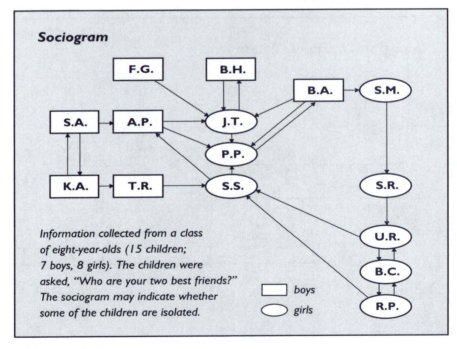

Sociogram

Information collected from a class of eight-year-olds (15 children; 7 boys, 8 girls). The children were asked, "Who are your two best friends?" The sociogram may indicate whether some of the children are isolated.

☐ boys
⬭ girls

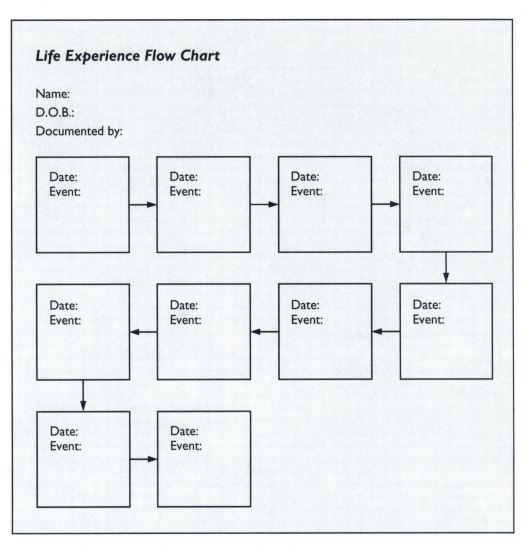

Life Experience Flow Chart

Name:

D.O.B.:

Documented by:

| Date: Event: | Date: Event: | Date: Event: | Date: Event: |

| Date: Event: | Date: Event: | Date: Event: | Date: Event: |

| Date: Event: | Date: Event: |

The depiction of an individual's significant life experiences may seem as simplistic as listing dates in history. To a historian the dates might offer a structure for understanding the chronology of events but offer no contextual information which might help in understanding why events occurred. The life experience flow chart gives an opportunity for identifying which experiences are "key" and labelling and sequencing the events. The flow chart can be written by an interested party and can help individuals acknowledge structure and patterns in their lives. Teachers and caregivers can be supported in their task by appreciating the child's cultural identity, traumas, life stages, and joyous experiences by putting together a life experience flow chart. It may lead them to have greater sensitivity to the child's needs and increased understanding of the child's perception of her reality.

Social Maps

Advantages	Disadvantages
Relatively easy to draw up.	Heavily dependent on professional sensitivity.
Gives visual overview of situation/context/environment.	Can be simplistic and insufficiently supported by contextual information.
Families usually helpful in supporting access to information.	Relies on accuracy of information collected.
Subjectivity not easily detected.	Requires objectivity of recording.
May appear clear and concise.	Influences may be difficult to draw.
Provides easily accessible information.	Training may be needed to analyze family patterns.
May enable individual and group contexts to be examined.	Inaccurate assumptions may be made by unqualified people.
May include the child's involvement.	If support is not available the child may be unnecessarily vulnerable.
Process of drawing up maps may have therapeutic purpose.	

Mappings

Sensitivity to the planning, set-up, and use of the child's environment leads educators and caregivers to want to evaluate what they provide. Part of a qualitative assessment of the use of space will be in the mapping out of the room or outdoor space to see how well the room is meeting the needs of the children. The evaluation might consider the effectiveness of the learning environment, how aesthetically pleasing the space is to children and adults, the contrasts of activities in different areas, how well the space allows for appropriate mobility and safety, flexibility of use and the construction of the environment based on an agreed philosophy of care and education.

Mappings can allow for tracking the movement of groups of children to see how they interact, move, and use the differing parts of the environment. By tracking an individual child, you might be able to notice what interests her, her mobility, her concentration span, and her range of movements between activities. The adult's role within the room or playspace can be evaluated by tracking his movements within the available space.

A simple line on a map can follow the movement of a child. Arrows can explain the direction in which the movement occurs. Movement back and forth in the same place can be represented by (<>) arrows in both directions depending on the number of times the space was travelled. Moments that capture the child staying in the same space can be shown with a circle containing the number of minutes or seconds she stayed at that activity. More than one child can be tracked on the same map if the observer has sufficient skill and uses a different colour line for each child.

A narrative description of the details of a tracking can help to explain what is recorded. This dual technique offers the possibility of elaborating the "tracks" so that a more qualitative evaluation can be made.

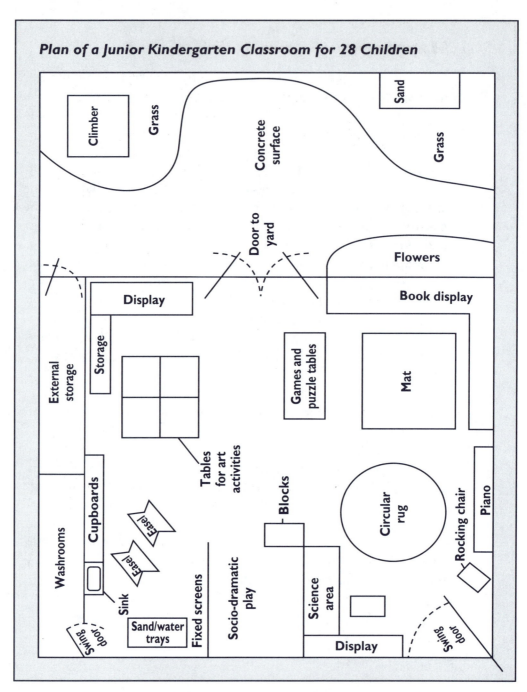

Plan of a Junior Kindergarten Classroom for 28 Children

Climber

Grass

Sand

Concrete surface

Grass

Door to yard

Flowers

Display

Book display

External storage

Storage

Games and puzzle tables

Mat

Tables for art activities

Washrooms

Cupboards

Easel

Easel

Sink

Fixed screens

Socio-dramatic play

Blocks

Science area

Circular rug

Rocking chair

Piano

Swing door

Sand/water trays

Display

Swing door

At the beginning of the year, the new teacher sat down with a map of the previously used set-up to start evaluating the use of space. He wondered about the wisdom of having the construction play in the centre and if all curriculum areas could be included.

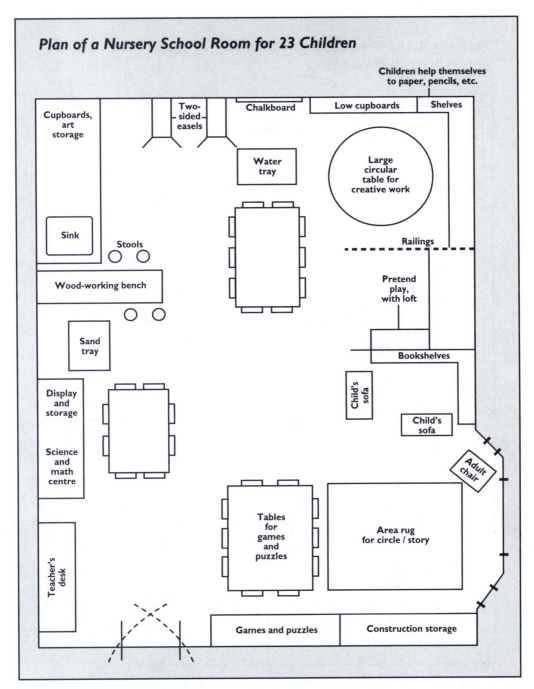

Plan of a Nursery School Room for 23 Children

Children help themselves
to paper, pencils, etc.

Cupboards,
art
storage

Two-
sided
easels

Chalkboard

Low cupboards

Shelves

Sink

Stools

Water
tray

Large
circular
table for
creative work

Railings

Wood-working bench

Pretend
play,
with loft

Sand
tray

Bookshelves

Display
and
storage

Child's
sofa

Science
and
math
centre

Child's
sofa

Adult
chair

Teacher's
desk

Tables
for
games
and
puzzles

Area rug
for circle / story

Games and puzzles

Construction storage

*(11 full time, 12 part time a.m., 12 part-time p.m.) The plan was drawn up as a "blank"
and copied so that each child's movements could be plotted while the teacher observed
the children.*

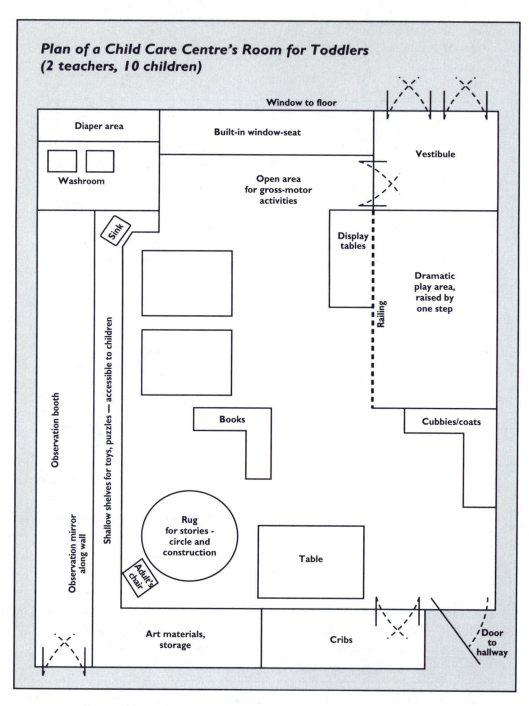

Plan of a Child Care Centre's Room for Toddlers
(2 teachers, 10 children)

Window to floor

Diaper area

Built-in window-seat

Vestibule

Washroom

Open area
for gross-motor
activities

Sink

Display
tables

Dramatic
play area,
raised by
one step

Railing

Observation booth

Shallow shelves for toys, puzzles — accessible to children

Books

Cubbies/coats

Observation mirror
along wall

Rug
for stories -
circle and
construction

Adult's
chair

Table

Art materials,
storage

Cribs

Door
to
hallway

Plan used for evaluating the toddlers' safety and to maximize what can be seen from the observation booth.

Tracking in School-age Program

Name: *Peter D.*

Age/D.O.B: *7 yrs. 2 m*

Observer: *R.D.*

Context: *Peter has recently come, with his sister Kate (six years), to an after-school program in a housing complex. Both started the program less than three weeks ago. Mom and Dad have recently separated and there is now nobody at home until approximately 6:00 p.m., when Mom returns from work.*

Reason for observations: *We tracked Peter's movement to help us determine the level of his interaction in the program. There were concerns about Peter remaining in an onlooker role while other children were playing.*

Narrative account of tracking: *Peter came out of the room just after 4:00 p.m., a few minutes after arriving from school. Standing at the door he looked around outside at the children. Walking to the storage room he said "hi!" to his sister, who was talking to some girls. After a moment Peter came out of the storage room carrying a ball, bouncing the ball as he walked. Peter looked up to see where everyone was and dropped the ball. Standing momentarily he watched a girl playing catch by herself against the wall. When she finished, only a moment later, Peter took over her position and bounced his ball against the wall. A boy called to him from a swing. He went over to the swing and had a conversation about school until the other swing came available. Snack arrived a few moments later so Peter left the swing in response to the caregiver's request. Walking slowly to the picnic table, he sat down, but was sent in to wash his hands. Following instructions, Peter came back after a few moments, ate a snack which was offered to him, but declined the drink. Walking around the backs of three seated children, he went to sit under a tree for some minutes as he watched the others staying at the picnic table. Another boy came up to him. They talked and walked together to the baseball diamond.*

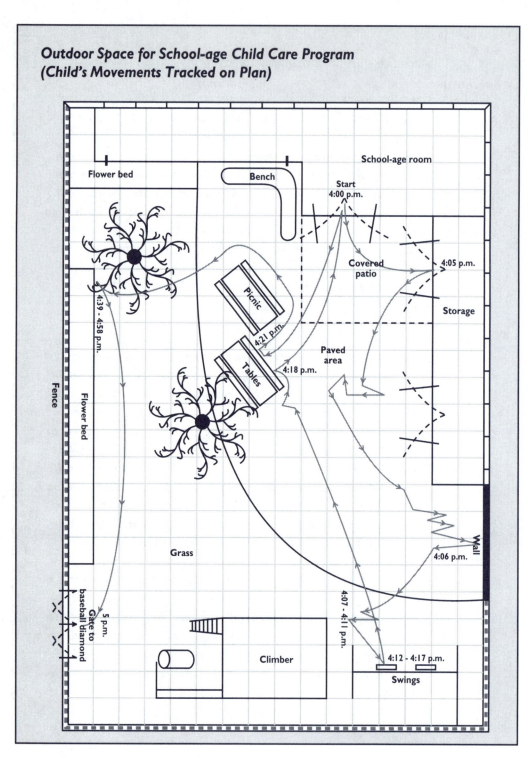

Outdoor Space for School-age Child Care Program (Child's Movements Tracked on Plan)

Flower bed

Bench

School-age room

Start
4:00 p.m.

Covered patio

4:05 p.m.

Storage

4:39 - 4:58 p.m.

Picnic

4:21 p.m.

Paved area

Tables

4:18 p.m.

Fence

Flower bed

Grass

Wall

4:06 p.m.

4:07 - 4:11 p.m.

5 p.m.
Gate to baseball diamond

Climber

4:12 - 4:17 p.m.

Swings

Mappings

Advantages	Disadvantages
Easy and efficient to record.	Space/room needs to be "mapped" beforehand.
Can focus on individual child or group action.	Difficult to record action of more than one child at a time.
May be used for traffic analysis, use of space, or safety consideration.	Qualitative evaluation difficult without accompanying narrative.
Can help to identify a. mobility b. interests/motivation c. attention span d. child-adult interactions e. child-child interactions f. participation in specific areas of the program.	Reasons for behaviour may not be revealed. Requires inferences to be drawn on little data. Participants in a program may find it difficult to make an accurate tracking.
Maps can be layered to show evidence of change, compare activity levels, or identify traffic problems.	

Interpretive graphic representation

Rather than direct observational material, the interpretive representations are concerned with demonstrating numerical results, percentages, comparisons, variables, proportions, or other quantifiable outcomes from observation or evaluation. The reason to read and use pictorial representations is to be able to understand and analyze the content of assessment data. While there can be a danger of over-simplifying such information without appreciating its context, the intention is to support the conceptualizing of large amounts of information.

Graphic representations are, generally, mathematical and statistical ways of presenting data in a clear and objective way. A wide variety of techniques might be used. Often easier to understand than to create, they may require some practice before being relied on for accuracy.

Charted tally marks can form simple graphic representations. Block graphs, **bar charts**, flow diagrams, **pie charts**, graphs, picture diagrams, genetic maps, percentile charts, and picture symbols can all help by providing ways of presenting data.

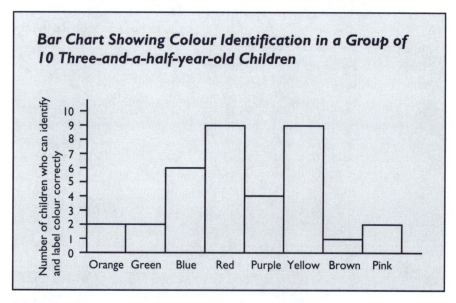

Bar Chart Showing Colour Identification in a Group of 10 Three-and-a-half-year-old Children

Information charted is not designed to show which child knows which colours; the intention is to determine the number of children who can identify each colour. The bar chart can be used for a variety of data presentation.

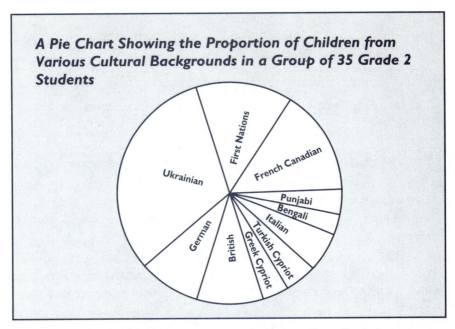

A Pie Chart Showing the Proportion of Children from Various Cultural Backgrounds in a Group of 35 Grade 2 Students

This particular chart indicates heritage rather than origin or place of birth. A pie chart may need a key to explain the items. This is a quick and easily understandable presentation but the "whole" must be identified, otherwise the proportions of the whole are meaningless. Percentage can be written into the pie for extra clarity.

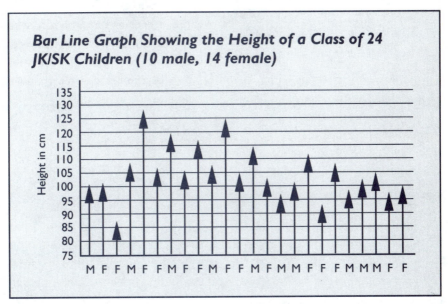

Bar Line Graph Showing the Height of a Class of 24 JK/SK Children (10 male, 14 female)

This presentation does not identify particular children or order the results. In this case the axis doesn't start at 0; if it did the chart would be cumbersome.

Interpretive Graphic Representation

Advantages	Disadvantages
Can offer simple, easy-to-understand information.	Relies on valid and reliable data information collection.
May offer trends and comparisons.	May need understanding of statistics to interpret.
Mathematical approach to data analysis may be more objective than anecdotal reports.	Results are quantifiable rather than qualitative.
Can provide means to put together information from various sources.	Open to inappropriate use a. may encourage comparisons with other children rather than changes in own performance. b. can be used for unwise program planning. c. may foster unnecessary parental anxiety. d. trends may be analyzed on basis of information that offers no context. e. may be more usable for research psychologists than practitioners.

Curriculum Planning Models

Striving for developmentally appropriate practice, teachers need to find ways of using observational information as the central means for determining the programming. Translating what is observed into plans for meaningful activities and experiences is challenging for many reasons.

1. Observational information can only indicate what is the child's current competency level – this does not, of itself, dictate what skills need enhancing or what new ones could be acquired.
2. Observation and evaluation techniques require detailed analysis of the data if accurate inferences are to be made -this requires training and practice.
3. Naturalistic observation puts the emphasis for evaluation on the shoulders of the recorder; there may be little built-in qualitative or quantitative assessment.
4. Because a child is functioning at a particular level does not mean that the child will always develop in a particular sequence within a time frame or that she will always progress and not regress.
5. Programming for groups of children, each of whom is at a different developmental level, can be challenging if the variation is such that the needs differ. Open-ended programming in which the child can operate at his own level can be an answer.
6. Where teachers believe that programming needs to focus on developmental needs they may find that working towards determined learning outcomes or a curriculum of a school board or other authority is not only limiting but impossible.
7. A process needs to be established so that there is a sequence of steps to take the observational information into programming. This is a time-consuming activity that requires observational recording and analytical skills.

For a variety of reasons, teachers may decide on a topic for focus or look at what children should be learning rather than start where the child is. The most effective planning models are rooted in appropriate evaluation of the child. This can be used to indicate current competence in each developmental domain, predict the acquisition of sequence of skills, and provide open-ended experiences from which the child can consolidate or build skills.

Processes for planning need to be established to ensure that the needs of the child and the goals of the program are met. Some teachers think that students learn to program effectively if they use a process involving the setting of goals and objectives. This procedure usually relies on the student being focussed on curriculum areas rather than on developmental needs or interests. Some goals may be set within a developmental context, but the presumption will be that the goal should be set at the next "stage" of development. What that "next stage" should be is open to debate. The educator may make incorrect assumptions or set a path to failure because mastery or refinement of presently demonstrated competence might be more appropriate than a big jump to acquire a new skill.

Various webbing models for planning take into account the child's observed performance and curriculum goals. These plans can generate many good ideas for constructing the learning environment but although they are intended to factor in observed information, their structure does not allow for it in any clear manner.

Sequential models make assumptions about the stages in which component parts of a competence are acquired. These can work well in some areas of development but they work most effectively when planning to support physical skills. Even with a clear step-by-step explanation of the stages through which the child will develop, there is little sensitivity to concepts of learning readiness or maturational levels. Children cannot always master skills even when the stages are specified and the necessary experiences are provided.

When serving administrators and officials, you may sometimes find that expectations regarding specified curriculum, competencies, or goals are not a "good fit" developmentally. If you program for the goal rather than the child, you may be unsuccessful. While less than desirable to those of a child-centred philosophy, a compromise can be reached in an input/outcome planning model which factors in both the child and the expectations. This may be an expedient model for teachers under pressure to conform; they need not lose their integrity in their developmental focus. Ongoing observation of the children, which is well documented, may lead the administrator to change the expectations so that unrealistic or inappropriate outcomes are dropped.

Topic-based planning may be based on notions of what is appropriate or desirable for the child to learn. This approach does not encourage optimal learning because it is not growing from the child's needs, interests, and abilities. The child may well get something from the topic but it is likely to be limiting. Thematic approaches may have similar limitations but do, at least, acknowledge the necessity to make learning experiences interrelated. Where the theme focus lends itself to open-ended activities, the child can operate at his own level if the tasks capture his interest and can be achieved using current competence.

The gap between what the child can do independently and what the child can do with support should be understood when planning experiences (see "Vygotsky's Zone of Proximal Development," Chapter 1). The role of the teacher is as important to the curriculum as the materials and set up. The examples of planning models may help you in your responsibility.

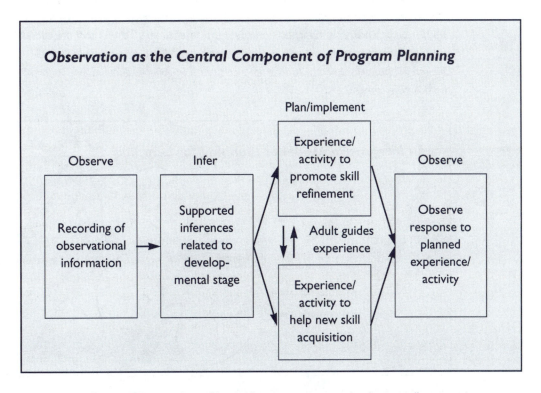

Observation as the Central Component of Program Planning

This model is one desired by teachers practising in a developmentally appropriate program, who use naturalistic observation as their primary tool for evaluation. The planning and implementation of learning experiences is supported by the adult's guidance.

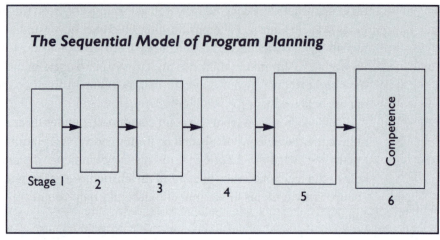

The Sequential Model of Program Planning

Stage 1 2 3 4 5 Competence 6

This is a long-term planning model for a particular curriculum area, which is designed to provide experiences that enable the building of skills in a sequence leading up to a specific competence. This model acknowledges the developmental stages that are considered necessary in progress towards a competence but it relies on the principle that all children will progress similarly. It does not incorporate on-going evaluation/observation of the skill development.

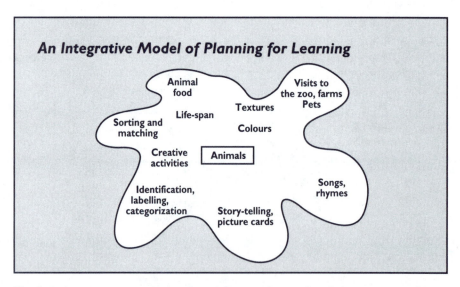

An Integrative Model of Planning for Learning

Animal food

Visits to the zoo, farms
Pets

Textures

Life-span

Sorting and matching

Colours

Creative activities

Animals

Identification, labelling, categorization

Songs, rhymes

Story-telling, picture cards

The focus here is not on particular curriculum areas but on the whole experience of the child to related thematic provision. This model plans experiences and learning environments but does not determine expected outcomes because the children will make of the experience whatever they are motivated and developmentally ready to do. It offers open-ended activities for a wide ability range.

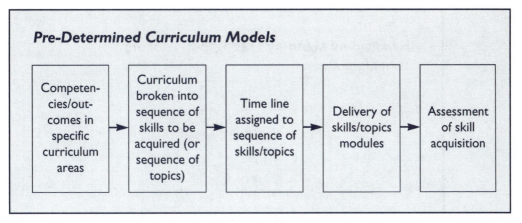

Pre-Determined Curriculum Models

| Competencies/outcomes in specific curriculum areas | Curriculum broken into sequence of skills to be acquired (or sequence of topics) | Time line assigned to sequence of skills/topics | Delivery of skills/topics modules | Assessment of skill acquisition |

This model requires a valid and reliable determination of competencies or outcomes in the curriculum areas. Planning its delivery requires a knowledge of the sequence of learning which is typical. The time line is assigned in what is considered to be an average or appropriate framework for most children. Delivery of information is the focus rather than a broader open-ended experience (but teachers can make this experiential in nature). Each component needs to be evaluated for its success for each child. Remediation is offered if a child does not keep to the model. This model can be challenged for its developmental appropriateness at each of its stages.

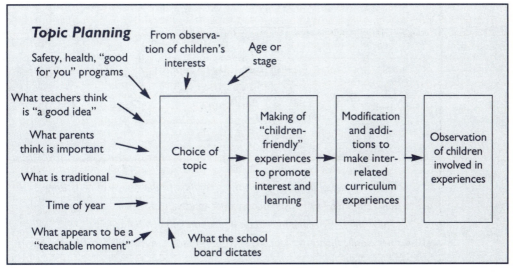

Topic Planning

From observation of children's interests

Age or stage

Safety, health, "good for you" programs

What teachers think is "a good idea"

What parents think is important

What is traditional

Time of year

What appears to be a "teachable moment"

What the school board dictates

| Choice of topic | Making of "children-friendly" experiences to promote interest and learning | Modification and additions to make inter-related curriculum experiences | Observation of children involved in experiences |

This model is commonly used by teachers and caregivers but frequently runs into problems because it starts with the topic plan and ends in observation rather than the other way around. The real reason for the choice of topic may be anything but developmentally appropriate; the model may provide experiences from which the children can gain but it does not consider how children learn.

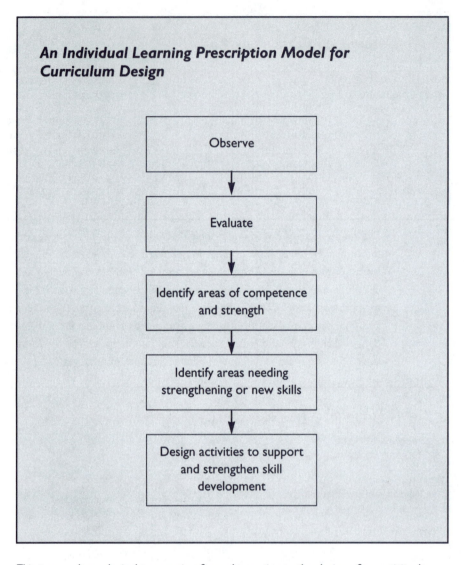

An Individual Learning Prescription Model for Curriculum Design

> Observe

> Evaluate

> Identify areas of competence and strength

> Identify areas needing strengthening or new skills

> Design activities to support and strengthen skill development

This process has a logical progression from observation to the design of an activity. It requires thorough analysis of observational data to identifying areas "needing strengthening" or "new skills." This depends upon a presumption of what is to be "next," which needs further clarification or validation. There is merit in the model's focus on the needs of an individual child.

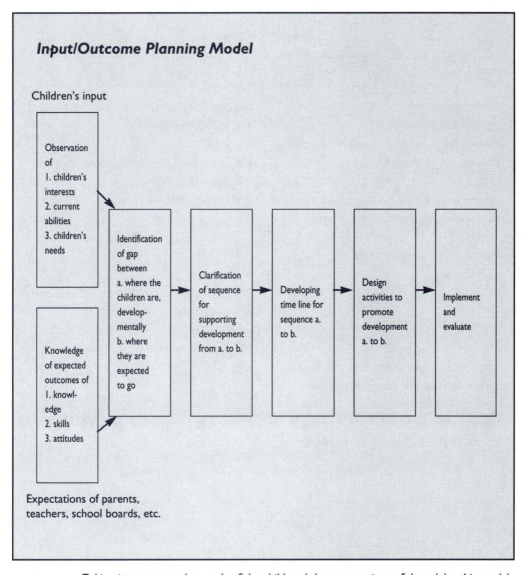

Input/Outcome Planning Model

Children's input

Observation of
1. children's interests
2. current abilities
3. children's needs

Identification of gap between
a. where the children are, develop-mentally
b. where they are expected to go

Clarification of sequence for supporting development from a. to b.

Developing time line for sequence a. to b.

Design activities to promote development a. to b.

Implement and evaluate

Knowledge of expected outcomes of
1. knowl-edge
2. skills
3. attitudes

Expectations of parents, teachers, school boards, etc.

Taking into account the needs of the child and the expectations of the adults, this model acknowledges the constraints put on the practising teacher. It relies on clear observations and knowledge of expectations, which help the teacher find direction. The sequences of stages of skill acquisition also depend on a thorough understanding of child development.

Planning Models

Advantages	Disadvantages
Visual presentations enable teacher to conceptualize plan easily.	Depends on a theoretical understanding of curriculum design.
Plan can offer programming process rather than random "good ideas."	Easiest options may be the least developmentally appropriate
	-plan may be too abstract
Shared team work planning can be effective when using common planning model.	
	If plan is based on observation perceptions may vary.
Model can be selected to fit program philosophy.	
	Planning models may be used without realization of their underlying premise.
Model may offer planning for developmentally appropriate experiences while being seen to be meeting program outcomes.	May not conform to needs of administrators.
Most models are circular and ongoing. Model may easily build in a component for evaluation of its success.	Model may be insufficiently flexible.

Assignment options

I. Skill building and practices

Individual tasks

1. Ask your family members and research old documents or registers to enable you to chart your own family tree.
2. Observe an infant for a day and record her rhythms of sleep and wakefulness, feeding and excreting.
3. Try to write a personality rating scale
   a. list attributes
   b. attach a 1 – 5 scale relating to the degree to which the attribute applies.
   c. give a copy to a friend and another to a family member, asking them to grade the same individual.
   d. analyze the difference between the responses
   e. list your concerns related to using your rating scale as an evaluation tool.
4. Critique the tracking observation in the assignment options to evaluate its usefulness in establishing Michael's mobility and interests.
5. Look at the sample sociogram at the end of the assignment options. What use could this information be to the children's teacher?

Group tasks

1. Draw a clear map of a pre-school room. Copying the map onto transparent paper or acetates, use the map to track as many different children as you have adults in your group. You will need to start and finish together and ensure you record all movement within the designated space. Compare your results by overlaying the trackings. What do you notice about the children's interests, mobility, concentration, and use of the space?

2. Using the videotaped sequence of play, design curriculum plans using the different planning models offered in the chapter. Each student should use a different model. What are the similarities and differences in your planning? Which model is the most effective?

3. Look at Bronfenbrenner's ecological model and discuss its implications. Choosing a child (or adult if that is not possible) who is known to each member of the group, try to determine the individual specifics of the ecological model for that person.

4. Interview the teachers whom you work with for your practicum or work experience to ask them how they plan their curriculum. Compare and contrast your answers.

5. Debate the motion, "The most important element in curriculum planning is knowing what the children must achieve at the end of the year."

6. Role play a situation in which you, the teacher, are challenged by a school board representative or ministry official about your lack of planning for achievement of curriculum goals.

II. Practising charts, scales, and pictorial representations

1. Using both a flow diagram and a chart, record the routine of a child's day. Compare the two – which gives the most useful information?

2. Draw a map of a public outdoor play space. For 15 minutes track children's movements and represent this on the map. Elevate the use of the space.

3. From questions you ask and sensitive observations of the choices they make, draw a pie chart which depicts the favourite activities of a group of school-age children.

4. Using the input/outcome planning model, design a curriculum experience for any group of children.

5. Interview a school-age child about his or her key life experiences. With the child's assistance, put these events on a flow chart.

6. Devise a rating scale that lists and evaluates children's learning styles. You will need to research the various styles of learning, format the styles into statements or questions, and allocate a grading system. The scale will need to be tried out and evaluated.

7. Make two block graphs. The first will depict the birth countries of all children in a grade 1 or 2 class. The second will show the perceived culture of the parents of the children. You will need to ask the parents this question or alternatively ask the teacher for his own perceptions of the cultural groups to which the children belong. Compare the two and make some valid inferences from the charts.

8. Ask each member of a primary class whom they most like to play with or work with in class. Represent the data you collect in the form of a sociogram.

Example to Critique #1

Tracking Observation

Setting: *Takes place at child care centre*
Time of observation: *2:45 p.m. -3:35 p.m. (50 minutes)*
(2:45) Michael starts off in room 2 eating snack. (after nap time).
(2:50) He cleans up his dishes and walks over to the counter to put them away. (2:51) He then walks over to the door and runs into the hallway into room 1. (2:52) Michael skips over to the carpet area and pulls the Lego container off the shelf. Michael sits down on his knees and picks up pieces of Lego (using pincer grasp) and puts them together. Also, he used palmer grasp while searching through Lego to find the pieces he wants. (2:57) Michael completes his masterpiece to his satisfaction. When asked by a teacher what he has made, he replies," a supersonic plane." (2:58) Michael leaps up from his kneeling position and puts his right arm with the plane in his hand up into the air, as though he is flying the airplane. Michael then walks quickly with small steps over to the book area. He sees the school caretaker (whom he knows) and taps with his left index finger on the window to get his attention. He waves Hi! with his left hand. (3:00) Michael flies his plane (again taking small quick steps) back over to the carpet. He squats down and picks up a few pieces of Lego with his right hand. The plane in his left hand, he adds on these pieces (also, with his right hand). (3:02) Michael again leaps up and flies his plane around block area, then over to the round table where a teacher is sitting. "Look what I made" (to the teacher) "Oh, Michael, that's so

creative, did you do that by yourself?" " Yes, I can do anything if I want to." (3:06) Michael quickly turns and flies his plane back to the carpet area, dodging other children on the floor, making quick, sharp turns, so as not to run into anyone/thing. (3:07) Michael sits down cross-legged and starts to pick up the pieces of Lego, creating another plane. (3:12) Michael gets up and climbs over the picnic table and walks up to another boy, Arron (who is also on the carpet) with his plane in his left hand and the new one in his right hand. He sticks out his right hand with the plane in it and says to Arron, "Here, I made you a plane so you can play with me." Arron says, "But I'm playing with the link-chains, want to play?" Michael says,"Okay" and sets down both airplanes beside him, saying, "I'll save them for you so we can play later." (3:15) Michael says, "You be the dog and I'll be the master." Michael sits beside Arron, on his knees, and starts building onto the other end of the chain (he uses pincer grasp and whole hand to manipulate the links). (3:19) Michael says, "Okay, I'm putting on your leash." He goes up on his knees and wraps the chain around Arron's waist and shoulders. Two other boys come over and watch. Michael says, "Want to play?" The boys say yes, and Michael replies, "You have to be the dogs, I'm the master." He makes the chain longer and puts the chain on the other two boys. (3:22) Michael stands up and says, "Let's go for a walk." He takes the leash in his right hand and walks (with long strides) around the long table, over to the sink, then to the dramatic area. (3:26) Michael takes the chain off the boys using both hands and says, "I'll feed you and brush you." He takes three bowls out of the stove and puts them down using both hands, in front of the boys on the floor. (3:28) Michael picks up a brush (belonging to a dust pan) in his right hand and manipulates the brush in an up-and-down movement on the boy's back, with full arm movement. (3:31) Michael puts the leash on one of the boys and whispers in his ear. He walks over to the teacher and says, "Want to hear a joke?" Teacher says yes. Michael says, "Okay, what does sandpaper feel like?" He points with his right index finger to boy, boy barks "rough." Michael then says, "What's on top of a house?", points to boy again, boy barks "roof." Michael walks away, pulling the leash, and the boy laughs. (3:35) Boys are told to clean up for outdoor play.

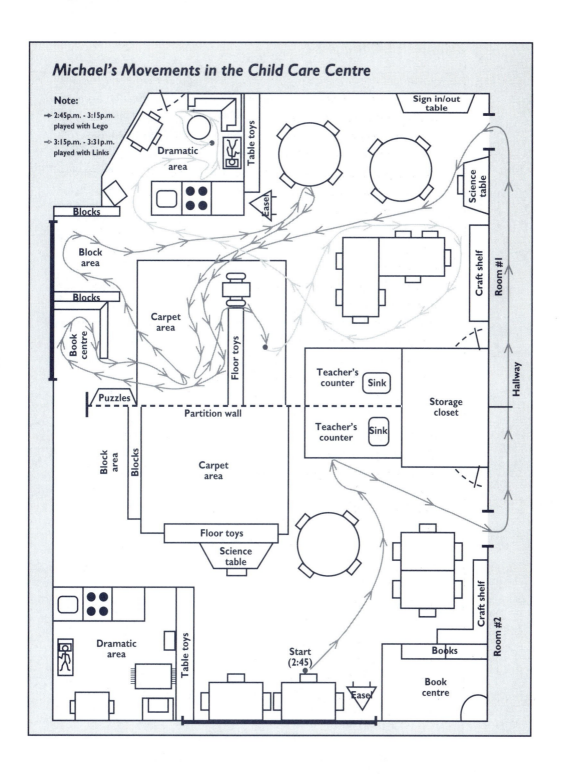

Example to Critique #2

Preparation of the Sociogram

The group of children were interviewed on April 13, 1993 with the verbal permission of the E.C.E. teacher of this group. The interview was done in a confidential manner at the corner of the school-age room with no disturbance from other children and it was done on a one-on-one basis. The interviewer told the children all their answers to the following questions would be treated confidentially. She also asked the children not to tell the other children of their answers.

The following questions were asked:

-Who is your best friend in this group? Why do you say he/she is your best friend?

-Who is your second-best friend? Why?

-What do you like to play most in this group?

-Do you think the other children in this group like you?

The following is a report on the answers given by the children:

Karen (six years old)
- *"Alice is my best friend. She likes me and always plays with me."*
- *"Cecilia is the second-best friend."*
- *"I like the game 'hide and count.'"*
- *"Yes." (She thinks the other children like her.)*

David (eight years old)
- *"Danny is my best friend. He always plays with me."*
- *"Mark is my second-best friend but he is not in the daycare any more."*
- *"We play spy, and we play it on the playground. We climb up the slide and try to kick people down."*
- *"Tag is my most favourite game."*
- *He thinks other children like him.*

Cecilia (eight years old)
- *"Rowena" (her best friend)*
- *"I play with her a lot in the daycare and I could trust her. We play games and walk around here."*
- *"Alice" (her second-best friend). "She is funny and is nice. We play cards and play in the drama centre."*
- *"Yes." (She thinks other children like her.)*

Alice (seven years old)
- *Mabel and Vincent are her best friends.*
- *"They play with me all the time."*
- *"'We play 'tag,' 'shiny rocks,' and 'drama centre.'"*
- *"Yes ."(She thinks she is liked by others.)*

Vincent (six years old)
- *His best friend is Alice and second-best is Mabel. But he cannot answer why they are his best friends. He just said, "I don't know."*
- *He likes playing in the drama centre with both Alice and Mabel.*
- *"Yes." (He thinks others like him.)*

Lora (seven years old)
- *She stated that her best friend was Alice and second-best was Mabel.*
- *"They are nice. They like to play with me a lot."*
- *She likes playing "tag" finger games and in the drama centre.*
- *She thinks she is liked by others.*

Jack (six years old)
- *He stated that his first-best friend was Danny. The reason he gave: he always plays with me.*
- *His second-best friend is David. The reason he gave is as follows: "He draws for me, lions and bunnies."*
- *The games he likes are tag and puzzles.*
- *He thinks he is liked by others.*

Rowena (eight years old)
- *She stated that her first-best friend was Cecilia and the reason she gave was: "She is in my class. She's nice to me and we play together."*
- *Her second-best friend is Alice. The reason given was: "Because she is a girl."*
- *Her favourite activities/games: 1. "Tire," – she usually plays the game with Cecilia (Tire is an outdoor game.) 2. " Tag," – she usually plays this outdoor game with Alice.*
- *She thinks the other children like her. She also states that she doesn't like boys, but she likes girls.*

Danny (eight years old)
- His first-best friend is David. When asked the reason why, he said that David was his first-best friend. He said, "Most of the times, he comes to my house and plays with me. I like him."
- He said that there was no second-best friend for him. He said, "I don't know" when asked to give name of his second-best friend.
- The game he likes is "Spud" – an outdoor game.
- When asked if other children like him, he said, "Yes." He also states that the girls are bothering him because they sing in the room.

Mabel (seven years old)
- Her first-best friend is Alice. The reason she gave: "She always plays with me."
-Her second-best friend is Cecilia.
-She likes playing "tag."
-She thinks the others like her.

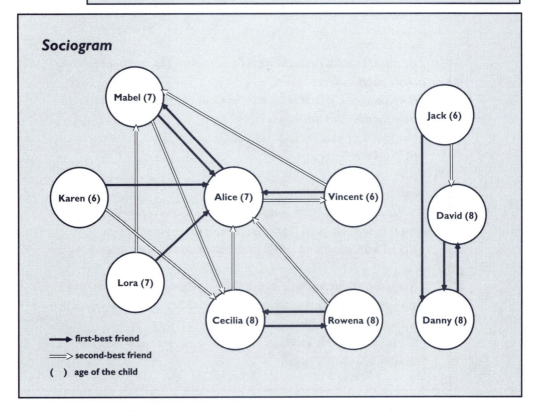

Sociogram

→ first-best friend
⇒ second-best friend
( ) age of the child

Answers to focus questions

1. A flow chart might be a useful way of depicting the sequence of events. Teachers or caregivers can devise charts which can be completed during the day which identify patterns of wakefulness, sleep, play, feeding, and so on. Infant charts may include more health and nutrition information. Charts recording an older child's routine might include play activities, teacher-directed times, choices, and transitions.

2. A curriculum planning model provides a format for thoughtful program design. The use of a particular process for program development helps the educator in his task because the procedure has been chosen to be in line with his preferred philosophy. Some models work more effectively than others; teachers need to evaluate them for their effectiveness and suitability as well as their underlying philosophy.

3. Inferences must always be checked out for their validity and reliability. It is necessary to ensure that they are made on the basis of objective information, that they match the findings of others, that they are carefully recorded, and that they are supported by theoretical explanations and reference to accepted norms. Patterns of behaviour involve some repetition of observed behaviours. When a particular behaviour is repeated it may reveal a changing response to the environment, a change in the environment, a cause, or trigger, or an emerging or refining of a skill or competence. You would need to look at the type of pattern and kind of behaviours to determine the progression or regression of development that you observed.

4. Standardized measures are scrutinized very closely and may have published data regarding their validity and reliability. Standardization is one way to evaluate a prepared rating scale but there are further criteria. You may find it significant to try out the scale to see if it gives consistent outcomes; in particular the scoring may need to be explored to ensure that it is clear and constant. Accurate use may depend on training and the understanding of terminology. The scale items need to be suitable for the age/stage of the children to be assessed. Finally, you may look at the inventory of items to be measured to check that they actually fit your theoretical understanding of the attributes being rated.

5. A bulk of observational information can be difficult to interpret. It needs some collation and quantifying. A variety of graphs and pictorial representations of information can be helpful. Simple tallying on a chart may be all that is needed but data can be transferred to time lines, block charts, sociograms, ecomaps, genograms, flow diagrams, pie charts, or graphs.

6. A variety of professionals could use a family tree to help them identify any of the following: genetically inherited diseases, family patterns, life cycles, family size, history, cultural identity, or origin. These can offer the professional a useful piece of contextual information.

◆ ◆ ◆ ◆ Key Terms

scales
graphs
quantitative analysis
family trees
mappings
trackings
observation charts
syllabuses
integrative curriculum models
sociometry
genogram
forced choices
graphic scales

interpretive graphic representations
competence
tally mark
numerical ratings
pictorial or graphic representations
semantic differential
sociogram
life experience flowchart
bar line charts
pie charts
sequential models
topic planning
input/outcome planning model

6 Media Techniques

We think we remember the growth of our children, and we remember the high spots. The triumphs and minor tragedies. But how much we miss with the camera of our memory. For the life of a child is a kaleidoscope of changing moods, aptitudes, activities and developing personality and physical growth. Photographs help us capture these facets and enjoy ourselves and to pass onto our children and our children's children. But we must realize that the pictures we can chortle or sigh over tomorrow we have to take today.
George Hornby (1977)

Oral reading tapes (audio recordings) provide excellent records of children's development in reading. A teacher or parent will find it more informative and interesting to listen to a tape of a child reading a story than to review reading scores.
Brenda S. Engel (1990)

A video recorder can be unobtrusive and help students in learning to observe. Here an in-class observation opportunity is recorded so that re-play can assist in making accurate inferences.

Focus Questions

1. What benefits might you have from using tape recordings of a child's language rather than writing down what the child says?

2. What kind of photographs of children are useful to the educator and parent?

3. How could you reduce the possibility of children acting to the camera when videotaping or taking photographs?

4. What special issues of confidentiality need to be recognized in using the newer technologies for recording observations?

5. Can you think of suitable ways of storing videotapes, cassette tapes, and photographs that contain observational data?

6. If you record observations on videotape, how might you use them to help you understand the child and to program successfully?

◆ ◆ ◆ ◆ **History Notes**

Peeking through the lens of a camera can make you see the subject in focus rather differently than you might without the camera. Having a recording device pointed at you may also make a difference to your behaviour. Bearing these two points in mind, we will look at how these media technologies have changed how we see.

In 1824, Joseph Nicephore produced, in France, the first black and white photographs. The first colour photographs were probably made by mistake with accidental combinations of chemicals, but the first recorded presentation of colour photographic images was in 1961 by a young British physicist, James Clerk Maxwell. In 1877, Ducos du Hauron from France made one of the earliest known colour prints. Joly and McDonough made early photographs of live subjects using a "taking screen" to produce a positive colour transparency made up of separate spots of colour. The 1940s saw great advances in the chemical processing and accessibility of photographic techniques to the public; although expensive, it was possible for ordinary people to own and use a camera for colour photographs.

If you enjoy photography of children and are interested in a visual history of photography you will enjoy *Children in Photography : 150 Years* by Jane Corkin and Gary Michael Dault. This Canadian book is a wonderful monument to photographic images of both passive and active children. Jane Corkin comments:

> They capture for us in the moment a quality unique to the photographic art, where the observer and the observed spontaneously collaborate – no matter how contrived the setting – to reveal something new about our relationship to the qualities of the child within each of us – to newness, to innocence, to vulnerability, to wonder.

Instant cameras were invented by Dr. Edwin H. Land and marketed in 1948 for the first time. In 1969 a second generation of camera-producing colour images became available. Land was president of the Polaroid Corporation, which keeps the monopoly on instant photography to this day. The novelty of instant photos has meant that this medium is frequently used for fun rather than professional purposes.

The movie camera was invented at the end of the 19th century. Since then, more than 300,000 movies have been made. Movies are based on an optical phenomenon which creates an illusion of movement in the displaying of a stream of still images in quick succession. The main difference between **video** and film cameras is that the video focusses the image on a tube which converts the image into an electrical signal, which is then recorded onto tape. Film requires photographic emulsions to create its long series of images. It was not anticipated that video would gain such popularity. The professional use for which it was designed was reconsidered to make it accessible to the home market. In 1976, Sony introduced Betamax as the choice for families. After debate as to whether Betamax or VHS was preferable, the latter came to dominate the market. Prices came down as competition and popularity increased. Videodiscs became available but have not taken a strong hold of the market because of their expense and some technical limitations.

We have come to expect to be able to record sound and vision simultaneously and also to have available cameras that can do this with the minimum of fuss and expense. Today's **camcorders** or **palmcorders** are straightforward devices.

Thomas Edison invented the **phonograph** in 1847 in the U.S. The first words recorded for public replay were "Mary had a little lamb." The Edison company made cylindrical phonographs, but other companies found ways of manufacturing cylindrical systems for recording sound, which were called **graphophones** or micro-phonographs. They were based on the same principle, which was tracking indentations with a stylus. The vibrations recreated sounds. The disc version of this came to be known as a **gramophone**. Although copied, it became a generic name. A succession of variants were tried out over the years using different materials on which the indentations were made. A wire recording device that used magnetic fields was explained in 1888 by Oberlin Smith in Britain, but it was Danish physicist Valdemar Poulsen who first made it work. In 1898 he applied for a Danish patent on what he called the **telegraphone.** American, German, and British inventors each attempted to perfect a tape recording technique. Not until the 1920s was a "Blattnerphone" made to synchronize sound with motion pictures. In 1925, Bell Telephone Laboratories in the United States developed an electrical sound recording device using a **microphone**. Large, cumbersome **tape recording** machines were manufactured for the public by the mid 1940s. Gradually scaled down in size and price, they became popular for personal recording uses and the replay of commercially recorded music. The quality of recording increased considerably from the 1940s onwards. The **compact disc**, which has superseded the record as a means of recording music, is not a useful addition to our accessible recording techniques because the audio CD is not generally available for recording.

Technological advancements in the last few decades have been only slowly adopted by those working with children. Typically, the resources have not been available or their application for record keeping has not been appreciated. In many instances the only photographs taken have been by a hired photographer for an annual picture for the child to take home. Photographs may have been taken by staff from time to time but more for sentimental than educational purposes. Systematic record keeping using photographs has been used by some for child identification systems and as an addition to written observations. But few agencies incorporate photography into their organization of information collection.

Moving pictures were first used for educational purposes as a learning tool for teachers before they became used for record keeping about individual children. Research workers could see the application of the movie for their purposes. These old films can offer us insight today as their content may still be valid. The work of James and Joyce Robertson, on

The complexity of some play activity can be a challenge to record. These school-age children play a game involving rules. Video recordings can capture this better than any other method.

separation, is such an example. Their films, made in Britain, centred on the separation of children from their parents in a way which would not be recreated today. Today these recordings have been transferred to a video format.

The video camera is much easier to use than the older movie camera. A gradual increase in its use for observational purposes has been evident but this has been done more by researchers than practitioners. Relatively few agencies have organized systems for video-recorded observations. Where they exist they have been used successfully for working with parents and sharing information about the child's development.

Observational use of the tape recorder has been common among language researchers. Its obvious application allows language samples to be gathered and replaced for analysis. Teachers and caregivers use this type of device for keeping segments of the child's language and music either for record keeping or for the child to replay to increase her awareness of her sound production. Language pathologists and speech therapists have used tape recordings for thirty years or more as a diagnostic tool or to support their therapy.

Educators are beginning to realize the usefulness of technically assisted recordings for their purpose. Reduced costs may help them to find these and other techniques a viable alternative to pen and paper, and offer some advantages in speed efficiency and replay.

Media techniques: Definition

Any method of recording or storing observational data that is achieved by mechanical, electronic, or technical means.

Features of technically assisted observations

An ever-widening range of methods of observing and recording information is becoming accessible to those working with young children. Each of the techniques offers the possibility of gathering information more quickly or effectively if it is used properly. They require the same degree of sensitive perception as traditional methods because the choice of who and what is to be observed and recorded remains the decision of the observer. Varying amounts of skill are necessary for the use of the different media techniques. The automatic functions of, for example, many cameras or camcorders can mean that little training is necessary to start; practice is the most effective way of improving the quality of productions.

Media techniques can serve us by enabling a quicker, more efficient, more accurate, more detailed, more readily replayable, and possibly more long-lasting and meaningful record of the child. These features are not always applicable and it should not be assumed that a technically assisted observation is, of itself, preferable to narratives or samplings. They are a useful addition to our range of information-gathering tools.

It is tempting to let a videotaped observation "speak for itself." When it was recorded it is quite possible that it was self-explanatory but the observation will become increasingly meaningless if it is not labelled, dated, explained, summarized, and analyzed as one would with any other significant data. Appreciating the usefulness of the media techniques while acknowledging their limitations will mean that we can choose the most effective method for observing and recording.

Most frequently used aids to observation are cameras, video cameras, or "camcorders," and tape recorders. In time these will be enhanced or superseded by a range of other devices with additional facilities. Although it is not a recording device, in itself, we may see the photo CD system (e.g., Kodak Photo CD), which allows developed photographs to be transferred onto a compact disc for replay on television, used as a major information storage and retrieval system. With each CD holding a hundred pictures, it has great potential to be an educational record keeping device.

Computer software has been developed that enables teachers to keep academic and other records. The major computer companies currently offer packages that meet the needs of the school community for **summative** record keeping. It is entirely possible for software to be designed to accommodate educators' need for creating formats for recording observational information. To date, programs for child care agencies have tended to focus on administration and formalized record keeping.

Linkages between the different recording devices such as camcorders and computers are quite possible but are usually expensive. It is the cost of the technology which prevents us from using the technique for observation and recording. A Video Spigot from SuperMac Technology or Video Vision board from Radius offer combined audio and video facilities. Recording video onto a hard drive is difficult because the video signal contains more information per second than the hard drive can record. The Video Spigot does not digitize the audio signal, so that you would need to use additional software to overlay the sound track. The technology will "make your movies smoother, more colourful, and more compact on your hard drive" (Pogue, *Macworld,* Oct. 1992). As the possibilities increase, we can be excited by their obvious application but may need to await the time when the price drops and they become more widely available.

Voice-responsive devices have been used in work with children with special needs for some while but their application for wider use, particularly as an observation recording device, is hindered by their high cost. Many of us would delight in the possibility of recording our observations onto a portable machine, like a tape recorder, which would have the additional feature of recording in print.

To be realistic, the majority of us consider ourselves fortunate to be able to use tools for observing and recording that are more sophisticated than pen and paper. This chapter will concentrate on working with the camera, camcorder, and audiotape recorder, as these are the media you are most likely to use to support your educational purposes.

Photography: Uses for Recording Information

You will need to consider your intentions and the possibilities associated with the use of photographs. It is likely that one of the following uses is helpful to you in performing your responsibilities or supporting your learning about children.

1. As part of a life book to support the child's appreciation of their own "'story."
2. As evidence of the child's changes in physical appearance, and growth.
3. For recording significant life experiences and rites of passage.
4. To support traditionally recorded observations.
5. As part of the child's developmental portfolio.
6. To record episodes of the child's activity.
7. To keep information about the products of the child's activity.
8. For file identification.
9. As a safety measure to ensure security.
10. To aid the child's memory of situations.

General principles for photography for observational purposes

Some basic guidelines might be helpful if you choose to use photography to support your child observations.

1. Choose a camera which fits your level of competence and the purpose for which you will use it.
2. Keep the camera loaded with film, stored safely but close to the place it will be needed.
3. Always have spare film ready.
4. Get lots of practice in taking pictures.
5. Have the children become familiar with you taking photographs.
6. Be aware of your reasons for taking a photograph and ensure that you avoid subjectivity.
7. Adjust your camera to choose film according to the lighting available.
8. Design and use a format for selecting, labelling, and storing the photographs.
9. Ensure every photograph is considered to be a confidential document.

How to take photographs you can use for educational purposes

Taking photos for use by professional agencies involved in child care and education is not substantially different from family photography. Your family snaps will be regarded as records of significant events or stages in life, as are the professionally used photographs. The essentials of recording are that you manage to capture what you believe to be pertinent in a way that is accurate and easily understandable. Some people have a natural flair for photography, while for others even the "idiot proof" camera presents challenges!

Here are some suggestions for increasing your skill and artistry.

Choice of camera

Many good pictures have been "lost" because of the time it took to set up a complex camera's speed, angle, and focus. The gifted and skilled photographer will get some marvellous results using expensive paraphernalia and lots of time, but adults working with children want to capture the moment spontaneously. They may prefer to choose a camera which has automatic functions, is relatively small in size, has an in-built flash, and is loaded with a film likely to be adequate both indoors and out. You can often take an adequate photograph with an automatic pocket-size camera, which might have been missed if you had to fiddle with the attachments. A camera fulfilling the following specifications is ideal and equally usable by any member of the work team.

a. small, pocket-size with firmly attached cord for wearing around neck or tying to something
b. automatic loading
c. automatic wind on
d. automatic shutter/exposure
e. automatic flash
f. clear indicator for # on roll of film
g. battery tester buzzer
h. clear and accurate indicator of image through lens of image
i. relatively inexpensive

Film facts

These points will help you with film choice:

- colour films and the human eye have different colour sensitivities
- film is not capable of a "perfect" representation of colour but colour film is much more accurate than it used to be
- dyes that form the characteristics of colour films differ from colours in nature
- the choice of what is quality film is, in part, subjective
- "professional" film is very similar to "amateur" but it may be fresher
- exposed but unprocessed film is open to image decay
- slight temperature variations may damage film
- high speed films (above ASA 250) permit shutter speeds that enable you to take pictures with a hand-held camera even under dim light
- slow films have the finest grain and produce negatives of the highest contrast but may require use of a tripod

The importance of lighting

Adjust your technique to the lighting available. Ensure there is sufficient light or supplement it with flash if necessary. Avoid taking photographs while looking towards the sun. If evident, the sun should be behind you, preferably not casting long sharp shadows. The degree of light can be deceptive: light in snow and evening sun are particularly difficult to evaluate without a light meter. Indoor lighting can seem stronger than it actually is and can also make your photograph turn strange, unpredictable colours. You may not know this until you have your pictures processed.

When to take a picture (being natural)

With some familiarity with being photographed children become desensitized to what you are doing and usually continue about their daily business without being affected by the "click."

Your purpose is likely to be to "capture a moment" of the child in action, to record their interests, playskills, relationships, learning, reactions, or some other educational consideration. Although patience may be necessary, try not to call the child to get their attention or disturb the activity in any way. The child's play and learning experience is always more important than the photograph. Recording the essence of the action is challenging but will not be achieved by trying to direct what the children are doing for the sake of the camera. If you start to do this you may be intrusive and contradict the professed philosophy of early childhood.

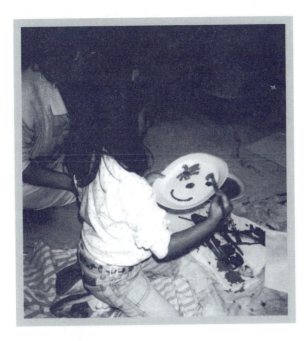

A photograph that depicts a part of the process of an activity can be a helpful addition to written observations.

To achieve naturalness, to record a child's interactions within his naturalistic setting, there is a longer list of what *not* to do than *what* to do. It may be helpful for the children to access "play" cameras or even offer opportunity for their own photography. This may help with acceptance of the adult's use of the camera.

Photographic recording of the child's development

Here the intention is to take regular and deliberate, rather than occasional or random, photographs of each child in your care. You might like to keep a chart record of the photographs you have taken so that you can check if you have selected each child at regular intervals.

Early use of photographic techniques by professionals frequently employed a static, impersonal, and posed technique. There are more effective ways of recording growth information than standing the child against a marked and measured wall like a police shot – a tape measure or scale can do that. What you want to do is take photographs of the child involved in typical activities.

Using photographs to supplement other observational recordings can be helpful because they can give a more real sense of "who" the child is when you review the data.

Instant cameras

Instant cameras are frequently called "Land" cameras after Edwin Land, who invented them, or Polaroid, after the company that developed, manufactured, and marketed them.

There are some obvious advantages of an instant photograph. They enable you to:

- tell immediately if you have taken an appropriate photograph without waiting for processing
- avoid waiting for film processing and sending, delivering, or collecting film
- date and label the photograph immediately and more accurately and rapidly share information with the subject of the picture, with parents, and with other professionals.

Against these points there are a few negative considerations:

- cost per photograph is increased
- quality of picture may not be as good
- photograph is thicker than a regular photo
- photograph may not resist fading as well as a traditionally processed film.

Capturing natural expressions

Getting down to the child's level is very important in understanding what the child is doing. The child's eye level is exactly where you need to be; the angle allows you the most open access to the child's expression and allows for personal eye contact which can help to personalize the moment, if that is what you wish. Less appealing is an angle which looks down at the child and distorts the action as the child sees it. You may need to lie on the floor, squat, kneel, sit on a child's chair, or adopt some other uncomfortable position.

When a child tries to pose it will not be the best picture taking time, as she will tend to over-act. If you take several pictures within a short period of time, you are more likely to get a more useful shot. At moments of discovery and engrossment the child is less likely to be influenced by you being there and this should be more successful.

Photographic processing

If you have a dark room and the appropriate equipment, you might want to develop and print your own film. More likely, you will use one of the processing services available in your locality or a service which accepts mail-in films for processing.

The cost of service varies considerably; in many instances it relates to the time you have to wait for the process. The faster the service, the higher the charge. Although photography experts may argue about the types of process and their results, it can be more a matter of personal preference than objective choice.

You will need to decide whether you wish to use an inclusive service in which you pay "up front" for the processing when you buy the film; you are then limited to using the place of purchase for the developing. Shop-front service may be quicker (processed in an hour), but may well be more expensive. Dropping off your film at a central depot or mailing it to the photography lab are often cheaper alternatives. Size of photograph, finish, and number of copies will be further choices for you to make. A good idea is to log the details of your photographs as you take them because there will be a time lag in having the photographs returned to you.

Storing photographs

You may wish to establish a photographic record system that uses a pre-determined labelling system. For observational purposes, it is often more helpful to have the photograph mounted on an accompanying form which can explain its context. Writing directly on the back is seldom successful because the photo suffers from being handled and the writing may rub off or show through to the front. Self-adhesive labels can be used successfully if you wish to cut down the bulk of paperwork, but even a pre-printed label does not help the picture from being lost in a file folder with other information. Photographs can be kept in albums for each child although this takes up a lot of space. Box files designed for file index cards can be used and form a wonderful gift to parents when the child leaves the agency.

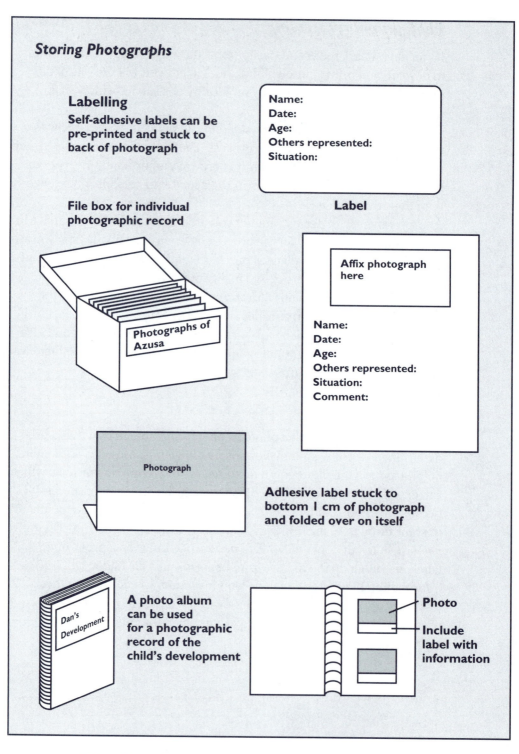

Storing Photographs

Labelling
Self-adhesive labels can be pre-printed and stuck to back of photograph

Name:
Date:
Age:
Others represented:
Situation:

Label

File box for individual photographic record

Photographs of Azusa

Affix photograph here

Name:
Date:
Age:
Others represented:
Situation:
Comment:

Photograph

Adhesive label stuck to bottom 1 cm of photograph and folded over on itself

Dan's Development

A photo album can be used for a photographic record of the child's development

— Photo
— Include label with information

Videotaping: Uses for Recording Information

There are a number of purposes for videotaping the child's activities or environment:

◆ for replaying when time allows for greater analysis.
◆ to share information about the child's development with parents.
◆ as a long-term record of an individual's progress.
◆ to assist in observing groups of children so that attention can be directed to each child's involvement and interactions.
◆ for research purposes.
◆ to record significant happenings or rites of passage in the child's life so that the child can review significant parts of her own life story.
◆ to support observations recorded in a traditional way.
◆ to recreate the activities and interactions of the individual to facilitate a multi-disciplinary evaluation.
◆ to assist in evaluating the child's environment.

General principles for videotaping

Skill can be gained quite quickly once you get started.

1. Survey the market of available recording equipment, identify the features you need, and adjust to your finances.
2. Familiarize yourself with your recording device and its functions.
3. Allow plenty of time and tape for practice.
4. Extend your vocabulary to include video terminology.
5. De-sensitize your subjects before you make recordings you intend to keep. You might have the children actively participate in videomaking.
6. Determine your purchase for recording.
7. Avoid subjective shooting that centres on what is "cute" or on children "acting up" to the camera.
8. Investigate possibilities for editing your video recordings.
9. Design and use a format for labelling and storing the videotapes.
10. Ensure every videotape is considered a confidential document.

The basics of video recording

To get started, you need some beginner's tips:

◆ read and use the owner's manual so that you can appreciate the camcorder's features.

- try using a tripod for holding the camera, or brace yourself against a firm object to avoid a bouncing effect.
- use an autofocus or practise focussing manually. Be aware that the camcorder set on autofocus will focus on the nearest object.
- practice your use of the **zoom** to prevent the feeling that you are lurching back and forth, but do not overuse it.
- compose your videotaping so that the context or background is clear before you go into close-up.
- set or move camera at different angles to the subject for more interesting images.
- use your camcorder to record movement that cannot be achieved by a still camera.
- hold static shots particularly at the beginning and end of a sequence.
- when panning across an area (L to R or R to L) go smoothly to direct the viewers attention but limit the angle of movement to 90 degrees.
- follow the child's action at their level for a more insightful view of the child's world.
- the pause button is a form of in-process **editing**. Practice using it.
- try to capture meaningful sequences of activity while being aware of the audio recording occurring simultaneously.

How to make videotapes for observation and recording purposes

To learn how to make video recordings, you may want to read "how to" manuals but your starting point will probably be trial and error. Awareness of the most common mistakes will not necessarily help you avoid them because you need to see how they occur before you can rectify them. Typical difficulties might be in camera bounce; you will notice this when you replay and you start to feel nausea! Becoming familiar with the functions of the camcorder is helpful and this you can do on a try-out basis. Short of dropping the camcorder or applying physical force to it, you are unlikely to do it any harm. Lewis suggests that the 14 basic skills of video can be learned in two days. He describes the sequence of skill development as:

skill 1	holding the camera
skill 2	camera movements
skill 3	moving with the camera
skill 4	zooming

skill 5	sound sense
skill 6	using lights
skill 7	composition
skill 8	a sense of direction
skill 9	space and time
skill 10	editing
skill 11	rostrum shooting (shooting two-dimensional subjects and copying onto video)
skill 12	animation (which, as an observer, you do not need)
skill 13	creating titles
skill 14	sound tracks

A weekend video making course is contained in Lewis's *Learn to Video in a Weekend* and offers the basics you need for the task. Despite the title, Hedgecoe's *Complete Guide to Video: The Ultimate Manual of Video Techniques and Equipment* is also easily understandable for the newcomer while providing detail that might be helpful.

Innovative features of camcorders that can help observers

Age subtitles: it is possible to program some camcorders to memorize an individual's birth date so that their actual age can appear on the video.

Date/time: camcorders usually record the date and time of recording on the screen.

Title superimposer: a memory in the camcorder can record a title or picture over a scene.

Self-timer: a timer allows the camera operator to "get into the action" for participant observation.

Insert edit: enables new recordings to be put over old with a sophisticated, dedicated insert edit facility you can pre-set to the point where you want to add new material.

Macro close-up/zoom: camcorders allow for varying degrees of close-ups. On some, this can be controlled automatically.

External mike socket: can help with sound pick up when the fixed microphone is too far away to pick up language.

Audio dub: replacing the recorded sound with a narrative is possible on some models.

Auto exposure: the iris diaphragm automatically adjusts size of aperture to suit available lighting.

When to make a video recording

When your skill is beginning to develop you will start to see opportunities for recording the activities of the children in your care. Such a flow of action will make it difficult to decide when and what to choose to record; the availability of your time may well dictate your choice. It can be a challenge to maintain your supervisory role, be a participant in the activity, and also manage to record what is happening. Resolution of this can happen if there are systems of shared care, cover, time designated for recording, or if your group of children is small enough or happens to be undemanding. Having said all that, educators who are committed to videotaping usually manage to do it.

You may want to record some of the more domestic and routine elements of the children's day. In only a short time these routines evolve as the child develops, and mere memories of them can be lost. Recording typical behaviours may be as rewarding as seeking "new advances" in development. The dated record will help you see developmental changes over a period of time. Capturing the child's spontaneous play activity can be the most revealing and meaningful element of videotaping. Having the camcorder available in the children's play area can mean that you can shoot what happens without any fuss. Indoors and out you can record a variety of play sequences and social interactions. Video recordings may be made centring on the activity of one child. Seldom does it happen that we record that child in isolation; most usually she will be involved with others. If we make a videotape, our decision needs to be about how to pick out the individual child's behaviour from the general flow. Editing facilities form the foundation of effective individual record keeping.

Videotapes

Blank tapes are not all the same. They vary in length, cost, quality, and type. Most of the guides to videorecording recommend using name brands sold by reputable dealers, and to buy them when the price is lowest. Alternatively read a video magazine or consumer report for the "best buy."

Videotapes need to be handled carefully. Using fresh tapes with a camcorder is desirable because the VCR tends to wear the tape. They need to be kept at a temperature and humidity which is average rather than extreme. Tapes need to be kept clean, in their sleeves or cases, stored fully wound and vertical, and kept away from magnetic fields. Labelling and dating is a common difficulty with videotapes because they offer little space for detail. A referencing system which is kept with the same counter numbering as the tape itself can accompany the video in its sleeve or box.

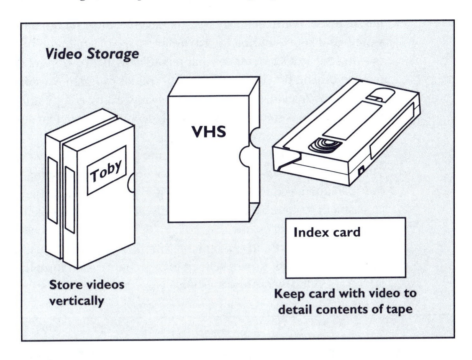

Video Storage

VHS

Toby

Index card

**Store videos
vertically**

**Keep card with video to
detail contents of tape**

Name:			Group:	
Date	Counter #	Context	Comment	

An information card can have a predetermined information category system.

Videotaping as part of long-term record keeping

Record keeping that forms a history of the children's development, activities, or festivals are relatively easy to make. Videotapes can be labelled, stored, and kept in chronological order.

An educator's videotapes that record activity of groups of children may require editing but can be very useful for program planning for the group. These can be stored fairly simply and accessed by staff when necessary. They may also provide very good teaching material for student educators and caregivers.

Most important is the record keeping done for the individual child. The recordings need to be kept with, or alongside, an observation file or portfolio and be considered as an integral part of the observation and assessment system. To make these individual tapes, it is essential to have an effective editing facility.

Confidentiality and professionalism must apply to the use of videotaped observations. You may need to use a permission form that addresses video recordings specifically (see Chapter 1).

Some suggestions of what your video recording might highlight

- any of the features of audio recordings
- play patterns
- body language/eye contact
- program effectiveness
- use of space
- group interactions/behaviour
- gross motor skills
- manipulative skills
- children's responses to activities
- discovery and curiosity
- experimentation with objects and materials

- mood changes
- independence skills/autonomy
- process of play and learning
- products of activity
- creative activity and artwork in process
- social groupings
- parenting styles
- separation or other anxieties
- any other aspect of development that could be revealed by other observation methods

> ### Audiotapes used as recorded samples
>
> You may have any of the following purposes in making audio recordings.
> - to support any traditionally recorded observation.
> - to record the educator's narrative description of the child's behaviour.
> - to record a child/children's verbal communications.
> - to facilitate close analysis of a language sample.
> - to record a child's/children's explorations and production of sound and music.
> - to keep records of the child's language, music, or reading skill development.
> - to communicate with parents in sharing direct recordings or anecdotal observations.
> - as part of the child's developmental portfolio.
> - for the student teacher to learn about language, music, humour, and thinking skills of the child.

◆ ◆ ◆ ◆ General Principles for Audiotape Recording for Educational Purposes

1. Consider your needs and purchase a tape recorder which is resilient and portable.
2. Set up the tape recorder in a convenient place but use its portable feature to go where the children are.
3. Give yourself lots of time to practise tape recording.
4. Familiarize the children with tape recording and have them become acquainted with recording and playback.
5. Organize time for replay and analysis.
6. Determine your purpose for recording.
7. Consider the possibilities of **splicing** and editing your recordings using specialized equipment.
8. Accept failures.
9. Design and use a format for labelling and storing the tape recordings.
10. Ensure every cassette tape is considered a confidential document.

Beginner's tips on tape recording

1. Try using an extended microphone with a jack to pick up sounds more clearly – a pair of microphones at least 9 inches (23 cm) apart can be helpful.
2. Avoid constant rewinding and re-recording because this may stretch and distort the tape.
3. Use the pause button for in-process editing.
4. Set up your recordings in an area which minimizes sounds of background activity.
5. Purchase brand name tapes in bulk when they are at a lower price rather than buy "cheap" brands.
6. Use a Dolby noise reduction system if one is built into the recorder – it will give you a better, clearer replay.
7. Keep tapes and recorders in a dry atmosphere, in moderate temperatures, and away from magnetic fields.
8. On occasions when the tape becomes unravelled, you can try to rewind it with a hexagon-shaped pencil, but damaged tapes might jam in the recorder.
9. If a cassette tape gets jammed in the recorder do not try to force it out. Take it to a dealer.
10. For educators working in well-designed environments with sound systems, try linking a mike with a recording device.

How to make audio recordings for observational purposes

You may be familiar with a range of audio recording machines: reel-to-reel, cartridge, and cassette systems have been available but the cassette is the most popular. The cassette protects the tape and makes threading a simple process. The production of cassette recorders has made possible the manufacture of small portable tape recorders suitable for an observer.

The set up of your recorder and microphones is important for success.

You will be frustrated sometimes that you missed some opportunities for recordings because you were not ready but you can limit these occasions if you are set up to record.

Laboratory schools and agencies which have in-built sound systems so that students and teachers can "listen-in" will be at an advantage. Not all of these systems are built for recording so you might want to check into this. A good sound system has microphones a little above the children's heads. The mics are fairly evenly spread across areas where the children are active. The observer listens from a distance, usually through a one-way mirrored observation booth with speakers or headphones. These headphones can allow the observer to select which microphone he wishes to use and therefore pick up the sounds he wishes. If there is an additional recording facility a lot of useful information can be stored.

Dangling microphones can be used if you are doing straightforward recording. One mic might give you a "flat" sound recording but having two or more give a stereophonic reality. If the two mikes are set up apart from each other, the effect is more like the human ears picking up sound. When further apart, the microphones can record a group of children more effectively.

Recording is better when the children are still. When they move around you might try the reporter's technique of following the children with a hand-held microphone. A propped-up mike on a table usually picks up too much white noise.

Batteries can be expensive. Rechargeable batteries may be a good choice. A recording machine that offers mains and battery power is useful. Re-winding can be done when the mains is being used because it uses up a lot of the battery power.

You will need to decide what to record according to your purpose. The children may become so familiar with the tape recorder that it does not bother them. Desensitizing them is often done by allowing the children to record and replay by themselves or, for younger children, for you to share your recordings with them. Squeals of delight are typical for the pre-schoolers but younger children may be confused when you re-play their language.

Choice of audiotape recorder

If you know the price you can afford and some of the features you might like, then to go to the store for a demonstration. Warehouse electrical suppliers might be cheaper than well-known stores but check that the guarantee they offer is good. Here are some features to look for in a basic tape recorder.

- easy hook-up to microphones/sound system
- resilient, robust design
- battery/mains operated
- simple operation
- a counter system
- Dolby noise reduction
- easy access to repair and servicing

Tape choice

The audio magazines debate the issues of what the best tape recorder might be. The higher priced tapes are often the best but try out a variety when they are offered at a discount. Avoid the cheaper copies of the well-known manufacturers' tapes. The brand-name tapes are usually superior because of their high frequency response, high output, consistency of magnetic characteristics, freedom from squeal, absence of stretching, and accuracy of reproduction of sound. However, they do vary.

When to make a tape recording

There are very many times in the child's day when you might like to make an audio recording. Try not to miss the normal, average, and domestic aspects of the child's day as well as the more structured peak programming times. Be prepared to make spontaneous decisions to record and also acknowledge that you will have to be patient. Here are some suggestions:

- circle times
- greetings, separations, and reunions
- group singing
- experimentation with sounds/instruments
- book corner – conversation
            – reading
            – story telling
- spontaneous play activities
- infant crib sounds

- infant interactions with adults
- sociodramatic play
- imitative play
- transitions
- bathroom routines
- conversations with adults
- individual singing or reciting rhymes
- music activities
- hearing children read
- bilingual children's conversation
- toddlers' emerging language
- problem solving activities
- outdoor play
- on outings, picnics
- at home with parents/siblings/friends
- formal assessments
- examples of school-agers' jokes
- portfolio assessment meetings

Storing audiotape recordings

As with any other observational material audio recording must remain confidential. You may wish to have general and group recordings. Remember that individual children's records are more effective in helping you to determine the child's developmental level and to program for her in response to her needs and skills. Where you have recordings of a group you will find it almost impossible to make copies for individual files. More successful is to make, from the tape, a written narration of the content. If the language is complex this will be difficult but it is possible to make written documents from tapes. They do, of course, capture all the detail and can be replayed many times so you can get it down on paper.

If you can organize taping so that you put into the record the child's "own" tape you will manage to gain some chronologically recorded bits of information for that one child. Using the counter and writing down the numbers is helpful to keep track of where you are on the tape.

Tapes must always be labelled, dated, and have an accompanying numbered log. They should be kept at room temperature in their boxes, having been re-wound. Tapes may be kept in the child's portfolio, or, because of their bulk, in a storage system kept near the portfolio.

Audiotape Recording Log

Name: D.O.B.:

Date	Counter #s	Sequence	Narrative documents		Comment
			Yes	No	

Some of the information that the audio cassette recording might offer

(This is not intended to be a comprehensive or ordered list, but some ideas of what you might be looking for in analyzing recordings.)

pronunciation
reading strategies
MLUs (Mean Length of
   Utterances)
pitch discrimination
experimentation with oral
   sound production
rhythm of speech
length of phrase
accent
phraseology
speech pattern
use of parts of speech
communication difficulties
egocentricity/egocentric
   speech
expression of ideas
articulation of concepts

over-extensions
grammatical errors
misunderstandings
social relationships
humour and incongruities
moral views/attitudes
social role play
cooperation with peers
developmental level of
   thinking skills
demonstration of feelings
solitary
   activity/isolation/talking
   to self
memory
sequencing of stories or
   events
imagination

use of rhyme
cultural patterns
musicality
concentration length
interests
play level
fantasy
realism
logic
friendships
peer interactions
imitation
conversation with adults
repetition
telegraphic speech
sibling interactions

Technically Assisted Observation

Advantages	Disadvantages
Offers detailed information recording not possible with traditional methods.	Cost.
	Availability.
Observation recorded may be more "objective" than those requiring observer description.	Training required.
	Can encourage quantity recording at the cost of quality recording, which is well-analyzed.
Can record quantity of information quickly.	
"Concrete" recording, which can be analyzed by many professionals individually and collectively after the event.	Knowledge of recording may influence the child and alter behaviour.
	Confidentiality issues challenging to resolve.
Can supplement and validate other traditionally recorded observations.	
	Storage and retrieval systems need to be established.

◆ ◆ ◆ ◆ *Assignment options*

I. Skill building and practising media techniques

Individual tasks

1. Write a narrative recording of a child's conversation with an adult or another child. At the same time use an audiotape recorder to tape the conversation. Transcribe the tape and compare it with your narrative recording. What did you learn by comparing the methods?
2. Examine photographs of children that you have taken in any situation. Consider ways in which they might have been taken that would have revealed more pertinent or lasting information.
3. Interview practising teachers and ask them about their needs and challenges in recording information about their children. Identify some media techniques that might assist the teachers in their responsibilities.
4. After a few days' work with a group of children (perhaps in your placement or work situation) identify the most significant features of activity that you saw. Then list five sequences that might have been recorded on videotape that highlight the children's skills.

Group tasks

1. Identify a particular gross motor skill and have each member of the group attempt to photograph a child demonstrating the skill. Share the photographs and discuss the features of the more successful images.
2. List the features of a video camera which fit the requirements of an observational task. Group members can research the cost and availability of such cameras and see if a budget can be met. If necessary make compromises to fall within the budget.
3. Review a pre-recorded play sequence of no more that five minutes in length. Attempt to make inferences regarding the children's social

skills, concentration, and the types of play demonstrated. Test the inferences for their validity.

4. Role play a situation in which you need to discuss strategies with parents regarding the anti-social behaviour of their six-year-old daughter. You have a video recording that shows examples of the challenging behaviour. Include your use of this material into the role play.

5. Imagine that you are in a situation in which you need to call in a language expert about some concerns about a child's poor speech. The child is three-and-a-half years old and is in full-time centre-based child care. What might be useful times of the day to record the child's language? When you carry out the audio recordings the language pathologist offers a diagnosis of aphasia. Research what this means and what might be done to support the child.

Practising media techniques

1. Take a series of six photographs that best depict the stage of development of any one child. Label them appropriately.

2. Use a video camera to capture the outdoor play experiences of a group of children. Evaluate the recording and re-record on a subsequent day, trying to improve your technique.

3. Devise a system of record keeping which incorporates a balance of traditional and media techniques and fits the need of a particular agency.

4. Make audiotape recordings of individual children singing. Attempt to identify each child's use of pitch and rhythm.

5. Investigate the use of computerized record keeping. Identify ways in which your recorded observations, health, and other information might be stored by a computer. Ensure that you explore issues regarding confidentiality.

◆ ◆ ◆ ◆ *Answers to focus questions*

1. Audiotape recordings can enable a student or practitioner to observe and continue to interact while recording the exact language uttered by a child. It will be more accurate than any other means of recording, can be replayed as many times as necessary, and you can enable those not present to be given objective information.

2. Images that record a child's significant life events, growth, changes in interest and abilities, their interactions, and their personalities are all suitable for the educator and parent.

3. Desensitizing the children by having them become familiar with the cameras is helpful. The constant presence of the camera may be part of the process. Answers to their questions need to be open and honest. The children may want to look through the lens or even take their own photographs. Videotaping and reviewing the children's activities can assist in the child's awareness of self. Taking photographs of the children involved in activities frequently prompts the memory of events. "Play" cameras may be useful additions to pretend play as they can be props that promote understanding.

4. It may be harder to ensure confidentiality with media techniques than with traditional methods of recording. Computerized recording must always be protected from inappropriate access and loss. Access codes may help. Individual discs can be filed in locked cabinets or with secure paper files. Where there are groups of children videotaped, the recorder needs to ensure that permission has been granted by the parents. Showing videos involving children, other than a parent's own, needs to be done with discretion even if a "blanket" permission has been given. The storage of all confidential information needs to be in compliance with freedom of information and privacy legislation.

5. Videotapes need to be stored in a video library or with the individual child's own portfolio. They should be labelled and dated. A log of the contents should be listed for ease of access. Audio cassette tapes can be kept in a similar way or, because they are smaller, might fit into the child's regular observation folder. Mounting photographs onto a preprinted form can assist in storage. They can be kept in albums for each child, in agency albums if the purpose is for recording the centre's history, in a child's "life book," or kept with traditionally recorded observations.

6. Videotaped observations can be used in the same way as other types of recordings. Frequently they offer a degree of accuracy of recording which supports their validity, they are non-selective in that they record whatever happens to occur, and they are non-interpretive. The summarizing and analyzing will always have to be done after the recording. Videos can be used to supplement a variety of recordings used for developmental profiles and program planning.

◆ ◆ ◆ ◆ *Key Terms*

instant cameras
video
camcorders
palmcorders
phonograph
graphophones
gramophone
telagraphone
microphone
tape recording
compact disc (CD)
summative
zoom
editing
splicing

7 Portfolios and Child Studies

Portfolios are powerful instructional tools. They offer children, teachers, parents, administrators and policy makers an opportunity to glimpse the sweep and power of children's growth and development. When carefully structured portfolios display the range of a child's work. Above all they integrate instruction and assessment.
Samuel J. Meisels (1993)

Learning is often hidden in a product; unless the teacher has observed the development of the product, the teacher will be unaware of what has been learned.
Ada Schermann (1990)

Parents and teachers like to capture special moments in the child's life. Such photographs can enhance child studies and life books.

Focus Questions

1. How could you gather information about a child in a way that offers objective recording but does not rely on standardized tests?

2. What kind of contextual data can help you to analyze observational information?

3. How could you ensure that your records about a child's development are as thorough and complete as possible?

4. What might a student learn from carrying out an in-depth child study?

5. On what basis would you choose to keep examples of a child's art work for later appraisal?

6. When would a child be able to contribute to record keeping about her own experiences and learning?

◆ ◆ ◆ ◆ History Notes

Child studies and **portfolios** are both methods of collecting and making sense of information about individual children. They have evolved from the studies of John Locke and Jean-Jacques Rousseau in the 17th and 18th centuries. In their original form they were collections of narrative descriptions of the child's behaviour and perceived characteristics. Although fascinating, early examples would not meet today's standards of objectivity and analysis.

Granville Stanley Hall's contribution to the study of children was most significant because it was more systematic and changed the focus of study to a more scientific approach. In the late nineteenth century he wrote *The Content of Children's Minds*, which altered the way in which children were studied in the U.S. A dominant part of his technique was to use questionnaires to get information directly from the children being studied, one of the methods used today for gathering data.

Baby biographies were a new methodology in 1890. Wilhelm Preyer, in Germany, devised an approach in which mothers studied their own children in an attempt to understand their thinking. He had spent several years studying his own son and became a master of narrative recordings in the child study method. His influence spread to the U.S., where he advanced interest in the newly emerging study of children.

The inclusion of mothers in the process of observing and recording was also made by Millicent Washburn Shinn, who carried out her own studies of a young relative and promoted this type of study. She believed in the usefulness of a biographical method in that it allowed for understanding of the individual's unfolding development. Combining this with an approach which involved checking out the child's responses to particular stimuli, Shinn's studies contained elements of today's child study, which is done for the purposes of academic inquiry.

Other significant figures offered approaches which compared observed behaviour with that which was considered typical, by means of set-up tests or recorded information on chart and measures. The child study that is undertaken in our time tends to pick and choose from a range of these techniques, often employing several so that a better picture can be drawn.

Recordings used for study purposes, planning, or information exchange with parents and professionals have altered considerably in the light of changing understanding about how children develop.

Forms of record keeping changed as teachers were trained to understand children's needs and appreciate the stages of development through which they progressed. The realization that parental involvement was important was only slowly recognized. School practices vary considerably today.

Some schools will provide term reports which offer little more than a vague percentage scoring and a brief comment like "satisfactory" against each of a list of curriculum areas. These were common in the 1930s and 40s and are used by some schools to this day. Meeting the parents' needs to "know how Sarah is progressing" cannot be achieved by this approach. An informed parent will want to know how the grade has been arrived at – by testing or by comparison with a class norm. The term "satisfactory" may indicate the teacher's feelings about the child's progress, but it doesn't offer anything more than that.

The developmental view, which requires a fuller appraisal of the child's skill development, has been picked up more seriously by child care workers and kindergarten teachers than by others in the education system. Over the last thirty years, early childhood programs have been refining themselves so that the children's individual developmental needs are met. To do this, teachers have had to make observations of the children in their care. A need for accountability within the education community has led teachers to support their philosophies with some concrete data in the form of developmental records. Educators must substantiate their statements about the need for the programs they run. Records have supported their claims and helped to shift societal attitudes to some extent. In the last decade it is the portfolio method which has received the greatest praise for its breadth and effectiveness.

There have been examples of schools, child care centres, and agencies for children with special needs that have kept portfolio records for the last thirty years, but these are a small minority. Some of these systems enable a flow of information to the parents about what has been going on for the child.

There have been many changes in practice in child care and education over the last ten years. Although there is growing confidence in the appropriateness of what is being done within the professional early childhood community, there is also a greater demand from outside for clearer measurements of children's progress. We now have a set of conditions that lead to the necessity for portfolio evaluation and record keeping. They address the need for accountability for what we are doing with young children, while holding firm to the principles of developmentally appropriate practice.

Child studies and portfolios are both methods of collecting information. They focus on one child and form a gathering of data in a variety of ways. Case studies, individual file records, **baby books**, journal recordings, **records of achievement**, **profiles**, and **life books** have some similar characteristics and can be included in this category of data collection.

Child studies: Definition

A child study is a thorough analytical project in which a student or practitioner collects information about a child. It will contain observations and may include a variety of other information gathering techniques that may be collected over a period of time. Typically it is used more for the benefit of the student in his enquiry into child development than for the child herself.

Portfolio: Definition

A portfolio is a record keeping device in which observations, health and social information, test results, work samples, and other significant information about an individual child are stored. The system enables child care professionals to keep records over a period of time, add items as necessary, evaluate the child's performance, evolve plans to meet the child's needs, and to review progress.

◆ ◆ ◆ ◆ Features of Child Studies and Portfolios

Although child studies are usually undertaken by students and portfolio records by teachers, they have many features in common. While the child study is undertaken primarily to support the student's learning, the portfolio is done to help the practising teacher to find out more about the child, for the child's benefit.

Contents of a portfolio or child study

Teachers and caregivers vary in their philosophies regarding the practice of record keeping. The portfolio approach is sufficiently flexible that all practitioners can adapt it to their needs.

The following is a list of suggestions of what a portfolio might contain. Those using the system will want to pick and choose those elements which suit them, their skills, the agency, and the child.

◆ health records (possibly a parent questionnaire, maybe information from a physician)
◆ contextual information (parent questionnaire, objective notes, genogram, ecomap, lifecycle flow chart, etc.)
◆ notes forwarded from previous caregiving agencies
◆ anecdotal records (see Chapter 2)
◆ **running records**/specimen records (see Chapter 2)
◆ development **checklists** (see Chapter 4)
◆ parental input in a variety of forms
◆ infant charts (see Chapter 5)
◆ event/time samplings (see Chapter 3)

- **rating scales** (see Chapter 5)
- assessment results from **standardized tests** (see Chapter 8)
- psychologist's reports
- social worker's notes
- photographs of the child (passive or in action)(see Chapter 6)
- photographs of special moments in the child's life
- photographs of things the child has made
- special items selected by the child
- art work samples
- samples of the child's writing
- audiotapes of the child's language, reading, or music (see Chapter 6)
- videotaping of the child's activities (see Chapter 6)
- the child's own records-of-achievement journal
- a **learning log** of the child's lifetime experiences
- questionnaire responses

The portfolio philosophy

A portfolio is much more than a collection of information; it is an attitude and a process. While it is relatively easy to describe a possible list of contents of a portfolio, it is more challenging to generate enthusiasm for the concept of portfolio evaluation and record keeping and to get each member of the team to participate in the process of data collection.

Several principles underlie the portfolio philosophy:

- the process of the child's experience is important, and individual to that child.
- the most effective way of recording information about the child's experience is to observe the child in her natural setting, i.e. home, child care centre, or school.
- information about the child is most usefully supplied by parents, teachers, caregivers, and other stakeholders in the child's life.
- portfolios provide for the opportunity to record data about the process of the child's experience and evidence of the products of the child's work.
- portfolios enable the stakeholders in the child's life to be involved with both formative and summative evaluation of the child's performance, skills, and competence, based on valid collection of data.

- portfolios encourage teamwork and cooperation among the stake-holders which support the process towards meeting of the child's needs.
- portfolios offer the possibility of recording family health and **contextual** information, which puts the behavioural data into a more meaningful framework.
- portfolios encourage (in the long term) the child's involvement in the record keeping process, selection of items for inclusion, and the child's sense of responsibility and ownership for his or her behaviour and a sense of control in determining the education experience.
- portfolios are flexible in meeting the needs of the stakeholders as they can contain a variety of types of information.
- portfolios may include input from a variety of additional professionals as may be desirable; psychologists, social workers, and others may add to the portfolio in ways that extend the information base and will frequently validate the findings of the primary caregivers and parents.
- portfolios encourage professional accountability in that they provide documentary evidence of evaluation processes and program planning. (These have been a significant challenge to those teachers who have had a child-centred philosophy.)

Through practice, teachers and caregivers will see the value of the portfolio process. Those who say they observe all the time but do not record their observations will see that portfolios can help them to do their job more effectively with only a little effort and time investment.

Furnished with information from a variety of sources, the teacher may be better able to understand the child's needs and see how his family and context should determine how the needs are met. Agencies that subscribe to the portfolio philosophy will usually find that the practice supports closer work with parents and a more cooperative style of teaching. At a time when parents, boards of education, and other administrative bodies are demanding greater professional accountability, the portfolio provides appropriate documentation of evaluation, planning, and practice.

Forms of Portfolio Records

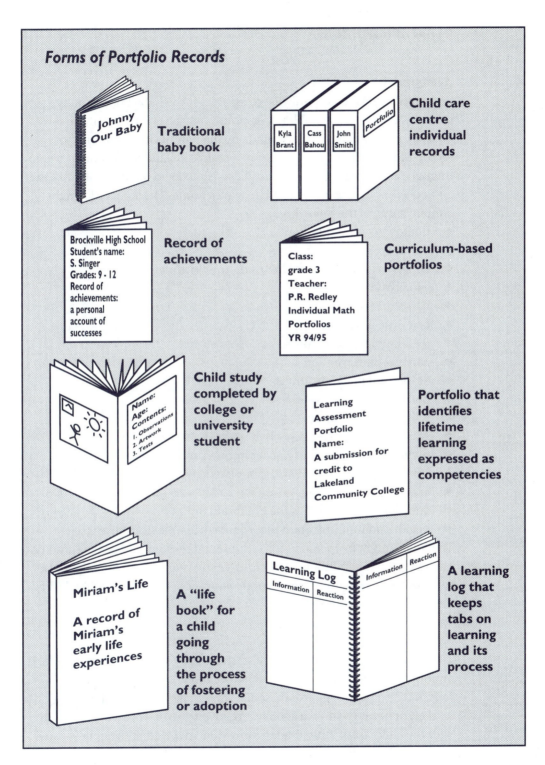

Johnny Our Baby — **Traditional baby book**

Kyla Brant | Cass Bahou | John Smith | Portfolio — **Child care centre individual records**

Brockville High School
Student's name:
S. Singer
Grades: 9 - 12
Record of achievements:
a personal account of successes

Record of achievements

Class:
grade 3
Teacher:
P.R. Redley
Individual Math
Portfolios
YR 94/95

Curriculum-based portfolios

Name:
Age:
Contents:
1. Observations
2. Artwork
3. Tests

Child study completed by college or university student

Learning
Assessment
Portfolio
Name:
A submission for credit to
Lakeland
Community College

Portfolio that identifies lifetime learning expressed as competencies

Miriam's Life

A record of Miriam's early life experiences

A "life book" for a child going through the process of fostering or adoption

Learning Log
Information | Reaction
Information | Reaction

A learning log that keeps tabs on learning and its process

Types of portfolios

A baby book

Perhaps the most commonly used portfolio is the baby book kept by parents. A ready-prepared book or album may be given as a gift to new parents. It might be bought or made by the parents in an attempt to record the significant happenings in a child's life and to map out developmental milestones. Some parents may wish to keep up the book until the child reaches school age or until he leaves home. These records might contain some of the following:

◆ homes/accommodation
◆ family tree
◆ copies of newspaper headlines on the "birthday"
◆ a lock of hair
◆ hand/foot prints
◆ favourite foods, toys, etc.
◆ feeding/sleeping records
◆ caregiver information
◆ developmental milestones
◆ photographs
◆ religious information
◆ gifts
◆ name information, naming ceremonies record
◆ "firsts" : words, at day care, school, to a party, etc.
◆ art work
◆ anecdotes, funny things the child said or did
◆ health and immunization record (dates of infectious diseases)

The items might be included for sentimental reasons and so that parents have a concrete reminder of the child's early years. The book might also serve as a way of keeping health or development information which may need to be accessed later.

A "life book"

This record keeping album can be started at any stage of the child's life. It attempts to capture the individual nature of the child's own story. Initiated by a parent, guardian, social worker, adoption and fostering worker, or other child care agency employee, the book can be passed on, with the child, from individual to individual involved in the child's care.

The child can benefit directly from the documentation of her life history. Changes, both happy and sad, need to be included so that the child can reflect on her own experiences and appreciate her personal story. Agencies may use this kind of portfolio to support mental health, particularly when the child is undergoing transitions in parenting, home, caregiving or other potentially traumatic change.

A life book may contain some of the following:

- photographs of the parents/guardian
- a family tree
- pictures of significant people
- pictures of significant places/homes
- small sentimental objects
- lists of favourites, such as foods, games, objects
- birthday greetings
- mementos from outings/special occasions
- developmental charts
- health information, immunization schedules
- letters from friends and family members
- cassette tape recordings of people, music, etc.
- religious affiliation records, initiations
- club membership cards, friendship souvenirs
- art work

A learning log

The learning log is intended to be a record of an individual's learning. While it is not in itself a full portfolio, it can form part of a meaningful record documenting a young person's learning. Written by a teacher, or later, by the child herself, the log keeps an account of the child's activity. There are two parts to this kind of log. One part records the program plan, curriculum activity, or experience as "provided" -the other forms a record of how the child responded to the experience – i.e. what he "learned." The log system requires a teacher to be diligent in record keeping. It can provide a detailed analysis of what the child is doing. For the child who has a diagnosed special need, this type of record keeping can provide data which can be interpreted and form part of the planning process. For teachers with large numbers of children in their care, or for whom curriculum planning is more spontaneous, this method might not be as useful.

Older children capable of documenting their own experiences may keep a log which is directed by the teacher but in which they record their responses to classroom or other activities

A Page from a Learning Log

Date	Curriculum experience	Response
May 27, '94	*Gross motor activity* *Introduced new hurdle activity to encourage Mark to climb and manoeuvre*	*Mark watched the others as they tried the hurdles. He did not attempt them until the the other boys had left.* *After making an effort to get over the first, he failed and left to sit and read.*
May 28, '94	*Gross motor activity* *Left the hurdles in the gross motor area but altered the 1st hurdle to to make it easier to climb.*	*Today Mark tried the 1st hurdle successfully but did not continue.*
June 1, '94	*Gross motor activity* *Cleared away hurdles and brought out the tricycles.*	*Mark complained that he wanted another try with the hurdles. I told him I would put them back in a few days.*

Child care centre/school individual records

An agency, with the support of parents, may choose what components of the portfolio the worker should use. A list of possibilities might be viewed and discussed so that the needs of the child, parent, and agency can be met.

Child studies

The student's assignment description may outline the necessity to make certain inclusions or focus on particular aspects of development. The child study enables the student to appreciate the complexity of the child's context and development. The student focusses on one child as objectively as possible, and also gets a more personal view of what that child's experience and development are like. Critics of the child study approach say that it tends to be subjective and gives non-statistically significant information. Where there is validity to the argument, it should not be used to claim that child studies do not offer educators important insights into the individuality of the developmental process.

Curriculum-based portfolios

There are records made by teachers which are based on formative evaluation of the children in particular curriculum areas. Formatted to record information about the curriculum experiences offered and the group and the individual responses to the experiences, the curriculum portfolio provides for documentation of the curriculum development process, evaluation of its effectiveness, and data on which to base further planning.

Curriculum-Based Portfolio

Date	Curriculum area/activity	Group response (anecdotal record)	Individual outcomes
June 9, '94	*Seriation* *Introduced story of three bears. Activity involving three bears in order of size on flannel graph.*	*Very positive but enjoyed story more than follow-up.*	*Seriated three bears* *M.T. "* *R.S. "* *L.P. "* *S.W. "* *N.H. "*
June 10, '94	*Seriation/matching* *Made up story to accompany four animals and their four homes in order of size. Flanel graph activity involved matching animals and homes, and ordering the sizes of the animals.*	*Children wanted to extend story and made up their own stories about the animals. They played with the flannel graph pieces, but did not match them.*	*M.T. Seriated four animals and matched four.* *R.S. Seriated three of four animals and matched four.* *L.P. Seriated two and matched four homes.* *S.W. Did not cooperate.* *N.H. Seriated four animals and matched four.*
June 11, '94	*Seriation/matching* *Used story again with four animals and homes. Directed flannel graph activity to seriate and match.*	*Children actively involved, tired of flannel graph after a while.*	*M.T. Absent.* *R.S. Seriated three of four animals and matched four homes.* *L.P. Seriated two and matched three homes.* *S.W. Seriated three of four, did not match.* *N.H. Seriated four animals and matched four.*

Learning assessment portfolio

This is an individual record keeping device. It can be kept by a teacher or, as the child matures, may be used by the child, adolescent, or adult to detail her own learning. In this portfolio, experiences as well as more formal learnings are documented. The recordings express experience in terms of the competencies that were achieved as a result of that experience. These learning outcomes are analyzed. In other words, the experience is reflected on with a view to establishing what it has enabled the person to do.

The learning assessment portfolio is a useful device for teachers and learners in all stages of their education. The process of recording experiences and examining them to establish what learnings have come out of them is an important critical thinking skill which forces the individual into active learning and self evaluation.

An early childhood educator may wish to log the experiences of a child day by day and evaluate the effectiveness of the provision by determining and recording the newly acquired competence. Practice in the use of recording behaviourial information is necessary, but, once mastered, the portfolio provides tracking of the child's learning.

An older child can, with help, log her own experiences and what she learned from them. For the child to identify what she has learned is a helpful part of the consolation of that learning.

More mature individuals may want to explore the experiences that they have had to learn to express the outcomes of that learning in the form of acquired competencies. Evaluating experience and determining skills is becoming more widely accepted as a means for gaining credit and access to college and university programs. It may be considered in a process of job evaluation. To start this process in early childhood settings can only be helpful to the child growing up in a changing education and work environment.

Reasons for including each portfolio entry

Health records

Health information should be updated as regularly as there is a need. The child's health history is not a static record but a document that needs new additions as further health and growth information becomes evident. Not only will this type of data help you to know the child better but it will also enable you to respond to her needs. Health conditions affect the child's development and are therefore an important part of the portfolio. With a strong correlation between growth, health, and development, it may be a good idea to include measurements as the child grows. A child health information questionnaire is best completed with the parent at an interview. An additional updating sheet is offered so that you can make extra entries when information becomes available. Refer to the chapter on charts (Chapter 5) for prepared formats for height, weight, immunization, feeding, and sleeping charts.

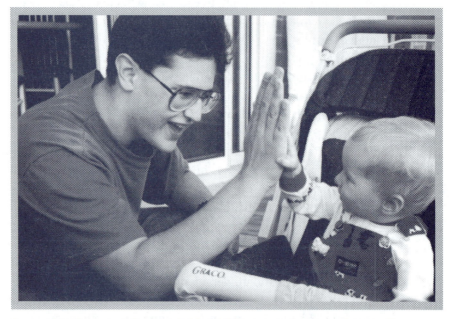

Interactions between infants and older children or teenagers can be revealing. Observations of children should be made in a variety of contexts.

Child Health Information Questionnaire

Please take time to complete this form. The information will help us to know your child better and respond appropriately to his/her needs.

Family information

Today's date: _____

Recorded by: _____

1. Child's name: _____
                           (first)   (last)

    "Pet" name, nickname: _____

2. Child's address: _____

    _____

    _____

    Home telephone number: (____) _____

3. Mother's name: _____

    Mother's home telephone number: _____

    Mother's home address (if different from above): _____

    _____

    _____

    Mother's work number: _____

    Mother's work address: _____

    Other contact during day: _____

    phone: _____

    fax: _____

4. Father's name: _____

    Father's home address (if different from above): _____

    _____

    _____

    Father's home telephone number: _____

    Other contact during day: _____

    phone: _____

    fax: _____

5. Child's sex (male or female): _____

6. Child's year of birth: _____

                               month   date   year

     Age yrs/months: _____

7. Other family members living at the child's address
(names and ages of children): _____

8. Previous child care/school agencies attended): _____

_____

_____

Birth history

9. Child's weight at birth: _____

10. Length of pregnancy (premature/full term # of months): _____

11. Were there any complications with the pregnancy or birth? If so, what?

_____

12. Did your child have any medical problems at or soon after birth? If so, what?

_____

13. Family physician's name: _____
Family physician's address: _____

_____

Family physician's phone number: _____

14. Paediatrician's name: _____
Paediatrician's address: _____

_____

Paediatrician's phone number: _____

15. Dental surgeon's name: _____
Dental surgeon's address: _____

_____

Dental surgeon's number: _____

Health status

16. Please give a complete history of your child's immunization schedule (this may need to be verified by your doctor).

Immunization type   Date given

_____   _____

_____   _____

_____   _____

17. What infectious diseases has your child ever suffered from? Please check boxes. (Circle Yes or No and add date if Yes.)

measles	Yes	No	Date: _____
rheumatic fever	Yes	No	Date: _____
chicken pox	Yes	No	Date: _____
pneumonia	Yes	No	Date: _____
mumps	Yes	No	Date: _____
meningitis	Yes	No	Date: _____
whooping cough	Yes	No	Date: _____
others:			Date: _____
			Date: _____

18. Has your child suffered any repeated infections (cold, flu, tonsillitis, etc.)?

_____

_____

19. Has your child ever received treatment in a hospital emergency room? If so, why?

_____

_____

20. Has your child ever been admitted to hospital as an in-patient? If so, why?

_____

_____

21. Does your child take any medication on a regular basis? If so, what?

_____

_____

22. Please offer any information about your child's health check-ups. Has your child recently been evaluated by any of the following? (Circle Yes or No and add result if Yes.)

dental surgeon	Yes	No	Result: _____
ophthalmic surgeon (eye doctor)	Yes	No	Result: _____
hearing specialist	Yes	No	Result: _____
paediatrician	Yes	No	Result: _____
other specialist	Yes	No	Result: _____

23. Does your child have any known allergies?   Yes   No
To what? _____
Severity of reaction: _____

24. (a) Does your child have problems with any of the following?
(Circle Yes or No and describe if Yes.)

asthma	Yes	No	Describe: _____
hayfever	Yes	No	Describe: _____
skin sensitivity	Yes	No	Describe: _____
reaction to the sun	Yes	No	Describe: _____
warts	Yes	No	Describe: _____
dairy products	Yes	No	Describe: _____
constipation	Yes	No	Describe: _____
easy bruising	Yes	No	Describe: _____
concentration	Yes	No	Describe: _____
mood swings	Yes	No	Describe: _____
sleep	Yes	No	Describe: _____
spasms, twitches, tics	Yes	No	Describe: _____
habits	Yes	No	Describe: _____
other	_____		

(b) Are there any genetic diseases in the family? _____

25. Does your child behave in any way that concerns you? If so, what?

_____

26. Has your child ever been exposed to any significant traumatic event (witnessed violence, divorce in family, moving home, death of relative, etc.)?
Yes/No   Describe: _____

27. Does your child play in a way that you would expect?
Yes/No   Describe: _____

28. Do you have any concerns about your child's speech, communication, or understanding? If so, what? _____

29. What is your child's height? _____
weight? _____
shoe size? _____

30. Describe your child's feeding/eating patterns (# meals, snacks, types of food/milk/formula, attitude to eating).

_____

Health update

Name: _____ Today's date: _____ Age/D.O.B.: _____

New immunizations (cross reference to immunization record card):
Immunization type   Date given

_____   _____

_____   _____

Recent health conditions: _____

Medication: _____

Physician's reports (attach if appropriate): _____

Updates on growth information
(also plot data on growth chart)
height: _____
weight: _____
shoe size: _____

Identified health needs: _____

Contextual information

A working portfolio makes much more sense and is likely to be interpreted more accurately if some background information is offered. Some of the entries might come from observation but you will probably need to rely on parental input for a large amount of information. An initial interview in the child's home can help forge links between home and the agency you represent. There is a fine line between asking for information which is pertinent and that which might be seen as none of your business. These interviews are better conducted as an informal chat rather than a long question-and-answer-type questionnaire process. If you can explain why the information is helpful to you before you ask any questions, the parents' response is more likely to be favourable.

"Why do you want to know that?" is a fairly typical and reasonable question. If you do not know why you need the information then you should not be asking for it. Some parents may perceive you as being nosey – back off on some questions and wait until you have built a relationship of trust before you return to them. Parents can decline to offer information. This must be respected.

The following questions may help you to know what to ask. Review the questions ahead of the interview time. You may need to modify areas according to legal requirements, your understanding of the necessity for asking the questions, and the parents' comfort level. This is not a questionnaire to be completed by a parent although they must be asked for input and allowed to access what has been recorded. Most jurisdictions have freedom of information and privacy provisions which you will need to be aware of as your information gathering processes must comply with such legislation.

A full set of contextual information may be put together with the inclusion of a sociological survey of the child's geographical location.

Background Information

Recorded by: _____ Today's date: _____

1. Child's name: _____
    last   first   middle   pet name

2. Current age: _____ D.O.B.: _____

3. Child's appearance: height: _____
    weight: _____ eye colour: _____
    skin colour, birth marks, texture: _____
    identifying features: _____
    hair colour, style, condition: _____

4. What does the family see to be their nationality, race, citizenship, ethnic origin?
    (In some jurisdictions this question may need to be altered or omitted.)
    _____

5. What is the language(s) spoken in the home? _____

6. Family composition (mention all those living at the same address and their
    relationship): _____

7. Proximity of extended family: _____
    communication system with family members: _____

8. Mother's occupation, if employed: _____
    Mother's hobbies/interests: _____

    Father's occupation, if employed: _____
    Father's hobbies/interests: _____

    Guardian (if not mother or father): _____
    Guardian's occupation, if employed: _____

    Is the child fostered or adopted? _____

    Family total income source: $ _____ month

9. Abilities/disabilities observable in nuclear family: _____
    _____

10. Accommodations/residence type: _____
    # bedrooms: _____   # bathrooms: _____   # people living in home: _____
    owner/mortgage/renter/squatter/unpaying guest, etc.: _____

11. Pets/animals living in home: _____

12. Locality of residence (describe – urban/rural, industrial, residential, etc.): _____

13. Play space available to child: _____

14. Availability of playthings/books: _____

15. Number of children cared for as a ratio to caregiver: _____

16. Transportation access (bus, train, car, etc.): _____

17. Family member needs that are not met: _____

18. Does the family require welfare, social insurance, grants, etc.? _____

19. What changes in the family have occurred since the birth of this child? _____

20. Does the family practise a particular religion? _____

21. Can family members trace their family tree? _____

22. What is the mom and dad's parenting style? _____

23. What kind of life style does the family enjoy? _____

24. Are there particular mealtimes/bedtimes or other rituals? _____

25. Does the "family" express or demonstrate particular attitudes, values, or bene-
    fits? _____

Changing circumstances – portfolio update

Child's name: _____   Date: _____

Age: _____   D.O.B.: _____

Entry made by : _____

Nature of change (move home, divorce, unemployment, etc.): _____

Identified need of the child: _____

Observations

This part of the portfolio is essential. The observations will be the core to which the other components are additions. The observation methods you select will be chosen on the basis of what developmental information they can reveal. A variety of styles will be necessary, some being repeated. Please refer to the chapters on different methods of observation to help you with your choices.

Unless you focus on what the child can do and observe her behaviour in her natural setting, you will not be able to make adequate evaluations. The central part of the portfolio will be observations contributed from both home and the care agency or school. Those written by the professionals should be objective and detailed; parental contributions should be valued even if they are not in the format and language of the teacher or offered in a completely objective fashion.

Not all your written observations would, or could, be included in the portfolio. Selection of material will be necessary. Choose the observations that offer the most up-to-date or significant developmental information.

Parental input

Having a set format for observations to be shared can be helpful. Copies of "blank" observation forms can be made available for parents to complete. Others may be more comfortable with giving you verbal anecdotes of what they have seen. You can record them on a parent sheet if that works best.

The spontaneous comments of a parent may not always be the best record. A mom may tell you about the child's reaction to catching her parents in an intimate moment, or may tell you how exasperated she is about her son's irritating habit of nose picking. These may not be appropriate to keep in a formal record. From another perspective, you might see the validity of including accounts of how the child first slept through the night, rejected the breast, or became more cooperative in play with her cousins. These are professional decisions based on understanding of what is significant.

If parents have been part of the portfolio process for a while, they might give you information about how a guidance strategy is working, how they are implementing a learning plan, or the information they have gained from a health professional or psychologist. While this is "second-hand" information, recording it can be useful. Notes must indicate the source of the comments.

A teacher-parent journal can be kept in a suitable place to aid both parties in communication. These contributions can focus on practical requests like "Please drop off more diapers," but a more analytical approach may include more thoughtful comments about the child's mood, interests, or development. This record book can be included in the portfolio and provides an interesting picture of changes.

Records from previous agencies

You will be fortunate if assessments, health records, and reports have been transferred to your agency. Treat the material with respect but be cautious in believing everything you read. You will want to think that the records are accurate and objective, but without some verification of the findings, avoid making programming decisions on the basis of them.

There are some legal requirements governing the transfer of this kind of information which vary according to the jurisdiction. Be aware of the legalities and policies that pertain to your situation. These may be by-laws, municipal guidelines, Board of Education policies, or procedures agreed to by agencies or local practices.

The content of the record may be a useful prompt to ask questions of the parents; they may wish to see the record themselves and to offer opinions on the content. Their rights may include the possibility of removal of items as well as the inclusion of further items or comment on the information.

Use the records to prompt some informal observations of the child as she settles into the new environment. Records can be obsolete by the time they get passed on. You may note considerable development and life experience changes in the time between leaving one agency and starting at another.

Some supervisors choose to limit access to child histories because they do not want to colour the attitudes of the teacher with direct responsibility for the child. Teachers are trained to be objective and professional and be aware of inappropriate influences. They should usually evaluate for themselves the content of records which they receive.

Professional reports

Assessment records, reports, suggestions, and plans from professionals contributing to the child's health, education, and well being may be included in the portfolio. In situations in which the caregiving agency requests a report from a specialist, the consent of the parents is usually needed. Parents may seek a specialist's help directly. Sometimes they might need to seek a physician's letter of referral or some other introduction. The report which results from such intervention may not always be accessible to you, the caregiver, or the student. For personal reasons that you may never know, you might have to deal with the frustration of being excluded from the information. It may not be a sign of mistrust that leads to a lack of access, but you might feel that you could help better if you had as much information as possible.

There are situations in which your input is crucial to the assessment process. If you agree to offer input, you will, even then, not necessarily receive feedback.

Assessment results will be helpful if they reinforce what you have already observed. If they do not, it may not be that either is "wrong," but that you are evaluating the child from a different perspective. Because the observations are carried out in a naturalistic setting, they are more likely to represent what the child can do everyday. When test results indicate a level of achievement below that which you have observed, it is likely that the test was inappropriate or presented in a way that induced stress or elicited unexpected responses.If the results duplicate your findings, you can feel that your inferences are more likely to be valid. You could, though, both be wrong. Ideally, the team will work together, parents will be involved, and outcomes will be commonly agreed.

"Products" of learning and experience

Evidence of learning is not only to be found in observations. These may enable you to glimpse the process of the child's learning but examples of the products confirm achievements. In keeping products, such as art work and writing samples, you will still value the process by which they were made. Concrete examples of the child's end products can help the professional to appreciate the stage of the child's development.

While remaining cautious about making invalid, unsupported inferences, you can be helped to evaluate a child's progress if you can look at representative samples of her work. With knowledge of the sequence of drawing skills and representation of the child's world in art, you can make pertinent comments about the child's feelings, skill level, and perception. Writing and math work can be analyzed on a similar basis. By looking at what the child can do you can attempt to appreciate conceptual understandings and have a glimpse of the child's construction of knowledge.

Selecting items for the portfolio can be difficult when the child creates a large a volume of products. You may be tempted to select "the best" according to your personal responses. What is more significant is what is most typical of the child's work at this time.

Media techniques

Photographs, videotape and audiotape recordings, and other media techniques for gathering information can be helpful to the portfolio process. They enable you to put together a more comprehensive collection of items than would be possible by using the traditional observation techniques.

Video and tape recordings of the child supplement the portfolio by adding a quality of detail of the child's activity and language which is often superior to a narrative recording. Remember that recordings, of themselves, are not interpretative unless narrated by a teacher or analyzed in detail after the event. Review Chapter 6 to help you use media techniques.

Photographing and processing photos has become much easier and the results more lasting in the last two decades. We are getting used to photographs being used for identification and record keeping. Having a loaded camera available near the children's activity will help you to be ready to "snap" the child in action. A variety of action and posed pictures is a helpful addition to the portfolio and brings it to life for the reader.

Inclusions made by the child

The sense of involvement and ownership of the educational process increases significantly when the child feels that she has some control of the input into her own record. In choosing pieces for inclusion, the child can identify the items that are particularly significant to her. When the item is too precious to be stored in the portfolio, it might be possible to photograph the item and include the photograph instead.

Assembling a portfolio

As a team approach, in which parents and practitioners work together is desirable, it may be a good idea to decide collectively on the system you will use for record keeping.

Organizing the content for storage

How you keep the portfolios will depend on the space available to you. File folders which open for the insertion of items are used most commonly. They can be too small to accommodate large pieces of art work. To get around this problem you might decide to take photographs of the art work instead of including flaking paint and unstuck macaroni! Box files can be expensive but may not give you the kind of privacy and storage space you need. A local manufacturer might be able to let you have boxes – shirt boxes or others of that size are useful. Pizza boxes (if clean) may provide an answer. Ring binders for each child allow items to be put in chronological order and removed when necessary. You do need to be aware that this kind of record keeping requires space that is accessible but secure.

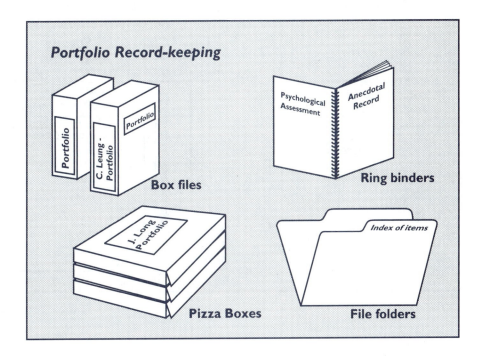

Including items in the portfolio

The portfolio box file, or whatever you choose, should be kept in an orderly fashion. It should be labelled on the outside and kept somewhere that disallows inappropriate access. Each item must be labelled clearly and dated. You should develop a system to ensure that you remember to make additions. From time to time you will need to meet with the child's parents and other professionals to review the contents and make assessments of progress. All such meetings should be documented briefly with the outline of what was discussed and decided. A set form can be helpful for this.

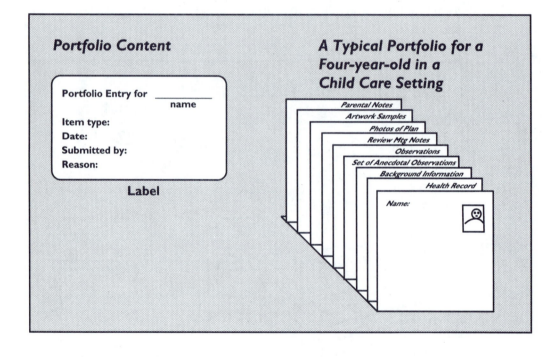

Portfolio Content

Portfolio Entry for _____
                            name

Item type:
Date:
Submitted by:
Reason:

Label

A Typical Portfolio for a Four-year-old in a Child Care Setting

Parental Notes
Artwork Samples
Photos of Plan
Review Mtg Notes
Observations
Set of Anecdotal Observations
Background Information
Health Record
Name:

Choice of content

What you put into the portfolio will depend on your philosophy and why you are keeping the records. These are some considerations that your team might like to discuss to help you decide on the context.

1. the purpose of each type of record
2. the space available
3. who will keep the portfolio up to date
4. who will access the portfolio
5. how the data can be analyzed
6. the cost of keeping the system
7. the philosophy of the agency (child-centred programs may have fewer standardized tests, some may focus on process of learning and accentuate observations, others may want to have more products included)
8. privacy and confidentiality
9. the time available to collect and process information
10. the attitude of staff and parents

Portfolio Review Meeting Report

Child's name: _____

Date: _____

D.O.B. and age: _____

Meeting called by: _____

Those present: _____

Intention of meeting: _____

_____

Review of recent additions to portfolio: _____

_____

Changed context, social, or family circumstances: _____

_____

_____

_____

Developmental summary given by: _____

Summary details: _____

Cognition: _____

_____

_____

_____

Personality: _____

_____

_____

_____

Language and communication: _____

_____

_____

_____

Emotional development: _____

_____

_____

_____

Physical development: _____

_____

_____

_____

Social skills: _____

_____

_____

_____

Curriculum implications: _____

_____

_____

_____

Program plan/strategies: _____

_____

_____

_____

Child Study as a Means of Learning About Development

Advantages	Disadvantages
Provides an opportunity to study one child in depth.	Focus on one child is not the basis for generalizations about all children.
Each aspect of the child's development can be seen in relation to the others.	Close connection with the child may mean that the inferences drawn are more subjective.
Contextual information helps the observer to make more valid inferences.	The process is time consuming and cumbersome.
Information gathered over a period of time enables the observer to appreciate the changing process of development.	Study may not lead to any direct benefit to the child studied.
A variety of observations and accumulated information can give a more accurate picture of the child.	All children in the group cannot be studied in the same depth.
Detail of analysis can surpass any other evaluation method.	Student may make inappropriate inferences that are not challenged.
Provides a strong learning experience which supports the student when later carrying out portfolio assessments in practice.	Large volume of material may not be evaluated in sufficient detail to be able to offer adequate feedback.

Portfolio as a Means of Ongoing Evaluation and Record Keeping

Advantages	Disadvantages
Provides for a comprehensive record keeping process.	Requires effort to keep updated and is time consuming.
Allows for a variety of observations and information to be kept together	Can become more of a sentimental memory box than a valid assessment tool.
Enables professionals and parents to access records and make additions.	May require use of substantial amount of file space.
The record can be used at any time.	Focus may be deflected from the process of the child's learning to over-zealous record keeping.
Information is stored over a long period of time and can be passed on from one agency to the next.	Information may be stored without having been evaluated on a regular basis.
Process includes deliberate parental involvement. Provides for the most rigorous, thorough, and developmentally appropriate assessment because its contents are so diverse.	Criteria for inclusion of items in record may not be clear.
Informal and formal records may be kept alongside each other which helps identify program intentions.	Teachers need training in what to look for when choosing samples. Teachers need not to be trained in portfolio assessment as an attitude.
Provides opportunity for ongoing assessment. Allows for more immediate responses than some other assessment procedures.	Meetings may need to be organized for team work planning.
System can be adapted whatever the child's needs or abilities.	
Allows for recording both the process and the product of the child's experience.	
The child values the portfolio assessment process which validates the importance of her activity.	
Accommodates a wide variety of teaching and caregiving philosophies.	

Assignment options

1. Skill building

Individual tasks

1. Interview a teacher to find out what record keeping she does. Ask about its effectiveness and any concerns the teacher has about the process.
2. Ask parents if you can see a baby book that was made for their child. Ask why they made the choice to include what is in it. What use do you think the baby book might be as the child grows up?
3. Write a list of reasons why the caregiver or teacher needs to keep comprehensive records.
4. Fill in this chart with as many ideas as possible.

The ideal portfolio items to include	Reasons to make this inclusion in a portfolio
_____	_____
_____	_____
_____	_____

5. Keep a learning log of your experiences in your child development or observation classes. What challenges were there in recording your reactions to experiences? Did the process of writing the log alter the learning experience for you?

Group activities

1. Make a chart piecing together what you know about the different observation methods that could be included in a portfolio.

Observation method	Main features	Information it might access	Strengths	Weaknesses
_____	_____	_____	_____	_____
_____	_____	_____	_____	_____
_____	_____	_____	_____	_____

2. Debate the motion that "standardized tests give the most accurate and objective measurement of a child's development."

3. Discuss the advantages and disadvantages of doing
   a) a child study
   b) a collection of observations of different children
   What could you learn from each?

4. Identify and write on flip chart paper the aspects of a child's social and cultural background, health, religion, housing, geography, country of origin, friendships, or other background information you *would* include in a portfolio. Give reasons for each answer and say how you would find out the information and record it.

5. Using the criteria below, evaluate a whole portfolio made by a student or teacher.
   - confidentiality
   - professionalism of portfolio management and storage
   - dating of each inclusion
   - clarity of labelling items
   - stated source of each inclusion
   - appropriate flow of input over time
   - portfolio ordered chronologically
   - varied use of information gathering techniques
   - replication of information recorded in different formats
   - objectivity of observation recordings
   - validity of inferences made in analysis of data
   - documentation regarding parent meetings
   - observation information used to make appropriate developmental plans
   - evaluation of program implementation

◆ ◆ ◆ ◆ Answers to focus questions

1. The most effective way of gathering information about a child is to collect data in a range of different ways. A variety of observation techniques can be used by the caregiver or teacher; these will form the essential components of the collection of information. Background information about the child can be included, in the format of previously held records, health histories, contextual notes, and parent questionnaires. Photographs, audio and video tape recordings, and

examples of the child's work may also supplement the observations. These will offer a more diverse, realistic, appropriate, and objective view of the child than a standardized test.

2. Any information which helps explain why the child is who she is will help us to analyze her behaviour. Housing, family, health, culture, and religious background information may support our understanding but we should avoid making stereotypical judgments about what these might mean; it is the actual experience of the child that is relevant. The primary source of information would be the parent or the child herself. Every element of the child's experience of life, in relationships, location, exposure to attitudes and beliefs, and physical environment, is part of the child's context.

3. Record keeping should aim for a fair representation of the child's interests, abilities, growth, changes in circumstances, and development. To be complete and thorough the records should be made regularly, systematically, and in a way that tracks significant changes as they occur. Documentation should always include a range of observations made at different times. The most successful records are portfolios that include a variety of information gathering techniques and samples of the child's work.

4. If the student avoids making inappropriate judgments and assumptions about other children on the basis of the child they studied, they will have learned some significant things. Students usually gain an appreciation of the individuality, humanity, and special characteristics of the child on which they focus. This takes the study of child development further than that of norms and theories and enables the student to become more sensitive to all children. Understanding the child's background may assist in an increased awareness of the reasons why the child behaves the way she does. The student can take that awareness to the work they do with other children. The complexity of a child's life, his innocence, vulnerability, dependence, and amazing curiosity are frequently commented on by students observing the child in a variety of settings or situations. In acknowledging the impact of the environment on the child, the student may be moved to take responsibility for the child's experience. Communicating with a child's family can help a student's interpersonal skills and help the student to gain insight into the role of parents and their strong bond with their children. A child study can help a student to explore aspects of the child's development and see changes

over a period of time. Explanations of how development occurs and the influence of growth and maturation on that development are frequently revealed. The student may want to refer to "norms," stages and theories to understand the development through which the child is going, but is more likely to take in some pertinent information about how each area of development is interrelated.

5. Samples of the child's art work may offer insight into the child's perception of her world, her reactions and feelings, and give an indication of her skill level. The art work may involve some degree of creativity but this is not always evident from seeing the sample without knowing something about the process of how it was made. Examples of the child's work may be chosen on the basis of what the child typically produces. Special choices may be made when some significant, amazing, or even disturbing piece might be kept. The child might want to be a part of the decision-making process. The adult needs to take responsibility for analyzing the pieces included. Rhonda Kellog's work is particularly useful in helping to explain a child's art work.

6. As soon as a child is aware that records are kept, the children should be able to make contributions. Four-year-olds may offer pictures for inclusion. Some very young children may want to know what you are writing about them. Frequently you might be able to share your observations with a child – this gives her a sense that you value what she is doing. School-age children who have some basic writing skills may be able to contribute to a learning log and will want a place to keep their "best work."

◆ ◆ ◆ ◆ Key Terms

child studies
portfolios
baby books
records of achievement
profiles
life books

running records
checklists
rating scales
standardized tests
learning log
contextual information

Screening and Assessment

The basis of screening is the comparison of the baby's level of development with that of an average baby of the same chronological age; it follows that a thorough knowledge of the 'average' or 'normal' is essential.
R.S. Illingworth (1973)

The ultimate goal of testing should be to help a child in some way – physically, developmentally, educationally, or emotionally – if this is not the case, why do it in the first place?
Virginia E. McCullough (1992)

An ECE student supports a group game while being a participant observer. Teachers and caregivers need to be observing the children continuously.

Focus Questions

1. What efficient method of recording information would let you see if one or more of a group of children are in particular need of attention?

2. How can you decide if a ready-made test is any use to you?

3. What difference is there between an observation and a test?

4. If you were to read some test results that a psychologist had determined about a child in your care, how might you react?

5. Can you be as objective as a visiting psychologist or other professional assessor in evaluating a child in your care?

6. Why should parents and teachers be wary of standardized testing results that do not match what they know about a child?

◆ ◆ ◆ ◆ History Notes

Evaluation of the child's development was always made by informal observation before more scientific measurement methods were devised.

In the 18th and 19th centuries, Rousseau, Pestalozzi, and Froebel focussed on indentifying the characteristics of children and their consequent needs. Their work encouraged innovation and change but brought about little evolution in practice within their lifetimes. They had not advocated testing for individual children but had acknowledged the necessity for assessment of the child's needs. It is unlikely that they might have considered formal measurement of development a desirable way of finding this information but they, with other educational pioneers, precipitated a more scientific approach.

Scientific measurement has been accepted practice in the natural sciences; the inroads made by the behavioural psychologists transferred a scientific approach to the study of animals to human behaviour measurement.

Frequently considered the "father of human development," G. Stanley Hall (1844-1924) was the U.S. pioneer of developmental psychology. Using the first psychological laboratory in America, he devised and carried out experiments in the study of behaviours in systematic investigations. Designing a questionnaire to gain information about children's thinking, he got information directly from the child. Nearly 200 different questionnaires were devised by Hall and his followers. Lewis Terman, Arnold Gesell, and John Dewey were notable psychologists from Clark University where Hall had been the first professor of psychology. Gesell first outlined the chronology of behaviours of young children. Terman was the leader in the design of mental **tests**.

Standardized tests were first developed to be used as scholastic aptitude tests to help evaluate university applicants. Educators saw a need to make further evaluations of children within the school system. Americans were drawn to the idea of measurement more strongly than their European counterparts. For a long time in Britain, the selection of pupils for different types of secondary education at the age of 11 was the most significant **achievement testing** carried out. Most states in the U.S. held on to testing procedure within their schools. For some, the outcome might mean streaming into achievement levels, for others, depending on their location, it might mean individualized learning support, grade level changes, or curriculum re-planning. By 1965 Britain was withdrawing the selection testing with a view to more **formative assessment.** The acknowledgement of systemic bias and parental pressure were factors which affected the educational change. It is significant that Americans have become increasingly aware of the inherent dangers of testing procedures and gradually demonstrated concern about state-wide tests but when opportunities have arisen educators and policy makers have been reluctant to let testing go. Practice varies widely from state to state but the acceptance level of testing procedures on the U.S. continent appears much higher than in Europe.

The evolution of educational practice in Britain has involved a move to **benchmarks** as reference points for assessment with the development of a National Curriculum. This represents something of a return to formal assessment techniques after a period of plateau. The systems of testing in schools in Canada vary from province to province but commonly rely on a standardized curriculum, which is used as a guide for progression as the student develops.

Many Canadian educators fear that the mistakes made in the U.S. and Europe will be, or are being, repeated in Canada. Boards of Education are bending to the notion that accountability is dependent on testing. The two are obviously related but standards do not, of themselves, improve because outcomes are measured. If precious time and resources are spent on testing when they could have been spent on more valid pursuits, children's time is wasted. The tests used for **assessment** are frequently unsuitable for Canadian children because of their inherent biases, and even when more valid and reliable, they are often used inappropriately. In societies that cater for an ethnically diverse population over a wide geographic area, educational standards must be improved in a way that is regionally and personally sensitive.

Educators who concern themselves with the importance of **developmentally appropriate practice** are increasingly concerned about the "trickling-down" to child care and early education of negative elements of educational practices employed in later childhood. The dubious systems which are heavily dependent on over-structured curriculum and testing designed to train children to perform narrow competencies are being translated into developmentally inappropriate infant, toddler, and preschool curriculum and assessment. Anxiety over achievement levels is influencing teachers and caregivers to use methods which will reduce quality rather than improve it.

The younger the child tested, the greater the cause for concern. Readiness tests have been widely used with pre-school and kindergarten children to evaluate their skill level and consequently their apparent "readiness" for the next step. Many educators express alarm at the trend but the proponents of higher standards claim that these measures are necessary.

Screening: Definition

Screening is a process of evaluating behaviour, health indicators, growth, skills, or performance in specified tasks to identify individuals in particular need, whose development is delayed or abnormal, who require further testing, diagnosis, or medical intervention. Screening procedures usually involve use of standardized tests in assessing a large population of children in a brief, relatively inexpensive manner. They are usually carried out by medical professionals, psychologists, or diagnosticians. Informal screening techniques are used by child care workers and teachers as they identify children whose development is in some way atypical.

Assessment: Definition

Assessment is a process of gathering information about an individual's behaviour, health indicators, growth, sensory levels, performance in specified tasks, intellectual abilities, social relationships, receptive and expressive language, personality traits, motor skills, spontaneous play activity, potential, or other pre-determined criteria. The process may take many forms, including informal observation, standardized tests, teacher appraisal, developmental checklists, parental observations, the individual's own evaluation, medical diagnosis, or any combination of these or other methods. Assessments may be carried out by a variety of professional parties such as health science professionals, psychologists, social workers, teachers, caregivers, early childhood specialists, and parents; the most effective process involves a team.

Features of Screening and Assessment Instruments

Formal testing as a method of evaluation is the focus of this section. Even if your Early Childhood philosophy emphasizes evaluation through naturalistic observation, you will need to appreciate the strengths and weaknesses of standardized testing by being able to critique tests and evaluate the data they provide. There has been a trend to use a wide variety of standardized tests to determine "**readiness**," "skill acquisition," "developmental stages," "learning disabilities," and so forth. You need to acknowledge the reasons why some teachers think this is desirable and useful; you do not have to agree with the approach or follow the trend if you think you can gain the information more easily, naturally, effectively, and cheaply by other means. Underlying the belief in standardized testing is a philosophy that values some or all of the following ideas:

◆ that a test can measure what it purports to measure.
◆ that a child's behaviour can be evaluated by comparison with an expected "norm" or "stage."

- that a test situation can elicit objective information.
- that the outcome of a test is a predictor of later development.
- that children evaluated to determine deficits in development can benefit from improved programming.
- that the teachers and other professionals are able to determine behavioural goals and learning on the child's behalf.
- that test data can increase an agency's accountability.
- that evaluation of published information regarding "**reliability**" and "**validity**" of tests can filter out possible bias or inaccuracies.
- that testing procedures are advantageous to curriculum development rather than detrimental.
- that test results can be interpreted accurately and successfully by teachers, caregivers, and parents.

Professionals frequently use tests to aid their work, in the belief that they will offer more objective data than other sources of information. Considering the way in which the data are collected it is doubtful whether it can be objective; children may not perform the same way in a "test" situation as they might in their natural surroundings. Some tests are administered by someone other than the regular caregiver. Here the child might be affected by the strangeness of the test or the tester. Without appreciation of the child's regularly displayed behaviour patterns, you can tell little about the overall progress of the individual. With little understanding of the family background, current issues in the child's life, or a view of what is normal for this individual there is limited scope for effective evaluation. Comparisons with "norms" determined from a general population may give you some reference point but, even if accurate, the norms will tell you little about what to do if a deficit is identified. Particularly worrisome is the undetected cultural bias of many of the well-used standardized tests. Results that reflect acquired skills may not give you more than a quick "snapshot" of current development – in themselves, they do not determine appropriate curriculum.

If a test has a well founded theoretical basis it may indicate the stage through which the child might next progress. When the child will develop particular skills is as much a matter of maturation as a response to the adult's strategy. All that was needed was the adult's construction of the appropriate learning environment and responsiveness to the individual's adaptations to that environment. The test served little purpose.

A key issue in evaluating a test is to determine what exactly it does measure. The title or naming of the test items does not necessarily indicate the content so that you can be assured that it actually tests what it is meant to test. For example, an IQ test may not test intelligence but problem solving, which is only one component of IQ. Another example is the "Readiness Test" – it may involve evaluating a set of skills which the test designer believes important in determining readiness for, say, kindergarten. In fact, it may reflect skill acquisition in some areas, but not all: social skills are commonly left out.

The appropriateness of the use of tests with particular language and cultural heritages, ages of children, personality differences, interests, motivation, powers of concentration, and so on must be considered before a test is administered. There are so many possible in-built biases. Many obvious ones include skill assessment in one developmental domain being dependent on expressive language, which may not be the area tested. Test items may be reliant on familiarity with particular domestic items unknown to a child because of her culture. Questions may rely too heavily on logical thought, which may be an unfavourable approach for a creative mind. A child's self esteem may be evaluated as "poor" because the test did not allow for differing emotional responses.

The administrators and teachers who wish to use tests on children to prove their own effectiveness work on the premise that quality programming is measurable in the short term. Only if the "before" and "after" are measured is there any significant data; and then only if the data are viewed in terms of stages of growth rather than adherence to timeliness. There are many other, more successful ways of determining quality programming. Why not spend the time with the children and the money on the learning environment?

Choosing a test

If you do appreciate the concerns regarding testing you may not wish to use a standardized test. But these following criteria will help you to choose a test which best fits your purpose.

The most effective evaluations of a child's skills are achieved in natural settings. Absorbed in a creative experience, this young person with Down's Syndrome demonstrates a longer-than-expected concentration span and extraordinary attention to detail.

How to Choose a Test

1. **Determine your role in the testing procedure.**
   Are you to be receiving the test results as a teacher, supervisor, administrator, parent, child care worker? You will want information that is useful to your role and in a way that you can easily understand and interpret. The role of tester may be appropriate for you if the test you choose fits your qualifications and experience. If you need to find a tester you will need to factor this into your decision making. Consider the possibility of receiving training to administer a test.

2. **Identify your reason for wanting a test to be carried out.**
   Will you be wanting very specific information about one child, screening for all children in your care, or establishing an assessment system to be used over a period of time? Whatever your reason, you will need to evaluate the tests available to you to see if they can give the screening or assessment data you wish. Are you sure a test measures what you want it to measure?

3. **Determine the type of assessment you need.**
   Are you focussing on health, development, or particular skill development? You will need to find a test that contains the criteria for evaluation that fit your needs.

4. **Ensure that the test covers the age and developmental stage levels that you need.**
   Are you choosing a test because the title sounds correct but the span of developmental stages is insufficient? To re-use a test over a period of time, you will want to check for the inclusion of a wide developmental range.

5. **Check that the test will offer information in each of the developmental domains or skills you are seeking.**
   Are you sure that these domains or skill areas are sufficiently detailed to give information about the quality as well as the presence of the behaviours you want tested?

6. **Review the test material for objectivity, use by others, and published critiques.**
   Have you only read the information produced by the writers and publishers of the test material or have you checked it out more thoroughly? Here you will want to look at test validity, reliability, and usefulness.

7. **Find out if the test can be easily obtained, and how much it costs.**

Do you have a budget that allows for the testing you want? Many testing procedures require updating or use of duplicate forms which have to be purchased after the initial kit is obtained. Loss of pieces of the testing equipment may also occur, so check that you can replace these easily. Some tests have copyright prohibition so you are prevented from copying the evaluation forms. A few tests may need computer access for scoring; you will need to ensure that your hardware is compatible. Most of the recognized tests and inventories require a verification of professional qualifications before materials can be bought.

8. **Evaluate the test items for possible bias (cultural, gender, or language).**

Will the test be appropriate for the particular children you have? You will need to consider test items to ensure that they are not faulty in their expectation of Euro-centric responses or strong dependence on English language skills. If there are such items as a doll in the assessment kit, could you change the type of doll to reflect the ethnicity of the child to be tested? Look to see if there are any in-built biases that might be relevant in tasks such as sequencing a story line or identifying similarities or differences that might be perceived differently by children from various cultural heritages.

9. **Consider the test's ability to give you results that are easily understood.**

Can you interpret the statistical information and understand the terminology of test results? Money is wasted in buying testing procedures that are probably quite valid in themselves but have scores or outcomes that the teacher cannot use. This type of information may lead to impressive record keeping but very little help in program planning.

10. **Think about how you will use the test results.**

Do you intend to use them for screening or across the group for evaluation? What will you do when you identify a child in need of further assessment or an **individual program plan**? You need to work out if you can make the necessary responses. What will you do with the information on the progress of each child?

If you use a test with caution and understand its limitations, it helps you to be more sensitive to the individual's needs and leads you to to modify the learning or social environment. If it enables you to work with your colleagues and the child's parents more effectively, you may have chosen an ideal method of testing. You might, though, have collated better information through informal observation and achieved your intentions more effectively and inexpensively by using a parent-involved naturalistic assessment. The most effective assessments involve the use of a variety of information-gathering techniques. Each player in the life of the child can contribute informal observations. The professionals may offer more detailed structured observations and tests. The child herself may be empowered by being able to add her own selection of anecdotes or examples of her work to the **portfolio assessment**. This ideal form of evaluation includes a careful selection of observations of the child's spontaneous play, social learning activities, some interpretive checklists of skill development, and the inclusion of any necessary screening or test results, examples of the child's art, evidence of academic skills in the child's products, photographs of the child's activities or constructions, video recordings of play, tape recordings of language and music and any other samples that reflect the child's processes and products of learning. From these a more accurate, broad, and contextual picture of the whole child can result. The perceptive teacher can select the methods most pertinent to his/her skills, time, budget, team of colleagues, context, parental involvement, and the child's stage of development.

The Brigance offers a systematic approach to developmental assessment. Testing procedures can be done in the child's familiar surroundings.

Standardized Tests

Advantages	Disadvantages
Are usually designed and tested by psychologists.	May be carried out by adult unknown to child.
Provide uniformity of administration.	Child may not respond well to testing situation.
	Contextual information may not be available.
	Score may be open to inappropriate interpretation.
Give a quantifiable score.	Norm may not consider cultural or language diversity.
	Users of tests are not always aware of validity concerns.
May be **norm referenced.**	Reliability within a group does not determine intra-cultural reliability.
Tool will have been tested for validity.	Users may not have access to appropriate range of tests.
	Expensive to buy and administer.
Repeated use may increase reliability.	Training may be needed in administration of tests.
A wide choice is available.	Test scores should not be used alone to determine evaluation and construct program for a child.
	Time taken in testing might be better used for play or learning.
Offer specific information to parents, teachers, and psychologists.	May focus or end on what child *cannot* do.
	Skills not identified on test will not be evaluated.
	Child may be able to demonstrate skill in non-testing situation.
Test may be administered to individual or group.	Children may lose valuable learning time to test preparation.
Identifies what the child can do.	Lack of evidence of skill mastery may be incorrectly interpreted as inability to perform the task.
May support other informal assessment.	Test may provide insufficient evidence on which to base program planning.
	Most tools lack flexibility.
May identify potential concerns.	Test may not be based on current teaching principles.
	Some assessment/screening tools are not designed for diagnosis but are frequently accepted as such.
Results may help indicate appropriate **curriculum**/activity plan.	Outcome may result in inappropriate labelling.
	Screening and assessment tools may be seen as interchangeable (their purpose is quite different).
Results may be available quickly.	Seldom opportunity for parental input/observation.
	May be used by teachers as a "quick" method of evaluation in preference to naturalistic observation which can be time consuming but more effective.

A Selection of Assessment Instruments Used in Early Childhood Settings

Name: *AGS Early Screening Profiles (ESP)*
Author: *Patti L. Harrison*
Publisher/date: *AGS, Publisher's Building, 1990*
P.O. Box 99, Circle Pines, MN. 55014 USA
Administered by: *early childhood educators, teachers, hospital and clinic professionals (professionals and para professionals)*
Age range: *2 – 6 yrs*
Areas covered: *Profiles: Cognitive/language, motor, self help/social*
Surveys: articulation, health history, and home survey
Notes: *-screening tool to identify developmental concerns or potentially gifted children*
-takes less than 30 minutes for 3 profiles
-battery assesses the child's development in an ecological fashion, using multiple domains, settings, and sources
-three basic components, called profiles, supplemented by four surveys
-may be used in component parts or in entirety
-uses ASSIST scoring software
- needs some training to administer
- includes parental input
- may indicate need for further education

Name: *Battelle Developmental Inventory (BDI)*
Author: *J. Newborg, J.R. Stock, L. Wnek*
Publisher/date: *Houghton Mifflin, 1984*
The Riverside Publishing Co., 420 Bryn Mawr Ave., Chicago, Illinois   60631
Available in Canada from DLM Teaching Resources,
PBM Industrial Lts., Customer Service,
1220 Ellesmere Road, Unit 17, Scarborough, Ontario M1P 2X5
Administered by: *psychologists, specialists*
Age range: *birth – 8 yrs*
Areas covered: *personal – social, adaptive, motor, communication, cognitive*
Notes: *- a comprehensive instrument for screening, diagnosis, evaluation, and program development of children with disabilities*
- computer scoring available
- short form or screening available
- uses observation in natural settings
- can be used to screen a number of children within a group
-requires training to administer

Name: *Bayley Scales of Infant Development*
Author: *N. Bayley*
Publisher/date: *The Psychological Corporation, 1969.*
757 Third Avenue, New York NY 10017
Administered by: *Trained professionals*
Age range: *infants 2-30 months*
Areas covered: *gross motor and fine motor development*
Notes: *-takes approximately 1 hour with mother present*
  -used for assessing and recording observations of when child is tested
  -used to determine developmental delays
  -devised in U.S. but used extensively in Canada and UK (with some modification)
  -individual assessment tool

Name: *Boehm Test of Basic Concepts (The Boehm)*
Author: *AE Boehm*
Publisher: *The Psychological Corporation,*
757 Third Avenue, N.Y., N.Y. 10017
Administered by: *teacher/diagnostician/special education teacher*
Age range: *4 – 8 yrs*
Areas covered: *– concepts of time, quantity, and space*
Notes: *- takes approximately 30 minutes*
  - directions can be given in English and Spanish
  - score converted to indicate age/grade placement
  - can be used to assess group of children and determine program planning
  - does not predict later performance

Name: *Brigance Diagnostic Inventory of Early Development*

Author: *A.H. Brigance*

Publisher/date: *Curriculum Associates Inc., 1978.*
5 Esquire Road, North Billerica, MA 01862-2589
In Canada, Michael Preston, Publisher, 94 Asquith St., Toronto, Ontario

Administered by: *Early Childhood professionals supported by parents, no special training but demonstration essential*

Age range: *infants up to seven years*

Areas covered: *pre-ambulatory motor skills and behaviours, gross motor skills and behaviours, fine motor skills and behaviours, self-help skills, pre-speech, speech and language, general knowledge and comprehension, readiness, reading, manuscript and basic math*

Notes: *-parental input desirable*

-assessment instrument used to identify individuals' developmental strengths and weaknesses

-integrates processes of assessing/diagnosing, record keeping, and instructional planning

-individual assessment tool

-easy scoring

-results can be readily interpreted into program planning

-accompanying resources offered to assist program planning

-data may be stored in computer database

Name: *Cooperative Pre-School Inventory*

Author: *B. Caldwell*

Publisher: *Addison-Wesley Testing Service,*
South Street, Reading, MA 01867

Administered by: *teachers, early childhood educators*

Age range: *3 – 6 1/2 years*

Areas covered: *verbal and nonverbal skills in four areas:*
personal – 1. social relationships, 2. associative vocabulary,
3. concepts – numerical, 4 concepts – sensory

Notes: *-takes 15 minutes*

-easy scoring

-test available in English and Spanish

Name: *Denver Developmental Screening Test – Revised (DDST)*

Author: *W.F. Frankenburg, J. Dodds, A. Fandal, E. Kazuk, and M. Cohrs*

Publisher/date: *Denver Developmental Materials, 1975.*

Available from Teachers College Press, P.O. Box 939, Wolfeboro NH 03894

Administered by: *teachers, specialists, assistants*

Age range: *two weeks – six years*

Areas covered: *105 items grouped in four areas: personal/social, language, gross motor, and fine motor/adaptive*

Notes: *-takes 15-20 minutes*

    -parental input through parent report

    -available in English and Spanish

    -a screening used to identify children with developmental delays

    -devised for use by developmental paediatricians but has been used by ancillary personnel

    -individual test

Name: *Diagnostic Inventory for Screening Children (DISC)*

Author: *J. Amdur and M. Mainland*

Publisher/date: *Child-Family Clinic, 1984.*

Kitchener – Waterloo Hospital, 835 King St. W., Kitchener N2G 1G3

Administered by: *trained diagnostician*

Age range: *0 – 5 yrs*

Areas covered: *Fine motor, receptive and expressive language, gross motor, auditory attention and memory, visual attention and memory, self-help, and social skills.*

Notes: *-takes 15-40 minutes*

    -assesses skills on each scale with each of 27 age ranges

    -used for children who have been identified and referred for treatment

    -designed to help develop a treatment program

    -requires some parental support

Name: *Early Screening Inventory (ESI)*

Author: *S.J. Meisels and M.S. Wiske*

Publisher/date: *Teachers College Press, P.O. Box 939, Wolfeboro NH 03894 – available through Guidance Centre, OISE, 252 Bloor Street, Toronto, Ontario M5S 1V5*

Administered by: *teachers, psychologists, and assistants when trained and supervised*

Age range: *four years – six years*

Areas covered: *30 items in three areas: visual – motor/adaptive functioning, language and cognition, and gross motor/body awareness*

Notes: *- parent questionnaire available*

    - screens development rather than school achievement

    - used to identify children who need further evaluation

    - individual test

    - soon to include three-year-olds

Name: *Gesell School Readiness Test*
Author: *Gesell Institute of Human Development*
Publisher/date: *Harper and Row, 1978, 2350 Virginia Ave., Hagerstown MD 21740*
Administered by: *psychologists, early childhood specialists*
Age range: *pre-school*
Areas covered: *schooling readiness*
Notes: *- used to determine kindergarten readiness*
    - assesses current level of achievement; not a prediction of school success
    - claims to measure developmental age
    - individual test
    - concerns have been raised regarding test's validity, reliability, and normative information

---

Name: *Gesell Developmental Schedules*
Author: *H. Knobloch and B. Pasamanick (editors)*
Publisher/date: *Harper & Row, 2350 Virginia Ave., Hagerstown MD 21740 US*
Administered by: *trained diagnosticians*
Age range: *four weeks – five years*
Areas covered: *wide variety of test items including following direction, matching naming animals, writing, and copying.*
Notes: *- takes 30 minutes*
    - requires relatively high degree of training to gain reliability
    - Gesell's work was first published in 1925 and marked the first norm-referenced form of assessment.
    - although more sophisticated these schedules come from a maturational view of development
    -detects developmental delay

Name: *High/Scope Child Observation Record (COR)*
Author: *High/Scope*
Publisher/date: *High Scope Foundation, 1992, 600 N River St., Ypsilanti, MI 48198-2898*
Administered by: *teachers, early childhood caregivers (preferably trained by High/Scope foundation)*
Age range: *two-and-a half to six years*
Areas covered: *initiative, social relations, creative representation, music and movement, language and literacy, logic and mathematics*
Notes: *- allows for assessment of individuals and groups*
    - uses parent report forms
    - focusses on current abilities
    - relies on early childhood professionals' observations as they engage in daily program throughout the year
    - fits in with High/Scope philosophy but can be accessed by any trained observer
    - uses a system of anecdotal record with checklist assessment
    - has developmentally appropriate goals

Name: *Humanics National Child Assessment Form (1982)*
Authors: *Marsha Kaufman PhD*
T. Thomas McMurrain PhD
Publisher/date: *Humanics Ltd.,*
P.O.Box 7447, Atlanta, Georgia 30309
Administered by: *teachers and parents*
Age range: *Birth – three; ages three to six*
Areas covered: *social/emotional language, cognitive, gross motor, fine motor, hygiene, and self help (three to six only)*
Notes: *- a checklist of skills and behaviours arranged in a developmental sequence*

- items observed in a naturalistic manner or when necessary in "testing" situations

- designed to be used for instructional purposes rather than diagnostic or clinical evaluations.

Name: *Kent Infant Development Scale (KID)*
Author: *J. Reuter and L. Bickel*
Publisher/date: *Kent Developmental Metrics,*
     126 W. College Avenue, PO Box 3178, Kent, OH 44240 – 3178
Administered by: *caregiver*
Age range: *under one year*
Areas covered: *self-help, social, cognitive, motor, language*
Notes: *- easy scoring*
     - produces profile of strengths and weaknesses
     - English and Spanish versions available

Name: *McCarthy Scales of Children's Abilities (McCarthy Scale)*
Publisher/date: *available from Guidance Centre, OISE, 252 Bloor Street West, Toronto, Ontario M5S 1V5*
Administered by: *psychologists and special education teachers*
Age range: *two-and-a-half years to eight-and-a-half years*
Areas covered: *1. general cognitive index including a. verbal b. perceptual/performance c. quantitative 2. memory index 3. motor index*
Notes: *scores converted to a cognitive index (IQ)*

Name: *Peabody Picture Vocabulary (PPUT) Test – Revised*

Authors: *L. Dunn and L. Dunn*

Publisher/date: *American Guidance Service, 1981.*
Publishers Building, Circle Pines, MN 55014

Administered by: *teachers/ psychologists*

Age range: *two-and-a-half to 18 years*

Areas covered: *Receptive vocabulary*

Notes: - *takes 10 – 20 minutes*
- *quick simple test easily administered*
- *tests verbal understanding without need for expressive language*
- *items need to be within experience of child*
- *designed U.S. – U.K. version available*
- *individual test*
- *relies on adequate hearing, sight, and English*

Name: *PIP Developmental Charts*

Authors: *D.M. Jeffries, R. McConkey*

Publisher/date: *Hodder and Stoughton Ltd., Mill Rd., Dunton, Green Sevenoaks, Kent, U.K., for Hester Adrian Research Centre, University of Manchester*

Administered by: *teachers, specialists, para-professionals*

Age range: *unspecified, determines skill level rather than ability related to norm*

Areas covered: *3 – 5 subsections in each of the following: physical, social, eye-hand, play, and language*

Notes: - *developed from Parent Involvement Project, financed by the Department of Health and Social Security and the Department of Education and Science*
- *is skill- rather than age-related*
- *designed to identify skill development and needs in each domain*
- *uses flow charts to assist assessment*
- *easy to use*
- *involves parental input*

Name: *Portage Early Education Programme*
Authors: *S. Bluma, M. Shearer, A. Frohman, and J. Hitliard*
Publishers/date: *NFER Nelson (U.K. Version)*
a. NFER- Nelson Publishing Co. Ltd.,
Portage Project (U.S. version),
Danille House, 2 Oxford Rd. East,
Windsor, Berks,
SL4 1DF, England (1976)
b. Portage Project, CES A12, Box 504, Portage, Wisconsin, 53901
Administered by: *teachers, specialists, early childhood educators*
Age range: *6 weeks – 5/6 years*
Areas covered: *infant stimulation, socialization, self help, cognitive motor, and language*
Notes: *-includes parent observation and activities*

    -in process assessment of skills combined with specific objectives for a program plan and details of how to teach each behaviour

    -simple checklist referenced to card file

    -easy scoring

    -short training necessary for professionals

    -training can be offered by professional users to parents

---

Name: *The Schedule of Growing Skills*
Authors: *M. Bellman and J. Cash*
Publisher/date: *NFER – Nelson Publishing Co. Ltd., 1988.*
Darville House, 2 Oxford Rd. East, Windsor,
Berks. SL41DF, England
Administered by: *Health professionals – special training required*
Age range: *birth – five years*
Areas covered: *hearing, vision, speech, and language*
Notes: *-a health and development screening and assessment tool*

    -developed for use in the U.K.

    -uses set of objects and picturebooks (these could be adjusted for appropriateness)

Name: *STYCAR sequences (4th Edition)*
Author: *M. Sheridan*
Publisher/date: *NFER/Nelson Publishing Co. Ltd., 1976.*
Darnite House, 2 Oxford Rd East, Windsor, Berks, SC4 1DF England
Administered by: *Health and other trained professionals*
Age range: *Birth – five years*
Areas covered: *Posture and large movements, vision and fine movements, hearing and speech, social behaviour and play*
Notes: *-devised for U.K. use*
  -requires no special toys
  -is strongly norm-referenced
  -can be used as a rapid assessment tool
  -Stycar sequences can be used to aid objective interpretation of natural-istic observations.

Name: *Stanford-Binet Intelligence Scale (4th Ed)*
Authors: *R. Thorndike, E. Hagen, and J. Sattler*
Publisher/date: *Houghton Mifflin 1986*
Age range: *two years – adult*
Administered by: *psychologists/specialist*
Areas covered: *intelligence*
Notes: *- used to test cognitive abilities*
  - may be used to identify learning disabilities/brain damage
  - measures cognitive skills of hearing impaired
  - widely used internationally
  - individual test

Name: *Weschler Intelligence Scale for Children – Revised (WISC – R)*
Author: *D. Weschsler*
Publisher/date: *The Psychological Corporation, 1974.*
Administered by: *psychologists/specialists*
Age Range: *five – 15 yrs.*
Areas Covered: *intelligence – 12 subtests*
Notes: *- intended to assess intellectual ability*
  - used for clinical and psycho-educational purposes
  - used internationally, usually as part of a battery of tests
  - individual test
  - takes about one-and-a-quarter hours
  - scores converted to IQs
  - does not test achievement

◆ ◆ ◆ ◆ Answers to focus questions

1. A valid and reliable screening tool could offer information about a wide group of children and indicate those who were in some special need of attention. While screening using a standardized test might be helpful, it should not be considered the only method. Observation of each child can give more significant results in some cases.

2. In choosing a test you need to be sure that you understand your requirements. The test should be is affordable, accessible, and appropriate for the purpose. Appropriateness involves many components; it needs to be a test that offers developmental information that is relevant, can be conducted by an available person, whose results can be interpreted easily, and whose outcome should be readily translated into an action plan. It should contain culturally sensitive questions and be without bias. Literature about the test should claim reliability and validity but this may need to be confirmed by users of the test.

3. Both observations and tests can be forms of evaluation. An observation tends to be more open-ended and likely to be recorded in the natural environment of the child. Although an observer may look for specific behaviours, an observation is not constructed in a pass/fail mode. Observations tend to be accepting of the child's demonstrated behaviour and centre on what the child can do. Tests are "closed" in that they look for specific skills and behaviours. They tend to be carried out in more formally set-up circumstances which may not be the child's usual surroundings. Tests look at what the child can do but frequently pose increasingly difficult tasks. The testing procedure may end in items which are "failed." Both observations and tests can be appropriate methods of evaluation; they may help validate each other if the outcomes are similar.

4. The two main ways you might react to test results are in a feeling or a thinking way. If the results are in accord with your general perceptions, you will tend to think that they are "good." You must, however, consider the source of the information and the reliability of the results. It is quite possible that a psychologist offers an insightful objective assessment but you might tend to disagree with it if it goes against your own ideas. Meeting test results with respect but a healthy questioning mind is appropriate. You might wish to ask questions about the test itself or the implication of the results. Offering your own observations might be helpful to the psychologist. Hopefully, with the

parents' input you will arrive at an appropriate evaluation that will be helpful to each party.

5. Working with a child over a period of time offers a wide array of opportunities for seeing a child's patterns of behaviour and spontaneous play. The rich observations that you can make will be helpful in any evaluation process. The close relationship that you have with a child is an essential part of what you offer to the child; it gives you insight into his behaviour and allows you to know him and his family very well. Teachers should be objective in their work but should not rely merely on a scientific diagnostic approach. While psychologists are not involved in the day-to-day care of a child, their caring should not usually be discounted. No professional is able to disconnect from caring – nor should they. They can, however, bring a different discipline to the situation and be able to analyze behaviour in an alternative way. All parties involved in the care of a child need to offer input into the evaluation process.

6. Standardized tests can offer new insights or specific details of assessment that other forms of evaluation may not. They can be helpful in confirming what the teachers, caregivers, or parents have observed. Where there are discrepancies or wide variations between observations of the child's performance in naturalistic settings and test results, some explanation needs to be made. When the child's performance is "better" than expected it may be that the test highlights skills not normally seen spontaneously or which regular programming offers no opportunity for demonstration. The majority of differences lie the other way around, the test results appearing "poorer" than the performance of the skill in ordinary circumstances. Anxiety about testing can be a major factor in the discrepancy. The test may have been given in a way that demanded language or comprehension skills which acted as a barrier; it is possible that in less structured, self-initiated tasks the child might be able to perform the skill. Tests do not always measure what they claim to measure, so that a low score in problem solving or intelligence may indicate that the test itself did not adequately measure those areas. The child might have been sick, stressed, or having an "off day" on the day of the test. Observation usually takes into account contextual information which might affect what is seen; tests rarely do this. A test result relies on the demonstration of a behaviour at a particular time whereas observation can be

carried out at any time. Self-directed activity may promote skills and problem-solving behaviours not measured by a test.

If testing results are at variance with what is known about a child all parties should sit down together to discuss their perceptions. If consensus is not reached further assessment, both formal and informal, should be considered. Labelling and program planning should not be made on the basis of inconclusive or contradictory evidence.

◆ ◆ ◆ ◆ Key Terms

standardized tests
achievement testing
formative assessment
benchmarks
assessment
developmentally appropriate practice
readiness
reliability
validity
individual program plan
portfolio assessment
norm referenced
curriculum

9 Environmental Observation and Evaluation

A well-planned environment will be safe and healthful, will meet the needs of both children and adults, will facilitate classroom management, will enhance the process of learning through play, and will support the implementation of program goals and objectives.
Carol E. Catron and Jan Allen (1993)

In observing a program it is important to remember that no program can ever be perfect, and that a given day will never be repeated.
Carol Hilgartner Schlank and Barbara Metzger (1989)

Outdoor play spaces need careful design. Their safety depends upon satisfactory equipment, careful use of space, good supervision, developmental appropriateness, and suitable use.

Focus Questions

1. Why might you want to assess the child's environment rather than observe the child directly?

2. What aspects of the child's environment could be observed by a teacher or caregiver?

3. How could you record information about an aspect of the child's environment?

4. In what way could you observe and record information about how a group of children use a space?

5. What process would you need to undertake to devise a tool for observing and evaluating an aspect of the child's environment?

6. How can you check to see if an environmental evaluation tool fits your purpose?

♦ ♦ ♦ ♦ History Notes

Ecological psychology, or studying behaviour in natural settings, was a new approach in the early 1950s. It represented a move away from laboratory methods. The ecological approach is one that considers behaviour important in the light of the **environment** in which it occurs. The dual importance of behaviour and environment was underlined by psychological research showing how a child's development could be fostered by stimulating environments.

A new social science, sociology, became significant on both sides of the Atlantic in the 1950s and 1960s. This study of individuals and groups enabled sociologists to identify links between social class and achievement, determine the cultural elements of child rearing, and highlight the importance of the child's language environment. These and other research outcomes led both sociologists and ecological psychologists to understand that the environment was the strongest influence on the child's development.

A gradual awareness of the implications of the work of Jean Piaget became apparent in changed educational practice. Following Piaget's theory of development, which explained how young children pass through a series of stages, educators evolved their teaching style. The learning environment became important because Piaget explained how children learn through discovery. In a process in which the child builds an inner knowledge of his world, the teacher's responsibility was to determine that environment. Structuring the environment to maximize the learning experience became a dominant theme in teacher education in the late 1960s and 1970s.

Not only did practice within educational establishments change; the buildings themselves were reorganized to facilitate greater movement and **child-centred** activity. New buildings reflected this philosophy with the use of more open planning for flexible usage. Architects, social policy makers, and educators influenced a generation of educational establishments, creating very different learning environments to those of the early part of this century.

Conflict between traditional teachers and child-centred educators has been significant and has not lessened to this day. Many of the problems with these changed learning environments arose because their users did not always keep pace, or believe in, the new theories. Success in using a particular environment was consequently variable.

Much recent research focusses on the social and emotional aspects of the child's development. While perhaps more abstract, it has offered insights into the importance of the child's social **context**, bonding, attachment, and emotional environment. Bowlby's classic work on bonding has been superseded by a wealth of information on attachment, which has supported the notion that adequate caregiving can be offered both inside and outside the family home. Explanations of how children gain a sense of self, form social relationships, and gain moral awareness have helped us in the last decade to appreciate the needs of the child more fully. Not only is this helpful to appreciate the stages of the child's development, but it also helps to design, utilize, observe, and evaluate environments to ensure that they support development.

Some of the most up-to-date investigations involving **evaluation** of children's environments have looked at the components of quality. Researchers have taken several different approaches to the task. Some have evaluated the environment in terms of the child's acquisition of skills in various developmental domains; others have considered the role of parents, the health of the children, or caregiver satisfaction. Methods of data collection have been varied but the outcomes have some similarities. They agree that the child-adult ratio in the most important indicator of a quality environment. The particulars of what constitutes an ideal environment vary, but there is a common belief that the child's individual style, and familial and cultural background, must be appreciated and catered to.

Environmental observation: Definition

Environmental observation involves the identification of all aspects of the child's surroundings, including those elements that are designed and implemented deliberately and those parts that occur without planning.

Environmental evaluation: Definition

Evaluation of the child's environment involves consideration of the planned and unplanned aspects of the child's surroundings to ascertain their appropriateness or quality.

◆ ◆ ◆ ◆ Features of Environmental Observation and Evaluation

Previous chapters have focussed on the child as an individual and on the way in which the child behaves. This chapter moves away from this approach to observation and concentrates on the whole experience of the child. Here we look at a range of aspects of the child's environment and attempt to evaluate them on the basis of overall suitability. What constitutes appropriateness and quality features is determined by research.

Any individual understands the world through interaction with the environment. In the early years before abstract thinking, the child internalizes information about the environment in an accepting, non-comparing way because that is all that is known to her. With physical explorations of the environment the child makes some sense of everything she perceives. It is for the child's sake that you observe and evaluate her environment. Taking responsibility for her experience of the world necessitates an effort to see the world through her eyes while holding in mind what you think appropriate according to your own attitudes and beliefs about how children develop.

The context of the child

Wherever the child spends time is an important place. Any adult involved in the life of a child would do well to take time to find out about and observe the child in her different settings. The obvious scenarios will include home and a child care centre or school. There may be time spent in other places and in travel between them; these are significant to the child's experience of the world.

The child's context includes all factors that pertain to her family composition and life style, residence, geographic location, economic status, social relationships, culture, space, resources, exposure to values, attitudes and beliefs, personal belongings, safety, consistency of handling, religious practices, her peers, opportunities in education, and her caregivers, as well as the more concrete physical environment.

The child's curriculum

Every part of the child's life is her "**curriculum.**" **Experience** takes place at any time of the day or night. There should be few boundaries for caregiving and **nurturance**; emotional needs may be required to be met at any time. Physical safety is just as relevant indoors and out, at home or in child care. Routines of sleeping, eating, diapering, or independent self care are just as significant as peak programming time. **Spontaneous play** and discovery may bring about more learning than a designed curriculum activity and therefore need to be planned for and valued. All the adults and the other children in the child's life are important. These people, what they model, and how they respond to the child are also an integral part of the child's environment.

The view that acknowledges all aspects of the child's life to be important gives the adult a great responsibility.

Why observe the environment?

It may seem overwhelming to take on an observation of the child's environment. There are so many locations and aspects to that environment that it may seem to be an unmanageable task. Realizing this, you need to decide which components of the child's environment you can reasonably focus on. You may have one or more of the following reasons for observing an aspect of the environment:

◆ to help understand the family context (home life), cultural background, ethnicity, and sociological perspectives of the child so that appropriate sensitivity and accommodations might be demonstrated.

◆ to help understand the child's behaviour and its causes and provide appropriate guidance.

◆ to help appreciate the child's conception of the world and support her learning.

◆ to help understand the child's level of social competence and provide appropriate experiences and support to improve the social environment.

◆ to help plan new experiences based on the success or failure of previously planned learning environments.

◆ to facilitate a better routine for the day, to use space effectively, to minimize safety risks, and to promote health and healthy practices.

◆ to support the emotional development of children through improvement of the organization of groups, space, and time.

◆ to determine the interests of the children by identifying their interaction with the environment.

◆ to maximize the adults' interactions so that the language environment and nurturance are enriched.

◆ to identify the influence of climate, temperature, colour, space, and atmosphere on individual or group behaviour.

◆ to help appreciate the "**hidden curriculum**" pertaining to attitudes, beliefs, and practices that influence the atmosphere, self esteem, and success.

◆ to fulfill a regular process of program evaluation and upgrading.

◆ to ascertain that a balanced curriculum is being offered and to ensure that program planning can emanate from the children's interests and development.

Observation and evaluation of the environment

Ensuring objectivity when observing the child's setting is a challenge because we all perceive information according to what is familiar.

Family lifestyle, affluence or poverty, social relationships, and accommodation type can be difficult to observe objectively because we bring to them our own world view. Observations can easily be tainted because a bias is so ingrained that we fail to recognize it. What is overcrowding to one person may be spacious to another; one individual's poverty is someone else's affluence.

Separating observation from inference is useful when learning to observe contexts with the most objective eye. Practise this by making statements which are matters of fact. Return to the statements, and from them make valid and supported inferences. Dealing with observation and inference as different entities will help you to avoid subjective comments about children's lives, which can lead to inappropriate interactions with the family, unjustifiable attitudes, and incorrectly based planning.

The difference between observation and evaluation of the child's environment is that the first relates to what you see and the second to how you assess it.

What to look for in the child's environment

Anytime and anywhere are the times and places to observe the child's environment. If you observed the context of the child only in formal times of organized learning in a planned environment, you would miss most of the child's experiences.

Here are some of the things you might look for which constitute the "environment" in a broad sense.

Home and Family

nuclear family composition/size
birth order/siblings
health/abilities/disabilities of family members
extended family location
changes in family composition/moves
non-family adults/children (in child's home environment)
religious/cultural heritage and practices
mother's role/guidance
father's role/guidance
sibling/others' role in caregiving/guidance
daycare/school enrolment/attendance
memberships
play space/play materials
books/toys available
TV/VCR/videogames
employment of parent(s)/hours of work
finances
accommodation (rented/owned)
number of rooms (privacy/shared)
clothing availability
laundry facilities
kitchen/food preparation equipment
temperature/indoor climate
practical needs met/not met
safety of environment
outdoor space
transportation/access/mobility
need for social work/therapy or other support
family concerns

Much of the information regarding the context of the child might be gained directly from parents. Be certain to record information offering its source. Some parents may, quite fairly, resent your request for this information. Some initial interviews for child care are held in the child's home — if this is the case, avoid the clipboard checking-off approach, as this can seem clinical and offputting to parents. Gain the information through more natural conversation about the child's home situation, but be clear that you are recording some of the bits of information that the parents reveal.

Sociological/Geographic Context

nation/city of residence
urban/rural location
accommodations (rented/owned, etc.)
neighbourhood type
population density
building types/age/history
transportation/mobility
shopping amenities
local industry
community services and buildings
banks/finances/economy/taxation/benefits
cultural mix of local population
play spaces
schools
child care provision
community concerns
religious buildings/practices
health services
restaurants/cafes/fast food outlets
social organizations
communications
climate
prevalence of disease
demographic changes
employment
social services

Child Care Agency/School Environment

type of establishment

number of and organization of staff/full-time or part-time schedules/supply staff

funding/budget

age ranges/hours open/ size of group or classes/ratios

catchment area

staff qualifications/union membership/gender of staff/representation of ethnic groups

indoor space and organization

interior design of space

philosophy reflected in design

stated philosophy

variety of activities (name them)

washrooms – access; independence level for child

routines: meals, sleep, etc.

food preparation/snacks

policies/procedures/meetings/communications

guidance strategies

exterior space/equipment

emergency plans

safety precautions indoors/out/First Aid

transportation

car parking

resources, space and access or involvement by parents/parent education available

involvement with community – trips/in centre

relationships between staff and children

types of programs offered

expendable resources: paint, paper, soap, etc.

temperature/humidity

hygienic practices

sick child provision

staff liaison with child's home

entry/acclimatizing plan for "new" children

accommodation for children with special needs

cultural/ethnic mix of those enroled

referrals to other services when/if required

personal belongings/storage

structure/flexibility/expectations

How to record information about the child's environment

Looking at the child's world with the eyes of an objective and articulate child is one of the most effective ways to see the child's environment. To record the context involves much more than checking off the presence or absence of an element of that environment on a list. Compare the following (A and B) part of a family context.

Family Context Checklist (extract)

		Yes	No
A.	Checklist – extract		
	Child has own room		
	Child has personal storage space in bedroom		
	Child has appropriate toys		
	Child owns books		
B.	Narrative – extract		

Sian lives in a downtown third floor apartment with her Mom and two older sisters, with whom she shares a small bedroom. The apartment offers space for Sian to play between the kitchen and living room where Mom can watch over her. The three girls go to the library with their Dad alternate Saturday mornings when he has custody. The shared arrangement with the father is amicable according to Mom, who said she liked to have a little time to herself when the girls are out. Returning to sleep at home on Saturday night I observed Mom playing with Sian. Her toys are not all new but seem to challenge Sian without causing her much frustration.

You can see that the narrative offers much more detail and background than the yes/no approach of a **checklist**. While open to greater interpretation the narrative description also indicates pertinent information that explains the content of the checklist. Neither is incorrect but each tells a different version of the situation. Checklists can be handy when you want to record lots of information quickly, and serve as a reminder to look for particular criteria – the narrative takes much longer but is more open-ended so that it can include what the observer thinks pertinent.

A compromise between these two methods of collating information is possible. A series of directed statements, prompts, or questions can have a yes/no component but leave room for comment. Open-ended questions can be added to ensure there is the possibility of including information that comes to light.

Open-ended Checklist (extract)

14. small wheel toys, cars, trucks   yes/no/not applicable

    comment/description _____

    _____

15. carpentry/sewing/cooking equipment   yes/no/not applicable

    comment/description _____

    _____

16. child-sized furniture   yes/no/not applicable

    comment/description _____

    _____

17. outdoor play equipment   yes/no/not applicable

    comment/description _____

    _____

Visual representations of the environment can be made using photographs, video recordings, and floor plans. Any of these might be useful additions to checklists, **narratives**, or **rating scale** evaluations and offer a record of the context that may be quicker, more detailed, and lasting. Recording the environment in one of these ways enables the observer or evaluator to consider the depiction away from the site or after the context has changed.

Acetates designed for overhead projection can be used for floor plans and overlaid to make comparisons of the use of space. Alternatively a "blank" floor plan can be drawn and photocopied so that room arrangements can be planned.

Measuring the environment

The descriptive approach to observation or the checking off of lists of environmental components can give a relatively unbiased account of the child's environment. This can be desirable for the purposes of understanding what constitutes the child's context, but it does not offer evaluative information from which a social worker might determine intervention, a caregiver decide on compensatory measures, or an educator appreciate contextual barriers to learning. To make an assessment of the child's environment requires a much deeper understanding of all the component parts of the child's experience and how they interact. Merely painting a picture of it does not offer sufficient insight to make the assessment. To make a **qualitative evaluation** of any environment, there needs to be a clear understanding of the philosophy on which it has been constructed and is used. For example, it would be impossible to assess a curriculum for its **anti-bias** characteristics if the concept of anti-bias education is not appreciated.

The simplest evaluation format is that of a checklist. The items must be clear, understandable, focussed, and as complete as the writer can determine. A more open-ended checklist may have space for inclusion of "add-on" items. A rating scale can be attached to the listing of environmental criteria; this will allow for a more qualitative response than indicating only the presence or absence or a "good" or "bad" response to the item.

You might wish to write up your own checklist or rating scale according to your own philosophy and what appear to you as significant criteria. If, say, you believed that a positive learning environment was one in which the children are directed and redirected when their concentration drops, then your environmental items would read somewhat differently to the list of someone who focusses on child-centred activity.

Another type of tool open to you is the standardized scale of checklists prepared by an "authority." These are checked to be valid and reliable, but reflect a particular philosophy. The best-known, reliable, and user-friendly environment rating scales are Harms and Clifford, "Early Childhood Environment Rating Scale" and the Harms, Cryer and Clifford, "Infant/Toddler Environment Rating Scale."

The scales can be used in a variety of early childhood settings. The Infant/Toddler Scale was designed for the youngest children (birth to 30

months). These scales can be administered by a wide variety of professionals, including teachers and assistants. They include a rating of each
item 1 – 7 and space for comment. Results are transferred to a graph to
help identify strengths and weaknesses. Each of the major categories is
divided into several components, which have clearly identified criteria for
grading. The procedure is straightforward but good results would be
dependent on general early childhood training and familiarization with
some terminology. A further rating scale designed for family home day
care is usable for home-based child care.

Section from Harms and Clifford, "Family Day Care Rating Scale"

Name of program: *Friendly Child Care*

Name of teacher: *Bonnie Smith & Christie Lee*

Most children attending at one time: *12*

Number of children present today: *10*

Number of adults present: *2*

Ages of children enrolled (in months) 2 to *16*

Date: *1/10/90*

Name of rater: *Linda Miller*

Position of rater: *director*

1. Furnishings for routine care   1 2 3 4 ⑤ 6 7

2. Use of furnishings for learning activities   1 2 ③ 4 5 6 7
    need open shelves and something to keep
    toys separated

3. Furnishings for relaxation and comfort   1 ② 3 4 5 6 7
    small rug, no soft toys

4. Room arrangement   1   2   ③   4   5   6   7
   only one open play area

5. Display for children   1   2   ③   4   5   6   7
   few pictures, only one mobile

Total   *16*
Furnishings and Display for Children Items 1-5

6. Greeting/ departing   1   2   3   4   5   6   ⑦
   written record near sink

7. Meals/snacks   ①   2   3   4   5   6   7
   some bottles propped; babies put to bed
   with bottles

8. Nap   1   2   3   4   ⑤   6   7

9. Diapering/toileting   1   ②   3   4   5   6   7
   adults wash hands but do not wash children's
   hands

10. Personal grooming   1   ②   3   4   5   6   7
    children's hands not washed before feeding

11. Health practice   1   2   ③   4   5   6   7

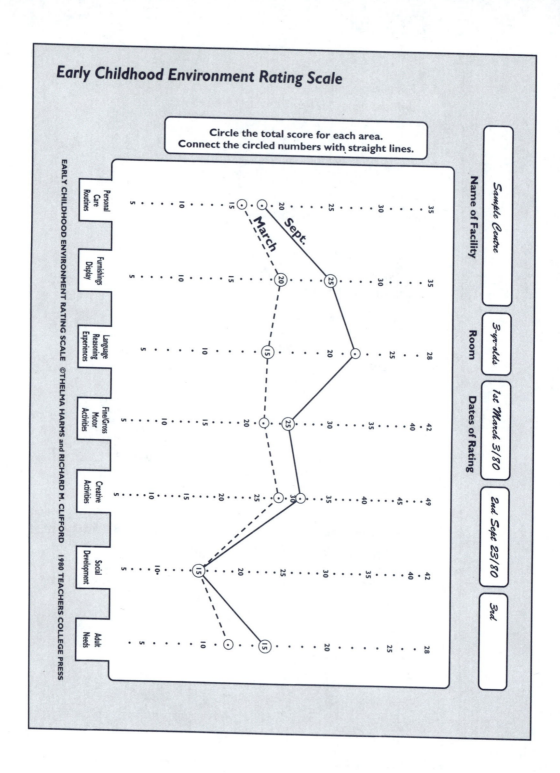

Early Childhood Environment Rating Scale

Circle the total score for each area.
Connect the circled numbers with straight lines.

Name of Facility: Sample Centre

Room: 3-yr-olds

Dates of Rating: 1st March 3/80 2nd Sept 23/80 3rd

Personal Care Routines: Sept. 18, March 17
Furnishings Display: Sept. 25, March 20
Language Reasoning Experiences: Sept. 22, March 15
Fine/Gross Motor Activities: Sept. 25, March 20
Creative Activities: Sept. 30, March 27
Social Development: Sept. 15, March 15
Adult Needs: Sept. 15, March 11

EARLY CHILDHOOD ENVIRONMENT RATING SCALE ©THELMA HARMS and RICHARD M. CLIFFORD 1980 TEACHERS COLLEGE PRESS

Checklist and rating scale results can be gained from both parents and professionals with an interesting comparison of the two. If the criteria are clear the perspectives of both parties may offer insight; frequently the outcome will be similar.

Quality Control: A Manual for Self-evaluation of a Day Care Agency offers a format for assessment covering all the functions of a child care centre. Supervisors and daycare operators may find this a useful way of over-viewing the centre's effectiveness in general. It may not offer sufficient detail to help educators examine the learning environment in a specific area. The steps identified in proceeding with a program evaluation are, however, clear and applicable even when using other evaluation systems. Another strength of the evaluation is that it includes parental input. Based on a rating scale attached to "Standards of Performance Statements," parents provide their scoring of program components including administration, facilities, staffing, admissions, and the program.

Appropriate environments

"Appropriate practice" in work with young children is a commonly used phrase in child care circles, but its meaning varies. An holistic and child-centred approach is the philosophy of the National Association for the Education of Young Children (NAEYC), who have identified the components of **developmentally appropriate** practice. Based on research into the determinants of quality programs, the NAEYC publication *Developmentally Appropriate Practice in Early Childhood Programs Serving Children from Birth Through Age 8* serves as a manual of good practice but can be used in a number of ways to evaluate an existing program or help develop provision from scratch. The age-stage-related integrated components of appropriate and inappropriate practice cover goals, ratios, and teacher qualifications as well as specific developmental practice. If each item were to be used with a rating scale continuum with appropriate practice at one end and inappropriate at the other, the charts become an evaluative tool. The items can be used as focus for discussion with parents or staff as well as in a more structured environmental evaluation.

Developmentally Appropriate Practice in Early Childhood Programs Serving Children from Birth Through Age Eight (NAEYC)

Integrated Components of Appropriate and Inappropriate Practice for 4- and 5-Year-Old Children

	Appropriate Practice	Inappropriate Practice
Teaching Strategies	◆ Teachers prepare the environment for children to learn through active exploration and interaction with adults, other children, and materials. ◆ Children select many of their own activities from among a variety of learning areas the teacher prepares, including dramatic play, blocks, science, math, games and puzzles, books, recordings, art, and music. ◆ Children are expected to be physically and mentally active. Children choose from among activities the teacher has set up or the children spontaneously initiate. ◆ Children work individually or in small, informal groups most of the time. ◆ Children are provided concrete learning activities with materials and people relevant to their own life experiences. ◆ Teachers move among groups and individuals to facilitate children's involvement with materials and activities by asking questions, offering suggestions, or adding more complex materials or ideas to a situation. ◆ Teachers accept that there is often more than one right answer. Teachers recognize that children learn from self-directed problem solving and experimentation.	◆ Teachers use highly structured, teacher-directed lessons almost exclusively. ◆ The teacher directs all the activity, deciding what children will do and when. The teacher does most of the activity for the children, such as cutting shapes, performing steps in an experiment. ◆ Children are expected to sit down, watch, be quiet, and listen, or do paper-and-pencil tasks for inappropriately long periods of time. A major portion of time is spent passively sitting, listening, and waiting. ◆ Large group, teacher-directed instruction is used most of the time. ◆ Workbooks, ditto sheets, flash-cards, and other similarly structured abstract materials dominate the curriculum. ◆ Teachers dominate the environment by talking to the whole group most of the time and telling children what to do. ◆ Children are expected to respond correctly with one right answer. Rote memorization and drill are emphasized.

Observing and evaluating a program can be achieved by turning performance objectives into questions. Schlank and Metzger developed an easy-to-use, open-ended tool that uses the minimum of jargon. The questions could be answered in a yes/no way but are likely to provoke a more explained response. This type of evaluation allows for parental input and is clear in its philosophy because each component starts with statement of intention.

Learning (physical)

It is important for young children to gain awareness of their bodies and to develop their physical capabilities. They may need help to feel okay about their differences in size, appearance, strength, and agility.

Is there opportunity for active physical play?

Does the caregiver encourage children to become involved in physical activities?

Is there large equipment such as a climber, large boxes, or a rocking boat for large muscle development? Is there adequate space indoors or outside for physical activity?

Are there activities to help children develop an awareness of their bodies in space? For example, are there activities such as walking on a line, moving to music, and jumping in place?

Are there materials such as blunt scissors, peg boards, and puzzles for the development of small muscle coordination?

Section from *A Roomful of Children*, C.H. Sclank and B. Metzger. Rochester Association for Young Children

---

Measurement of the home and family environment has intrigued many researchers, who have thought that there is a link between characteristics of families and IQ or achievement. Caldwell devised a measure of the environment called the HOME inventory (Home Observation for Measurement of the Environment). Interviewing and observation are undertaken with a parent about a typical day in the family, interactions with the child, and the material environment. The inventory has a series of Yes/No answers which are scored by the observer/interviewer. The intention was to see if the HOME Inventory Scores and the children's IQs were correlated, which they were. Replication of these studies has highlighted the importance of some of the components of the inventory but not all the reasons for the correlations are completely understood. They do, however, agree in that features of the child's home environment do have an impact on children's performance, competence, or IQ. While the inventory was designed for research purposes, it could be used for evaluation of individual families. Having assessed the inventory items, what to do with the results is less certain – intervention in the family style and interaction needs to be done only when there is clear dysfunction which is identified by the relevant professional.

Evaluation tools are devised as the need becomes evident. The use of a standardized procedure may fulfil your need but you might find it more useful to make a tool to fit your specific requirements. Modification or additions to existing measurement tools may also be helpful but you will need to be aware of the possible reduction of validity and reliability if you alter the tool.

◆ ◆ ◆ ◆ Devising Your Own Environment Observation or Evaluation Tool

1. Informal methods

A list of environmental components may be sufficient for your observation purposes. Serving as a reminder of things to look for, it may be helpful in refining your perceptions. As you form the list you will probably become aware of the philosophy behind the identification of the criteria; the fact that you include an item means that it is important to your belief system. You might want to explore the philosophy some more; this may help you to ensure that the listing is complete and organized. As you work, you may see the size of your task and decide to limit it to a more specific focus. You might also want to structure it under separate headings so that the parts become more manageable. As the list evolves you may like to phrase the items throughout more consistently as questions with a yes/no reply, or as statements to be graded. Trial use of the checklist or rating scale will be helpful and probably reveal some gaps and items which need to be restated. This kind of tool can be useful as it fits the setting well, but it must be remembered that it may not be as inclusive or objective as other tested tools, or may not be valid or reliable if used elsewhere.

2. Structured methods

An effective tool records or measures what it intended to measure. There is a process through which you would need to work to devise an effective tool for environmental observation or evaluation.

1. Identify need for evaluation.
2. Specify the area(s) to be observed/evaluated.
3. State goals of project and philosophy underpinning the tool.
4. Seek team/committee support.
5. Apportion roles and responsibilities of team members.
6. Clarify the process through which tool is to be devised.
7. Agree on time line.
8. Arrange for a trial of the tool.
   The methods for devising a tool may include any or all of the following activities separately or simultaneously and in any sequence:

◆ researching existing tools
◆ reviewing stated philosophies
◆ evaluating environment using different tools
◆ brainstorming ideas
◆ surveying parents/professionals/community to determine opinions/needs
◆ revising previously used tools
◆ identifying component parts of "environment," i.e. stating criteria
◆ editing
◆ trial runs with items used as checklists, rating scales, or open-ended criteria
◆ clarifying grading criteria

Advantages of using a more structured method for devising a tool are that it is more likely to fit the need, to reflect a common philosophy, be more detailed and inclusive than an informally put together checklist. It will probably have wider acceptance, and be more reliable in its use.

As fashions come and go and research supplies us with new information, you are likely to find your existing observation and evaluation tools to be less effective than you would want. Updating, changing, and recreating will continue to be necessary. The qualitative methods are most likely to need modification because the purely observational approaches make fewer inferences and are more open.

Aspects of the environment which are most frequently reviewed by caregivers, parents, and educators include the health and safety, quality, appropriateness, and effectiveness of the environment. You do not have to keep these categories if other concepts are more suitable. Each major category can have many component parts which may need to be identified. Where evaluation is made as an interpretation of observed information, the specifics will need to be clarified. For example, the definition of "high family involvement," "low ratio," or "type of accommodations for special needs" would have to be specific. A qualitative observation or evaluation relies on the recorder's consistent use of terms.

Indicators of appropriate environments for young children

These are broad components that warrant consideration when observing, evaluating, or planning group care environments. Specific criteria may be itemized according to needs and settings. When defined, these components may be used as a checklist, as the criteria for a rating scale, for a narrative description, for the focus of group discussion, or to form plans to create or modify an agency. The items are not prioritized.

General Indicators of a Quality Environment

◆ clearly stated philosophy based on researched indicators of quality
◆ small group size
◆ low ratios
◆ demonstration of meeting of individual needs
◆ appropriate/stimulating learning environment
◆ developmental appropriateness of design, activity, and guidance
◆ high degree of staff training
◆ high level of parental involvement and partnership
◆ positive quality of interactions with children
◆ effective teamwork with parents and professionals
◆ low staff turnover
◆ positive communications between staff
◆ optimal safety health and nutrition
◆ regular program evaluation

Every area of the curriculum needs to be assessed for its inclusivity. The effectiveness of an anti-bias curriculum can be measured by environmental checklists and observing the children within the setting.

Inclusivity: Indicators of an Appropriate Environment

- clearly stated anti-bias policy and practice
- welcome and inclusion of all children whatever race, appearance, class, **ethnicity**, ability, gender, origin, religion, or beliefs
- high level of staff training in **diversity**, anti-bias education, and acceptance of diverse life styles
- avoidance of superficiality, **tokenism**, **stereotypes**, and **touristic approaches**
- presentation of cultural and ethnic variety of music, images, scripts, artifacts, food
- sensitivity to range of familial backgrounds
- accommodations made for differing needs and abilities
- resources available for children with special needs
- support of first language and cultural heritage
- developmentally and individually appropriate activities/experience
- active encouragement of community involvement in program
- effective communication and partnership with parents
- knowledgeable and sensitive communication with all children, demonstration of respect to all
- access to support resources to aid inclusivity
- on-going evaluation of all books, images, toys, playthings, and materials for their appropriateness
- policies and practices that address racism, prejudice, judgmental behaviours, and exclusion
- effective communication with parents and involvement of families
- acknowledgment of a wide variety of parenting styles and child rearing practices

Physical Well-Being: Indicators of an Appropriate Environment

- good **hygienic practices** that control spread of infection
- policies, practices, and protective measures for physical and emotional safety
- minimizing of inappropriate stressors
- clearly stated policies and procedures for health, safety, and nutrition
- first aid provision
- demonstration of meeting of physical and emotional needs
- adequate kitchen equipment, food storage, preparation, and serving
- nutritiously healthy snacks and meals
- adequate space and opportunity for physical play
- positive role models
- resources and support available to parents on health-related issues
- provision for sick children
- toileting and washroom adequacy
- protection from extreme weather conditions
- health education for children
- regular program evaluations and review undertaken
- environment constructed for safe use and healthy development
- routine safety checks
- supervision adequate for well-being
- maintenance of a safe environment
- risk-taking encouraged with safety boundaries
- provision for rest, sleep, and quiet
- high level of cleaning, sanitizing, and sterilizing appropriate to building, furniture, and materials
- pollution monitoring
- appropriate waste management
- reporting to parents of changes in behaviour, health conditions, and general development
- effective communication with parents
- maintenance of appropriate temperature, humidity, and air quality
- confidential and complete health records
- adequate water supply
- community health resources accessed

- adequate training and professional development in health, safety, nutrition, and first aid for all staff
- compliance with local, provincial, and federal legislation and regulations
- parental wishes are considered sensitively
- accident and serious occurrence records kept
- documentation and sensitive handling regarding allergies and medical conditions
- regular and continuous observations made concerning health and behaviour
- early identification of behavioural changes and indicators of concern
- demonstrated positive attitudes to well being
- appropriate storage of materials
- accommodations for specific abilities and disabilities
- separation of areas for different purposes
- maintenance of health and management of stress of caregivers

Nurturance: Indicators of an Appropriate Environment

- small group size
- low child/adult ratio
- allows for personal space for belongings
- accepts individual styles and behaviour patterns
- provides opportunities for personal attachments
- demonstration of enjoyment, fun, and enthusiasm
- sensitivity, **responsivity**, and attunement to individual children
- positive **role models** that demonstrate the range of human feelings
- opportunity for play activity with peers
- provides for consistency of care-giving figures
- establishes **routines**/patterns that are flexible in order to meet individual needs
- stability of family and home circumstances

- positive approaches to changes in accommodation, care-giving, and parenting
- positive communications between parents and care-givers
- maintenance of stable, consistent program
- opportunity for family involvement in the program
- design of agency for contrasts to suit mood and temperament
- acceptance of cooperative and solitary activity
- play encouraged as therapeutic activity
- program is observed, monitored for its emotional climate and adapted as necessary
- demonstration that feelings are acknowledged and allowed
- encouragement of expression of feelings
- reality and fantasy explored openly
- positive communication with children about feelings, changes, crises, etc.
- empathy encouraged and modelled
- encourages objects that link home and agency
- support to develop strategies to cope with strong feelings
- acceptance of diversity in action and voice
- practical indication of support for self identity
- opportunity for self-categorization and self-discovery
- support for positive body image awareness
- fostering of creative thinking and success
- demonstration of support in separations and reunions
- catering to needs for privacy and quiet
- clear indication of parameters of behaviour and consequences of non-compliance
- opportunity for making choices
- open-ended activities that avoid correct/incorrect responses or winners and losers
- process-focussed activity
- authentic praise and encouragement
- adults provide support to each other
- caregivers share common philosophy of nurturing

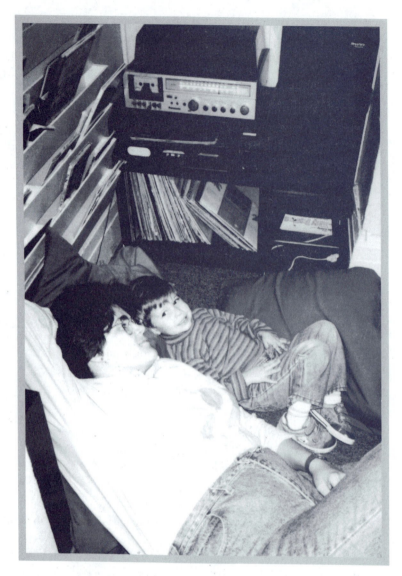

Opportunities for one-on-one communication, comfort, and quiet reflection contribute to the nurturance offered to a child. Environments should be evaluated in regards to whether they meet the children's needs.

Learning: Indicators of an Appropriate Environment

◆ designed to meet children's needs
◆ equipped with child-sized furniture and materials
◆ provides for opportunity for choices
◆ allows for self direction
◆ demonstrates value of spontaneous play
◆ focusses on process of activity
◆ enables freedom of movement
◆ developmentally appropriate programming
◆ caregivers observe individuals to help determine needs and programs
◆ provides for opportunity for experimentation/discovery
◆ sensitivity to the child's stage of understanding
◆ space organized for movement flow
◆ adults follow child's lead
◆ adults demonstrate enthusiasm for child's efforts
◆ adults extend (but not direct) activity
◆ curriculum evolves from child's interests
◆ activities allow for success and minimize failures
◆ encourages the communication of ideas
◆ program is open-ended and evolving
◆ offers stimulation in all developmental areas
◆ focusses on hands-on activity and participatory learning
◆ avoids limiting structure and rigid time-tabling
◆ families encouraged to contribute and participate
◆ encourages natural curiosity
◆ provides for imitative, fantasy, and sociodramatic play
◆ language supplied to help children classify and conceptualize new experiences
◆ adult interactions help children focus on learning
◆ extends knowledge from the base of the child's current understanding
◆ promotes language, print, symbols, and literature
◆ encourages child's need to order her world

- promotes sensory exploration
- offers children strategies to overcome challenges
- role models and supports moral understanding
- offers clear direction regarding expectations and behaviour
- program changes made at differing pace according to needs
- program includes wide range of traditional and non-traditional curriculum components
- acknowledges child's range of feelings
- promotes interactive learning and construction of knowledge
- encourages understanding of similarities and differences
- sensitive to different needs of members of the group
- plans for individual and collective needs
- includes **therapeutic** or **compensatory care**
- programming responsive to changing needs
- well-trained staff who share a philosophy of how children learn
- cooperation and communication in partnership with parents
- structures regular program evaluation
- plans regular observation of children
- plans learning from what is known to what is unknown
- provides open-ended activities and materials to encourage creativity
- curriculum makes appropriate and achievable challenges
- promotes higher order thinking
- encourages success and treats errors as a learning experience
- monitors skill development
- program can be justified in measurable ways
- uses community resources and maintains dialogue with community representative
- complies with all regulatory bodies

Assignment options

I. Skill building

Individual tasks

1. Research the topic of "Quality Care." List as many quality indicators as you can find, citing their sources.
2. Make arrangements to visit a kindergarten classroom or child care centre pre-school room. Kneel down and try to experience the environment as a young child might see it. Record your thoughts and feelings.
3. Plan ahead to "follow"a child for a day from waking in the morning to sleeping at night. List and then describe each of the situations or environments which the child encounters.
4. Find out by library search, interviewing, or calling municipal authorities, what the legal requirements are in your locality for childcare:
   a. adult-child ratios
   b. space requirements
   c. admission policies
   d. health policies
5. Carry out an exploration of a child care centre and its immediate environment. Look for these or any other pertinent information:
   - type of establishment
   - the building
   - staffing
   - children's ages and age grouping
   - range of equipment
   - program for children
   - schedule for staff

Add any other information which would help describe the placement. In addition, find out if the children live nearby. Gather information about the surrounding area. For example, look at the type and condition of housing, industry, transportation, services for families, local shopping and amenities, and any other information relating to the neighbourhood.

The style of presentation is not important. How you do this assignment is flexible. Use your initiative to present your work in a way which is meaningful and which helps the reader appreciate the environmental influences on the children.

6. Request permission to interview and observe a parent of a pre-school or school-age child. Use the questions below. Make clear appropriate comments on the left of your page. After your observation is over, consider your data and see if you can make objective inferences regarding a caregiver's need to respond to the child's home context. State these on the right but be very careful to avoid judgments and assumptions.

Interview/Observation

Name:
Age/D.O.B:
Date:
Observer:
Contextual information
The family

1. Parent(s)/guardian(s) of child, with whom the child lives
2. Siblings with whom the child lives
3. Other family members or non-family living at same address
4. Other family members or non-family involved with the child
5. Type of residence (house, apartment), location (urban, rural, local facilities/resources)
6. Description of accommodation (rooms, space, play space, etc.)
7. Pattern of time spent at home (and with whom)
8. Caregiving arrangements for the child (when, where, and with whom)
9. Particular challenges for the family

This is not a complete family profile but an exercise in writing observable information and substantiating inferences regarding the family.

Group tasks

1. A. In a small group, brainstorm ideas about components of environments which have

    i   a positive atmosphere for preschoolers
    ii   parental involvement
    iii   effective sensory experiences for infants
    iv   "green" ecological sensitivity

    B. From any of your lists of components (from A i – iv), group your items into several labelled categories.

    C. Formulate the components (from B) into a checklist or rating scale.

    D. Give your checklist or rating scale (from C) a trial and then re-evaluate it.

2. Formulate a questionnaire to find out what a wide variety of adults and children think that a child care, school, or home environment should be like.

3. Identify components of a child care environment that is sensitive to reducing, re-using, and recycling materials and provides a positive learning experience about ecology.

4. Read the listing of indicators of physical well-being given in this chapter. For each indicator, identify what you might observe in a program. For example, be specific about what the hygienic practices would be that control the spread of infection. You will need to check on local regulations and use various resources to support your answers.

II. Practising environmental observations and evaluations

1. Write a detailed descriptive account of the sociological environment of a child care centre or school where you work, where you are doing a practicum, or that is nearby your place of study. If two people focus on the same geographic area, compare your descriptions when you have finished. Take time to evaluate your language to ensure that you have excluded judgments and assumptions.

2. Use one of the lists of environmental components in this chapter (quality, inclusivity, physical well-being, nurturance, or learning) to develop a detailed checklist for use in evaluating a child care centre.
3. Give the inclusivity indicators given in this chapter a trial by using them as a checklist evaluation in any setting. What do your findings tell you? Would you change the checklist? What is the underlying philosophy behind it?
4. Attach a numerical rating scale to a safety checklist. Does it work effectively? What reason is there for your answer? What kind of items can be evaluated with a rating scale?
5. Draw a floor plan of a playground or indoor space used for indoor play. Observe the children's use of the space at 10 minute intervals. Use a time sample format or record each set of movements on a separate copy of the floor plan. Evaluate your observations on the basis of safety, use of space, and the type of activity the environment allowed.

♦ ♦ ♦ ♦ Answers to focus questions

1. Looking at the child's environment can give the educator some critical information that would be missing if the observer focussed only on the child. Evaluating the child's whole experience will enable the adult to acknowledge some of the child's personal context, understand the effect the child's experiences have on the child, and take responsibility for the creation, maintenance, modification, or change of any aspect of the environment over which they have control.
2. Observation of the child's environment is possible in any situation to which the adult has access. The most significant to the child are usually her home environment and a child care setting or school; other elements of the child's surroundings may be important but are rarely open to the educator or caregiver for evaluation. Assessment of a home environment is usually undertaken to assist the educator to appreciate the individuality of that context and to help make appropriate accommodations in the agency or school that help bridge the gap. Social workers may make home evaluations as part of an attempt to help the family make changes which would support its functioning. There are many components of the child's environment which can be evaluated. Most usefully, the educator might assess indicators of

quality, inclusivity, physical well-being, nurturance, and learning. Each of these should be addressed according to well-researched criteria. Agency or school environment evaluations help the teacher to set up and program effectively.

3. A wide variety of techniques can be used for gathering environmental data. Narrative observations, photographs, videotape recordings, mappings, trackings, checklists, rating scales, and questionnaires can all help the process.

4. Space assessments are done most efficiently by tracking, on a room layout plan, the actions of all adults and children using the space. The adult may wish to select specific times of the day to carry out samplings of the "normal" activity. Brief anecdotal accounts of the way in which space is used can support the evaluation. Questionnaires might/may be helpful if the children themselves are of an age that they can help with the assessment. A space evaluation needs to be designed to bring out the information which the adult requires. It may be that the space is being evaluated for reasons of safety or to maximize its learning or nurturing potential; the evaluator needs to determine the criteria for evaluation before starting. Access to materials, contrasts, sufficient space for specific activities, inclusion of all curriculum areas, meeting the children's physical needs, adequate supervision, and the integration of children with special needs may be some of the significant elements of the evaluation. A checklist of criteria may be written; attached to it could be a rating scale which might help qualitative assessment.

5. Determining personal or group philosophy of care and education is essential to undertaking the formulation of an observation and evaluation tool. Unless the criteria for assessment are commonly agreed the evaluation will be useless. You may wish to research existing environment evaluation tools and assess their use to you. You could use components of the tools that would be helpful or modify them to suit your purpose. Remember that permission may need to be granted by the publishers. Brainstorming ideas that reflect the stated philosophy may help in the process of listing environmental characteristics. Asking all stakeholders in the child's life to be part of the process can help give a wider perspective. When the criteria have been listed they will probably need some re-ordering and editing. Each item needs to be written so that a comment can be made or numerical score can be attached. The tool will only be as valuable as it is well researched.

6. For an environmental evaluation tool to fit your purpose its components match what is structured on a basis that fits your philosophy. All assessment tools have underlying principles and these need to be evaluated by looking at what they include and also what they exclude. It is essential that the criteria for evaluation offer you the opportunity to develop a plan for change. The components need to be sufficiently specific that they are understandable and observable.

◆ ◆ ◆ ◆ *Key Terms*

ecological psychology
environment
child-centred
context
evaluation
curriculum
nurturance
spontaneous play
hidden curriculum
nuclear family
checklist
visual representations
narratives
rating scale

qualitative evaluation
anti-bias
developmentally appropriate
ethnicity
diversity
tokenism
stereotypes
touristic approaches
hygienic practices
role models
routines
therapeutic care
compensatory care

Glossary of Key Terms

A

achievement test: test designed to measure level of progress in academic or school subjects

action: any activity or observable behaviour

analysis: a process of gaining understanding of recorded observational data involving study of the component parts, making inferences, and validating them

anecdotal record: a short narrative account of a child's activity

antecedent event: the event that occurred just before the example of the sampled behaviour

anti-bias: active opposition to negative or inappropriate attitudes towards or pre-judgment of groups of people, practices, or things

assessment: an evaluation of an individual's performance, which may be based on observations, tests, or the person's products

assessment portfolio: a collection of information about the child, used for evaluation, which might include samples of the child's work, and photographs, tapes, or videos of the child's activities, and informal observations of the child

assumption: a reaction to a behaviour that accepts as true an approach that has not been considered objectively or analytically

B

baby book: a book or album used for recording information about a child, frequently used by parents

bar chart: a graph that represents observational material as bars of varying heights along an axis

bar line graph: a visual representation of information using a grid and two axes

behaviour: the actions and reactions of an individual, i.e., anything a person does, whether deliberate or not

behaviourism: the school of psychology involving the objective study or responses of animals or human beings

behaviour modification: a technique that attempts to change, stop, or modify a demonstrated behaviour

benchmarks: checkpoints at predetermined points in time that are designed to measure an individual's achievement against set objectives or learning outcomes

bias: a view that is altered by the individual's perception and his or her values, attitudes, and beliefs

C

camcorder: a hand-held video camera

causality: a supposed connection between events that indicates what brought about one or more of the events

checklist: a listing of skill or other behaviours used as a guide for recording the presence or absence of each behaviour by a particular individual

child-centred: a philosophy of child care and education that emphasizes the importance of the child's need to direct activity, to make play choices spontaneously, and to learn at a self-determined level

child studies: a collection of information about a child, gathered by a student or teacher over a period of time, which may be used for record keeping, research, evaluation, or program planning

compact disc (CD) : a small disc that can record sound and/or a visual image, which is played back by using a laser beam

compensatory care: nurturance or education to address negative experiences or deprivations

competencies : a) the predetermined listing of skills, abilities, or learning outcomes ascribed to a particular stage of development or grade level b) the measurable and observable demonstration of skills and abilities of the child c) the predetermined listing of skills required to perform a particular role or function

confidentiality: the principle of privacy and the practice of storing information securely so that its disclosure is only made to those considered appropriate

consequent event: the event that occurred immediately after the example of the sampled behaviour

context: the circumstances, situations, or background in which an observation is recorded

contextual information: family, social, cultural, medical, geographic, economic, or other information about the background of the child, which enables a teacher or another stakeholder in the child's life to have some insight into the factors affecting the child's health, growth, or development

criterion-referenced: a test designed to measure the specified skills and knowledge of an individual

curriculum: the child's whole experience; usually used to mean the teacher's or caregiver's provision for the child's developmental needs

D

data: the observational facts from which inferences can be drawn

developmentally appropriate: the way in which a program or procedure is suitable for an individual's stage of progress

developmentally appropriate assessment: method of evaluation that takes into account the developmental stages through which an individual progresses

developmental psychology: the school of study that focusses on the individual's progressive change; it explains how that adaptation occurs in terms of a cognitive framework

diary recording: a recording made on a regular, usually daily, basis

diversity: a wide range (of people) of various abilities, appearance, ethnicity, gender, culture, belief, religion, or place of origin

duration: the length of time a behaviour is observed

E

ecological psychology: social science concerned with connections between the individual and his/her environment

editing: to put different shots together on one tape in a pre-determined order

emerging skill: a learned behaviour at a starting or incipient stage

environment: any part or parts of an individual or group

ethnicity: a label that identifies a perceived common culture or some significant aspects of it, such as language, religion, or origin

evaluation: a qualitative or quantitative appraisal

event: a way of categorizing an occurrence of a behaviour

F

family tree: a diagrammatic representation of an individual's ancestry

fine motor skills: learned behaviours involving the fine muscles of the body

forced choice scale: a rating scale that requires the observer to judge the degree to which a characteristic or quality is evident

formative assessment: in-process, ongoing assessment designed to indicate an educational progression from the identified skill level or to enable the educator to set learning goals for the child

frequency: the pattern or number of occurrences of a specified behaviour

G

genogram: a diagrammatic representation of a family structure, which may include historical and observational information about its style and functioning

gesture: a movement of the body or limbs that suggests meaning

graph: a diagrammatic representation of data frequently depicting the results of analysis of observational material

graphic scale: a rating scale that is designed to record judgments of characteristics or qualities on a continuum that has pre-determined word categories

graphophone: a version of the cylindrical recording play-back device

gross motor skills: learned behaviours involving the large muscles of the body

H

hidden curriculum: elements of the child's experience that are affected by the unstated attitudes and beliefs of the responsible adult

hygienic practices: all behaviours that promote cleanliness, sanitization, or sterilization of bodies, materials, furniture, buildings, or other aspects of the environment

I

Individual Education Plan (IEP): an individualized plan of goals and objectives, tailored to the child's needs

Individual Program Plan (IPP): a curriculum, activity, task, or educational plan designed for an individual child

inference: a deduction made from observational data

input/outcome planning model: curriculum planning based on observational information as well as pre-designed requirements such as competencies

instant camera: a specialized camera that uses film that can be processed within minutes by employing chemicals built into the photograph

integrative curriculum models: an open-ended curriculum or developmentally focussed form of planning based on the principle of child-centred activity

interpretive graphic representations: visual presentation of information analyses from data previously collected

J

judgment: a decision made on the basis of information

K

kindergarten: a term coined by Froebel, which translates as "children's garden." It is the name given to the place where pre-school children have early learning experiences

L

language: the complex means of communication that requires the acquisition of a vocabulary and the rules governing the structure of the method

learning log: a record keeping device used to record the objective description of experiences and process in which the student responded to the experience

life book: a book or album used to record significant people and experiences in a child's life over a period of time: a technique used by social workers and adoption agency workers

life experience flow chart: a diagrammatic representation of the series of key experiences in an individual's life

M

mapping: a diagram or map of an area where children are observed so that their movements are recorded or the program is evaluated

maturation: biological elements of the process of growth and development that occur naturally and sequentially over a period of time as a result of the genetic inheritance of the individual

microphone: a device that changes sound into equivalent electrical signals

N

narrative observation: a sequentially written, detailed description of a child's actions

naturalistic: observation of an individual in his or her natural, familiar setting (rather than in a set-up or testing environment)

negative behaviour: a behaviour judged to be undesirable, inappropriate, or socially unacceptable

normal patterns: the expected sequence of development of the individual; what is expected may be a result of personal experience of children or, more reliably, from a statistically significant sample of a population

norm referenced: the process of interpreting data according to an accepted range of performance

norms: averages (a mean, median, or mode) of demonstrated behaviours, skills, results, or measurements determined from statistically significant populations

nuclear family: immediately related individuals who reside together

numerical rating: a rating scale that requires the observer to quantify the degree to which a characteristic or quality is evident

nurturance: the whole care and experience of the child that fosters development

O

objective: a validated, unbiased position

objectivity: the pursuit of an approach that is undistorted, impartial, unbiased, analytical, and reliable

observation: the informal or formal perception of behaviour of an individual or group of people or the perceptions gained from looking at an environment or object

observation chart: a prepared chart with sections used for categorizing and recording behaviour at the time or soon after it is observed

observer bias: the observer's known or unknown perspective or point of view that has personal or philosophical values that influence objectivity

operational definition: a working, usable description of the behaviour to be sampled

P

palmcorders: a lightweight, palm-sized video camera

patterns of development: the sequence of skill acquisition in each developmental area

phonograph: Edison's invention of a cylindrical system for recording sound and playing it back

physical skill: the learned or required ability to perform bodily or motor behaviours

pictorial or graphic representation: a visual, often diagrammatic way of showing data so that it can be easily interpreted

pie chart: a circular diagram that represents "slices" to depict proportions or percentages

play patterns: the recurring sequences of activity that are directed by the child

portfolio: a collection of information about a child's development gathered over time, used by teachers for assessment and record keeping

positive behaviour: a behaviour judged to be desirable, appropriate, or socially acceptable

posture: the alignment or position of the body

preformationism: the theory that children are created as miniature adults

professionalism: the way of behaving that is appropriate for trained, skilled, and practising workers in performing their duties

profile: a term sometimes used interchangeably with "portfolio" — the profile may contain only some elements of the portfolio that relate to the child's present stage of development

progression: the advancement of skill development

Q

qualitative analysis: measurement of the quantity, amount, or range of specific criteria for evaluation

R

rating scale: a predetermined list of behaviour characteristics that is accompanied by a numerical, semantic, or other grading system

reaction: any response involving action

readiness test: a test designed to evaluate the individual's cognitive functioning

record of achievement: a record kept by the teacher or student that logs anecdotal notes regarding the student's skill development and achievements

regression: a reversion (or movement backwards) to a previously demonstrated level of skill

reliability: the degree to which a consideration or method can be consistent; the degree to which scores for a test or measurement tool remain constant, consistent, or reliable

role model: a demonstration of the behaviours associated with a particular task, employment, or responsibility

routine: a planned or responsive sequence of activity

running record: a sequential written account of a child's behaviour involving rich description and detail

S

sample: a selection, example, or portion of a behaviour

scaffolding: a term coined by Bruner that describes the adult's role in assisting the child in her learning

scale: a list of characteristics or qualities used to measure inferences made from observation

semantic differential: a rating scale that is

designed to record judgments of characteristics or qualities on a continuum, listing pairs of opposites

sequential: in order or sequence, i.e., from beginning to end

sequential model of curriculum planning: a diagrammatic representation of a plan to design learning on the basis of the breakdown of a competence into a series of stages

severity: the degree to which a behaviour has been observed, i.e., irritability might be described as mild, moderate, or severe (this involves making a judgment)

skill: a learned behaviour

skill acquisition: the process of gaining new behaviours or modifying or refining existing skills

sociogram: the diagrammatic representation of social relationships of those within a peer group

sociometry: the study of social interactions, which uses pictorial representations to record data

specimen record: an extremely detailed systematic narrative recording of an observation of one child made as the behaviours are observed: recording is made in a sequential manner and frequently uses coding devices to ensure that the particulars are accurate and complete

splicing: cutting, then reattaching sections of magnetic tape

spontaneous play: naturally occurring, unstructured activity of the child, which is directed by the child

standardized test: a valid and reliable tool for evaluation that specifies the method of administration, content, and scoring

stereotype: a description or image of individuals or groups that depicts them according to clichés, or exaggerated or erroneous criteria, without regard to actual characteristics or individual differences

subjectivity: an approach that is distorted, partial, biased, lacks analysis, or is unreliable

summative assessment: the total outcome of a range of assessment procedures or the total result of a particular evaluation tool

syllabus: a pre-set scheme of topics or focusses for study

T

tally mark: used to count the observed behaviour

tape recorder: a recording device that uses magnetic tapes

telagraphone: a wire recording device

test validity: the degree to which a test measures what it purports to measure

therapeutic care: nurturance, education, or special measures that attempt to address negative or missing experiences or trauma

time sample: the formal method of observing in which random or previously chosen behaviours are recorded at pre-set time periods

tokenism: the practice of exceptional favour, based on negative prejudice, to prove one's fairness

topic planning: planning for children based on pre-designated areas of learning

touristic approach: the practice of presenting cultural difference and places of origin in a superficial holiday, festival, or vacation style

tracking: a diagram or map of an area where a child is to be observed, onto which the child's movement is recorded; this may be used to identify interests, mobility, concentration span, or interactions

V

validate: to ensure that the inferences made from observational data are supported or confirmed by one or more reliable authority

validity: the degree to which a test or observation tool measures what it purports to measure

video: relating to vision

videotape: extra-wide magnetic tape for recording visual images

visual or pictorial representation: a visual, often diagrammatic way of showing data so it can be easily interpreted

Z

zone of proximal development: a phrase coined by Vygotsky that refers to the supposed gap between what the child can do presently in an independent manner and what the child can do in a supported way

zoom: to switch from a close shot to a wide one or vice versa, while videotape is rolling

Bibliography

Ainsworth, M. B. Individual differences in the development of attachment behaviours. In *Merrill Palmer Quarterly* 18 (1972).

Allen, J., E. McNeill, and V. Schmidt. *Cultural Awareness for Children.* Reading, MA: Addison-Wesley, 1992.

American Academy of Paediatrics. Health in day care: A manual for health professionals. 1987.

Beaty, J. T. *Preschool Appropriate Practices.* New York: Harcourt Brace Jovanovich, 1990.

Belsky, J., R. M. Lerner, and G. B. Spanier. *The Child in the Family.* New York: McGraw-Hill, 1984.

Bentzen, W. *Seeing Young Children: A Guide for Observing and Recording Behaviour.* New York: Delmar, 1993.

Boden, M. A. *Piaget.* London: Fontana, 1988.

Bowen, M. *Family Therapy in Clinical Practice.* New York: Aronson, 1978.

Brian, J. and M. Martin. *Child Care and Health for Nursery Nurses.* Chester Springs, PA: Dufour, 1986.

Bredekamp, S. (ed.) *Developmentally Appropriate Practice in Early Childhood Programs Serving Children from Birth through Age 8.* NAEYC, 1987.

Bredekamp, S. and T. Rosegrant (eds). *Reaching Potentials: Appropriate Curriculum and Assessment for Young Children.* NAEYC, 1992.

Bronfenbrenner, U. Ecology of the family as a context for human development: Research perspectives. In *Developmental Psychology* 22 (1986).

Brooks, J. B. *The Process of Parenting.* 3rd ed. Santa Rosa, CA: Cole Publishing, 1993.

Butterworth, W. E. *Hi-fi from Edison's Phonograph to Quadraphonic Sound.* New York: Four Winds Press, 1977.

Canadian Child Day Care Federation. National statement on quality child care. 1991.

Canadian Paediatric Society. *Well Beings: A Guide to Promote the Physical Health, Safety and Emotional Well-being of Children in Child Care Centres and Family Day Care Homes.* Toronto: Creative Premises, 1992.

Caplan, F. and T. Caplan. *The Second Twelve Months of Life.* New York: Bantam, 1985.

Carroll, C. and D. Miller. *Health: The Science of Human Adaptation.* 5th ed. Dubuque, IA: Wm. C. Brown, 1991.

Catron, C. E. and J. Allen. *Early Childhood Curriculum.* New York: Merrill, 1993.

CDCAA. Caregiver behaviours and program characteristics associated with quality care. 1992.

Chud, G. and R. Fahlman. *Early Childhood Education for a Multi-Cultural Society.* BC: Pacific Educational Press, 1985.

Cohen, D. and V. Stern. *Observing and Recording the Behaviour of Young Children.* New York: Teachers College Press, 1987.

Corkin, J. and G. M. Dault. *Children in Photography: 150 Years.* Willowdale, Ont.: Firefly, 1990.

Crain, W. C. *Theories of Development Concepts and Applications.* 2nd ed. Eaglewood Cliffs, NJ: Prentice-Hall, 1980.

Elkind, D. *The Hurried Child.* Reading, MA: Addison-Wesley, 1981.

Engel, B. An approach to assessment in early literacy. In *Achievement Testing in the Early Grades: The Games Grown-ups Play.* Constance Kamii (ed). NAEYC, 1990.

Erikson, E. *Childhood and Society.* 2nd ed. New York: Norton, 1963.

Froebel, F. *Education of Man.* New York: Appleton, 1826.

Garmezy, N. and M. Rutter (eds). *Stress, Coping and Development in Children.* New York: McGraw-Hill, 1983.

Godwin, A. and L. Schragh. Setting up for infant care: Guidelines for centres and family day care homes. NAEYC, 1988.

Goodwin, W. and L. Driscoll. *Handbook for Measurement and Evaluation in Early Childhood Education.* CA: Jossey-Bass, 1980.

Greenspan, S. and N. T. Greenspan. *First Feelings: Milestones in the Emotional Development of Your Baby and Child.* New York: Viking, 1985.

Hall, G. S. The content of children's minds on entering school. In *Pedagogical Seminary.* N.p., n.d.

Harms, T. and R. M. Clifford. *Early Childhood Environment Rating Scale.* New York: Teachers College Press, 1980.

Harms, T., D. Cryer, and R. M. Clifford. *Infant/Toddler Environment Rating Scale.* New York: Teachers College Press, 1980.

Health and Welfare Canada. Children with special needs in daycare. 1980.

Hedgeroe, J. *Complete Guide to Video.* Toronto: Stoddart, 1992.

Her Majesty's Stationery Office. Protecting children: A guide for social workers undertaking a comprehensive assessment. London: 1988.

Hills, Tynette W. Reaching potentials: Appropriate curriculum and assessment for young children. S. Bredekamp and T. Rosegrant (eds). NAEYC, 1992.

Hornby, G. *Photographing Baby and Child.* New York: Crown Publishers, 1977.

Illingworth, R. S. *Basic Developmental Screening 0-5 Years.* 5th ed. London: Blackwell Scientific Publications, 1990.

Irwin, M. D. and M. M. Bushnell. *Observational Strategies for Child Study.* New York: Holt Rinehart and Winston, 1980.

Katz, L. and S. Chard. *Engaging the Minds of Young Children.* NJ: Norwood, 1990.

Kostelnik, M., A. K. Soderman, and A. P. Whiren. *Developmentally Appropriate Programs in Early Childhood Education.* New York: Merrill, 1993.

Locke, J. *Some Thoughts Concerning Education.* London: Churchill, 1693.

Martin, S. Your child study: A new approach. In *Nursery World* (Sept. 1988).

McCullough, V. E. *Testing and Your Child.* New York: Plume, 1992.

McGoldrick, M. and R. Gerson. *Genograms: Family Assessment.* New York: Norton, 1985.

Meisels, S. Remaking classroom assessment with the work sampling system. In *Young Children* (July 1993).

Meisels, S. and D. Stele. *The Early Childhood Portfolio Collection Process.* Ann Arbor, MI: Centre for Human Growth and Development, University of Michigan, 1991.

Montessori, Maria. *Montessori Training Course*. Ann Arbor, MI: Ann Arbor Press, 1963.

NAEYC. Healthy young children: A manual for programs. 1988.

Neugebauer, B. *Alike and Different*. WA: Exchange Press, 1987.

Parten, M. B. Social participation among pre-school children. In *Journal of Abnormal and Social Psychology* (1932-33).

Pestalozzi, J.H. *A Father's Diary*. New York: Appleton, 1906.

Phillips, D. (ed). Quality in child care: What does research tell us? NAEYC, 1987.

Piaget, J. *The Child's Conception of the World*. Paris: Presses universitaires de France, 1929.

Piaget, J. *The Child's Construction of Reality*. London: Routledge and Kegan Paul, 1955.

Piaget, J. *The Origins of Intelligence in Children*. New York: International Universities Press, 1962.

Pinder, R. Not so modern methods. In *Nursery World* (Sept. 1987).

Pinder, R. SATs - Why the fuss. In *Nursery World* (May 1991).

Pogne, D. Quick time. In *MacWorld* (Oct. 1992).

Rose, V. Detecting problems with growth development charts. In *Nursery World* (Nov. 1985).

Rousseau, J.J. *Emile*. Translated by Barbara Foxley. London: Dent (First French edition, 1762).

Schaffer, L. *Mothering*. Cambridge, MA: Harvard University Press, 1977.

Schermann, Ada. *Child Care and Education: Canadian Dimensions*. Toronto: Nelson, 1990.

Schlank, C. and B. Metzger. A room full of children: How to observe and evaluate a pre-school program. New York: Rochester Association for Young Children, 1989.

Stevenson, M. F. and E. Zigler. *Children in a Changing World*. Santa Rosa, CA: Cole Publishing, 1993.

Toronto Observation Project, Board of Education for the City of Toronto. Observing children through their formative years. Toronto: 1980.

Vygotsky, L. S. *Mind in Society: The Development of Psychological Processes*. Cambridge, MA: Harvard University Press, 1978.

Watson, H.B. *Behaviourism*. Chicago: University of Chicago Press, 1930.

Whitbread, N. *The Evolution of the Nursery Infant School*. London: Routledge and Kegan Paul, 1972.

Williams, L. R. and Y. De Gaetano. *Alerta*. Reading, MA: Addison-Wesley, 1985.

Wortham, S.C. *Childhood 1892 - 1992*. Wheaton, MD: Association for Childhood Education International, 1992.

York, S. *Roots and Wings*. St. Paul, MN: Redleaf Press, 1991.

Young Children. The effects of group size, ratios, and staff training on child care quality. (Jan. 1993).

Index